Psychiatry as Medicine

Psychiatry as Medicine
Contemporary Psychotherapies

by

YEHUDA FRIED, M.D.

Tel-Aviv University,
the Sackler School of Medicine and
F. Brüll Community
Mental Health Center
Kupat Holim
Tel-Aviv

JOSEPH AGASSI, Ph.D.

Tel-Aviv University and
York University
Toronto

1983 **MARTINUS NIJHOFF PUBLISHERS**
a member of the KLUWER ACADEMIC PUBLISHERS GROUP
THE HAGUE / BOSTON / LANCASTER

Distributors

for the United States and Canada: Kluwer Boston, Inc., 190 Old Derby Street, Hingham, MA 02043, USA
for all other countries: Kluwer Academic Publishers Group, Distribution Center, P.O.Box 322, 3300 AH Dordrecht, The Netherlands

Library of Congress Cataloging in Publication Data

```
Fried, Yehuda, 1929-
   Psychiatry as medicine.

   Includes index.
   1. Psychotherapy--Philosophy.  2. Psychotherapy--
History.  I. Agassi, Joseph.  II. Title.  [DNLM:
1. Psychotherapy--History.  2. Psychotherapy--Trends.
3. Psychopathology.  4. Philosophy, Medical. WM 11.1
F899p]
RC480.5.F754   1983        616.89'14'019    83-4224
ISBN 90-247-2837-1
```

ISBN 90-247-2837-1

The text of this book has been electronically processed

PRINTED IN THE NETHERLANDS

CONTENTS

PREFACE

This volume is a sequel to yet independent of our *Paranoia: A Study in Diagnosis*, Reidel, Dordrecht and Boston, 1976. Whereas our first book centered on diagnosis, this centers on treatment. In our first volume, all discussions of nosology (theory of illness) and of treatment was ancillary to our discussion of diagnosis; similarly all discussion of this volume dealing with nosology – there is very little on diagnosis here – is ancillary to our discussion of psychotherapy. It is still our profoundest conviction that to speak of treatment without diagnosis is meaningless, if not irresponsible, since otherwise one does not know what one is talking about. Hence, our present study, though it centers on theories of treatment, links psychotherapy with psychopathology. It is the rationale of psychotherapy which is of importance, and the rationale dwells in this link.

We wish our present study to be self-contained and understood by readers who are not familiar with our first book – or with any specific literature. Our discussion of medicine in general, meaning the rationale of therapy in general, helps the uninitiated reader, as well as the initiated, we hope: it certainly has helped us. We did not see how else can we study a branch of medicine; we felt the need for some idea of how medicine is supposed to work. We found very little literature about medicine in general; we found very little literature about the two schools of medicine presented here – or even about one of the two schools of medicine in general; each of the volumes within the enormous literature on the subject belongs to one or the other school. Often no book is purely of one school, thereby raising questions about its consistency, since we can consistently present conflicting views together only when we are ready to contrast them. The contrasts, however, are studied by historians, seldom by clinicians. We hope to close a gap here. What we propose is that 'the cunning of History', to use an ugly expression of the notorious philosopher G.W.F. Hegel, is at work here: 'the cunning of Medicine' is not cunning, much less of such an abstract entity as Medicine or as History; it is nothing but the attempt of the honest thinker to muddle through. Not only honesty requires the examination of opposite views and gives them expression in the canonic writings of the professions; it is also the application of competing and mutually exclusive views in one's daily practice. The interest of the patient, after all, is shared by both schools.

The present volume is holistic in bias − very much in line with the philosophy of Mario Bunge, for example. It might, therefore, look like a defence of the holistic school in medicine, here labeled generalism. It is not. Moreover, holism has a bad name both amongst scientific researchers and amongst philosophers of science (with exceptions like Bunge, of course); it has a better reputation amongst circles not scientifically reputed. Regrettably we find this bad name justified. It is because of the victory of the opposite of holism, because of the victory of mechanism, and more so of its expression in medicine, here labelled externalism, that this volume is unbalanced: we deem the defence of mechanism in general and of externalism in particular quite redundant. Rather, we seek to rehabilitate and defend holism by showing that the interaction of generalism and externalism dialectically advances research. We confess ambivalence towards externalism, and we identify best with the remark Plato ascribes to Socrates in *The Apology:* the craftsman is wise in his craft but, alas, he is all too often willing to pronounce some foolish general judgements. We seek to supplement what we regrettably view as the philosophical narrowness of the externalist and mechanist by providing as a proper background to it a clean version of holism − philosophical and medical − and a clear description of the postive contribution of generalism to medicine. We suggest to replace the popular externalist contempt of holism and of generalism with more balanced a view. Nothing human is alien to us: contempt has no place in medicine, much less in psychiatry.

We began writing the present manuscript soon after the publication of our first work (December 1976) and finished it in Spring 1978.

Y.F.

J.A.

Tel-Aviv,

Spring 1982.

ACKNOWLEDGEMENT

We are grateful to Ms. Heather Korn for her dedicated hard work on the word-processor. We are grateful to the Tel-Aviv University Sackler School of Medicine and to Kupat Holim's F. Brüll Community Mental Health Center, Tel-Aviv, for their support of the preparation of the book for the printer.

SUMMARY AND CONCLUSIONS

I. MEDICINE:

1. Theory:

Medical theory is specifically nosology − theory of illness or disease − especially etiology − theory of the cause of disease. Two competing theories dominate the tradition of medical theory: generalism − illness is disharmony, ill-balance − and externalism − illness is the intrusion of (hostile) foreign agents or factors − both theories represented, largely, by internal medicine and by surgery. The success of each theory is reinterpreted by the other − at times successfully. The bias of externalism is mechanistic, of generalism holistic. The scientific revolution was mechanistic, contemporary science holistic. Holism is clearly superior, yet it could not win (in physics and elsewhere) before the Einsteinian revolution in physics, since the success of mechanism could not be properly handled by holists until Einstein took the method of approximation to be the standard of scientific progress: a new theory must explain the success of its predecessor by presenting it as approximate. Each mechanistic (externalist) success, thus, should be presented as an approximate to a holistic (generalist) theory − indeed sets of mechanistic approximations for diverse holistic situations are called for. Hence, from a modern holistic viewpoint both generalism and externalism are viable and indispensable with.

2. Practice

Medical practice is therapy, but, we contend, specifically diagnostic: after diagnosis the whole range of treatment agents is possible, from self-medication to treatment by nurses to treatment by a surgeon with golden hands. Diagnosis gains respectability from its repeatability, testability, and improvability (especially through the process of progressive differential diagnosis). It also gains respectability from both having theoretical rationale, however flimsy or well-founded, and having the empirical basis that permits it to survive the demise of its rationale. As to treatment, externalism directs etiology to the very cause of the illness, generalism invites sparse and at most symptomatic treatment, letting nature do the real job of healing. We tend to side here with generalism, though, of course, more in skepticism than in affirmation.

II. PSYCHIATRY:

1. Theory:

Psychiatric theory always was very conspicuously extremely externalist, yet it hardly ever was either medical or scientific: it usually was metaphysical, at times under the guise of commonsense − including the commonly accepted ideas of the society in which it was advocated, magic hardly ever excluded − at times under the guise of science − and so pseudo-scientific par exellence. Often one author exhibited both generalist and externalist traits, and then in extremist fashions. One author could also simultaneously employ both pseudo-science and metaphysics. This was conspicuously so with Pavlov and more so with Freud.

The only medically proper part of psychiatric nosology is the Freudian idea that the etiology of all psychic ills is that of an improper self-cure of anxiety, akin to a cutaneously healed yet subcutaneously still infected wound. Yet this defective cure is stable due to ambivalence, as Freud also noted. The idea that the object of ambivalence is exclusively sex, or anything else, is silly: it is never exclusive unless, perhaps, it is the patient's autonomy − in the abstract.

2. Practice:

No traditional psychiatric diagnosis is at all up to par except for the Freudian diagnosis of conversion hysteria and of clear-cut phobias (including hysterical blindness, and, by extension, la belle indifférence). In our *Paranoia* we have offered tools for diagnosing psychoses; in the present study we have slightly modified our proposal so as to add etiology to the picture. The etiology of all mental ills being as discussed above, the only treatment thus far advisable is the temporary symptomatic reduction of anxiety (like dentist's novocain) in order to facilitate dialogue between patient and therapist − or patient and anyone else for that matter − in order to treat anxiety on a somewhat deeper level. Our demand for psychiatric diagnosis to be more in conformity with high medical standards and our demand from treatment to be more dialogical, both together seem to us to hint at the proposal that psychiatric diagnosis be less mechanical and more anthropocentric.

INTRODUCTION

The present essay is not meant to be historical yet most of it is history, or rather most of it is that part of history which still is topical. It seems to us amazing how topical still is the ancient debate between the schools of Cos and Cnidus, with Hippocrates representing Cos, and the *Corpus Hippocraticum* representing both: indeed, our thesis is that medicine comprises both schools even today. The reader of the *Corpus* has constantly to be reminded that the reference of the ancient writings is so very different from today's. Consider the scalpel against which the Hippocratic oath speaks, and which treatises on surgery – which, together with the oath comprise the core of the *Corpus Hippocraticum* – speak in favour of. That scalpel is a very distant cousin of today's scalpel – unless both stand as mere symbols for the externalist school of Cnidus to which most surgeons traditionally today still belong. Quite appropriately the generalist school, to which most internalists traditionally belong, has no symbol: non intervention is best symbolised by no symbol.

Our concern is with psychiatry as medicine. The most bitter dispute in psychiatry is between the noninterventionist conservatives who speak of 'butchers-of-the-mind' and of 'chemical straight-jackets' and the interventionists who consider their opponents 'smooth-talkers' and 'quacks'. Our difficulty is to see both how exactly they differ and how exactly Medicine embraces both.

In addition to this, we have a genuinely historical thesis: the two schools , Cos and Cnidus, internists and surgeons, Iatrochemists and Iatrophysicians, Pneumaticists and Empirics, Methodists and Eclectics, are the same as Holists and Mechanists – we have decided to use the terms Generalists and Externalists because they refer to nosology (the theory of disease) and we see the heart of the historical debate as nosological. Amongst philosophers, though, the terms holist and mechanist are commoner, and for good reasons. Oddly, Holism views illness as imbalance, thereby also accepting for philosophers nosology as the heart of the dispute.

For the one school, the illness is an external agent; for the other, the root of the signs and symptoms – not the disease – lies in the general situation: the cause of the clinical picture is the patient's reaction to the external causes. For the two schools, then, illness is always the external agent or the inability to cope with the external agent, respectively. In psychiatry, the agent was the devil, and this gave the externalist school a bad name. In modern times the picture got more complex.

One methodological point before we start. Authors who at all discuss the matter, historically or otherwise, usually either side with one school or synthesize the two. We do neither. Also, most historians who at all discuss the matter, are concerned with actual continuity through possible or alleged direct influences. We shall not concern ourselves with this at all, maintaining that the disagreement is so universal and so important in all aspects of daily medical practices throughout the ages, that those not influenced by ancient ideas rediscover them. (For more details on this point, see I.M. Lonie, 'Cos Versus Cnidus and the Historians', *History of Science,* 1978.)

1. THE HISTORY OF IDEAS IN PSYCHOTHERAPY

This is a monograph of ideas, not of facts. It is hardly believable that one person could master all that was said about psychotherapy. But one can have an overview of key ideas, of their major developments, articulations, interrelations, etc; in order to both critically examine existing ideas, and help foreshadow and create new ones.

By examining the history of ideas in psychotherapy one quickly sees that many ideas are rooted in the way the therapist views the psychopathology of any specific case. Now this led us to study schools of psychopathology. But a given psychopathology itself is rooted in the way one understands disease in the broadest medical sense of the word, and so we began our study by representing *generalism* and *externalism* as the broadest schools of thought in medicine.

We did not particularly like the terms 'gereralist' and 'externalist'. Perhaps 'holist' and 'mechanist' are better. The main disagreement is between two philosophic schools. One approaches things, prima facie, strategically, and tries to see every defect, disease, problem, etc., globally: as involving the whole organism, system, etc. Only in special cases will the generalist agree to localize the trouble and concede that otherwise the organism or system is in order. The other approaches things, prima facie, tactically, and tries to see every defect, disease, problem, etc., locally, as involving a minor part of the organism, system, etc. Only in special cases will the externalist agree to view the trouble as global and concede that the whole organism or system as such is sick.

Hence the terms employed could be 'generalist' and 'specialist' or 'globalist' and 'localist' or 'holist' and 'mechanist' or 'organicist' and 'atomist'. However, we bow to convention and accept 'generalist' and stick to it by referring to its opposition as 'externalist' since the word 'externalist' imports another item, a new idea: the local approach postulates not only a localized defect, but also a specific external agent. For example, a small wound. It is a good example of externalism both as a localized trouble, and on the supposition that it was caused by a relatively minor brush with some hard object. In the popular mind often externalism is associated with external agents such as germs; yet the germ belongs to etiology — the theory of causation — not to nosology — the theory of disease. Nosologically, what seems to make the germs external, is the claim that germs attack specific seats: Corynebacterium diphtheriae germs attack the throat and gonorrhea germs, the genitals.

So much for terminology. Let us now turn to the controversy between the two schools of thought, the generalist and the externalist, which dominate — alternately or simultaneously — the whole history of medicine. It is not that anyone will contest that the deepest controversy lies here; rather, most writers prefer to pass over controversy in embarassed silence. For our part, following more modern methodology, we take controversy seriously and assume that the deepest and most metaphysical differences can and often do express themselves in practice — in research or even in healing.

To repeat, we consider generalism to the view of disease as a defect in the pattern of interaction between the organism as a whole and its environment, and its opposite, externalism, to be the view of disease as a local defect of the organism usually caused by intrusion from the environment. On the one hand we find it hard to pinpoint the difference between the two major schools: externalism assumes that the organism normally, naturally, interacts well with its environment (which is a generalistic view), and generalism will not refuse to view a foreign body, such as a bullet, as the specific cause of a specific disorder such as a flesh wound. Nevertheless, we contend, even if it is hard to locate the precise difference between generalism and externalism, even if in the last resort the difference may vanish, nevertheless the fact is that most surgeons are externalists and most general practitioners and internists are generalists. It is a fact that for many borderline cases — and these abound — the externalist physician or surgeon will recommend an operation or a medication quicker than the generalist. Similarly, on such borderline cases, researchers go their different ways.

It is here that our interest is kindled. There are the chemoiatric school and the psychiatric (psychological) school regarding mental illness. It is obvious that everyone admits that we can induce mental disturbances chemically and that most mental patients have great emotional strains and stresses in their anamnesis (the patient remembrance of his case). Yet on the one hand the chemoiatric school, being externalist, believed that removing some chemical obstacles will do the trick, or perhaps adding some missing chemical agents will do it. (Indeed, it is hard to say what is the difference between adding and subtracting a chemical: the externalist in psychiatry here bumps against the dispute between generalists and externalists in bio-chemistry.) On the other hand the psychiatric (psychological) school opposes chemotherapy. Clearly, both will agree that some cases will need psychotherapy even if chemotherapy helps, and some cases simply need chemotherapy (e.g. hyperactive children). Yet the controversy exists.

We shall try to present this controversy as clearly as we can, and while we follow chains of reasoning from nosology (theory of illness) to both etiology (theory of causes) and therapy (theory of healing).

Since the dispute between externalists and generalists is at the heart of the present study, we hope the reader indulges us one last clarification. The externalist looks at a machine as a collection of replaceable parts whereas the generalist sees it as a harmony.

The image the externalist uses is that of a machine, with parts having distinct existence and function: they are thus replaceable just because their roles are clearly defined, and their replacement is relative to those roles. The clear definiteness of the role of each part makes it utterly unrelated to other parts, even when these are similar and adjacent. When a motor-car operates in second gear, it matters not whether the car's third gear is in proper order or not, nor whether the model has three or four gears. The generalist image of a machine is that of an interconnectedness, of a harmony, of the resultant impossibility of utter replaceability. The whole design of a well-designed car depends on the number of gears it has, and when a part is changed the whole is different, since a part is a part of a whole, and a better designed car is more of a unity, a wholeness. The bias of the present work is holistic, yet it is for a combined or a compromised attitude: some parts are fairly replaceable, others not at all: by making generalism a matter of degree one can view externalist cases as low-level or poor integrations.

2. WHAT IS PSYCHOTHERAPY

When we sent a manuscript of a previous book of ours to an eminent European psychiatrist, he reacted to it by saying: why do you waste your time, energy and intellectual effort on a scholarly kind of work; who really cares today what said Sigmund, Anna, Melanie, or for that matter, Alfred, Carl or Ivan? He said that we are stupid to waste our time on such matters. We very much sympathize with his view, yet we do not share it. Our answer to his legitimate critique is as follows.

Psychiatry has still not even fully established a satisfactory clinical classification for mental disorders. The American Psychiatric Association changes its clinical classifactory criteria every few years; the World Mental Health Organization, i.e. the psychiatric branch of the World Health Organization, has in recent years seriously attempted to arrive at a world-wide concensus on what counts as schizophrenia. This attempt is as yet far from being successful. Antipsychiatry, in the mouths of its serious exponents, throws a very serious and heavy challenge at psychiatry. Yet antipsychiatry is not the movement exemplified by the Foucaults, Szasz's, Laings, Basaglias, et al. As an intellectual/critical trend antipsychiatry can be traced back to the French Revolution and placed well within psychiatry proper. Paradoxical as it may seem, Pinel precedes Foucault, Briquet precedes Szasz, Laing is the heir of Conolly, etc. Our contemporary antipsychiatry is novel merely in the sharpness of its condemnations, not otherwise. Hence, if we take seriously Pinel, Briquet and Conolly, we should likewise take seriously the challenges of antipsychiatry: Who is mentally sick? Who decides on this matter, and how? What are the criteria which demarcate the deviant from the normal? What is normal? Is normal identical with healthy? What is health? What is disease? What is normal healthy mental anguish as distinguished from the sick anguish which is part of mental disease? What about the diseased mental condition where there is no mental anguish? Is suffering a necessary condition for being mentally (and physically) ill? Is it a sufficient one? Is it either? Is it neither?

Once we arrive, closely or remotely, at the start of a serious attempt to find answers to these questions, the following ones inevitably and immediately arise too.

Which disease is medical, which is psychological, which is sociological? (Thank God, in sociopathology we have new kinds of disease (?) ! But the sociological — political? — approach is a challenge to be met, not a silly game to be easily dismissed.)

These questions are obviously immediately relevant to psychotherapy. If mental disease is, from the pathological point of view, medical, psychological, or both, or neither, then the very indication of psychotherapy as a means of healing (and the indication as to which psychotherapy — whether Freudian, Adlerian, Buberian, etc.) becomes very pertinent.

In medicine we say: the absence of an indication for a given treatment is (in itself) a counter-indication; if there is an indication, every effort should be made to offer that treatment to our patients; it is not a luxurious game, provided only to white, intelligent, rich neurotics. On the contrary, it should be considered criminal negligence to avoid available treatment if and when indicated medically or even only psychologically. And if psychotic patients are deprived of psychotherapy solely and merely because of a theoretical disagreement as to indication and/or techniques, it is vitally important then to deal with this disagreement. And if psychotherapy is indicated for the psychotics and yet denied them in prevalent daily hospital practice, it is a serious blemish on our medical/healing institutions. And if so, one should do something about it, be it on the intellectual level or on the organizational (or even political) level. On the other hand, if psychotherapy for the psychotic is neither here nor there, then why bother?

We propose that it is in an attempt at an overview, by looking from 'above' at the current situation in psychotherapy, medical or otherwise, that we might improve the state of the art. It is by examining one against the other ('compare and contrast' as Charcot used to say) the efficiency of our contemporary trends in psychotherapy, by examining (no less than) the very metaphysics of health and of disease, physical and mental, that a better handling of these problems can be attempted. By the same token, perhaps the examination should not be merely from the outside, from the Academy, from 'above'. It should be done, perhaps, by persons who are also in the inside, who face daily human suffering, mentally diseased people (patients), who feel passion and compassion for them.

Indeed, it is the passion and compassion for individual patients that gave birth and energizes the present, deliberately cold and detached, hopefully to some measure both disinterested and objective, admittedly too intellectual and too scholarly study. It is not what Sigmund, Anna or Melanie said, that concerns us. It is the fact (as we perceive it) that what they said, or did not say, what Pinel thought of, why, and why he or they avoided certain problems, certain facts and points of view, that assuredly deeply affect today's daily psychiatric practice in hospitals, in clinics and elsewhere. Psychotic patients, and/or (neurotics) severely disturbed (up to and including those suffering from actual physical or mental paralysis), are but a fraction of the population of the sick in general. Fortunately, the sick constitute only a fraction of the population in general. So far so good. But having psychiatry as a medical speciality, forces us to consider it part and parcel of the issue of health — surely one of the most important issues in the world. Otherwise doctors would not function as they do: their medicine is not only their craft and/or art; it is also their commitment. It is a commitment towards oneself and towards the other — to think rationally, criticaliy, to admit that the whole issue of one's own commitment is so very problematic, possibly even an illusion and sheer self-deception. This admission should not be avoided even when − particularly when − it complicates matters. But commitment − even if it is a mere phantom − is still here; and notoriously there is no better way to sift the real from the illusory than through a critical overview. Indeed, we suspect that it is the unwillingness to take a hard look at the history of the field that makes some practitioners dismiss it. For, the same practitioners will gladly endorse a benign overview and historical survey that only enhances their self-satisfaction. We do not wish to quarrel with them but to explain: it was dissatisfaction that took us to where we are now.

Let us, therefore, begin by examining medical thinking, models of medicine, general principles of health and disease; pathology; psychopathology in general; schools of psychopathology; psychotherapy; psychotherapies; chemotherapy (in brief); and, in conclusion, we shall try to review the state of the art. It is possible that at the journey's end we shall offer no novelties nor surprises; a person familiar with therapeutic practices in psychiatry, be he a theoretician or a clinician, may say, well, is this all you have arrived at? We hope, then, that the way itself is interesting enough, and we hope that by following, as we did, the flow of the (natural?) history of ideas in psychotherapy, the reader will find, as we did find, some additional insights, some sparks conducive to the birth of new ideas, some unexpected question marks emerging, and, perhaps, hopefully, some additional understanding both of the marvels and of the pitfalls of the psychiatric profession: of psychotherapy. At least, the kindly disposed reader is requested to view this book as a study in the history of ideas regarding psychotherapy; or as a mere footnote to existing psychotherapy, examining schools of psycholtherapy, both as theoretical systems and as medical practices. We hope we offer something both to readers who would decide that this study aims too high as well as to those who would decide that it aims too low. What this book aims at, and invites the favorably disposed reader to improve upon, is the effort to use cold reason for the compassionate end of improved psychotherapy.

I. GENERALISM vs. EXTERNALISM: THE CONCEPT OF DISEASE

1. INTRODUCTION: ANTIPSYCHIATRY

Every profession has an inner opposition from time to time, yet the opposition psychiatry has recently met is more than a mere expression of some inner dissatisfaction. This new movement has gained popularity outside professional circles, where it is known, somewhat inadequately, as antipsychiatry. Inadequately, because antipsychiatry is not opposed to psychiatry in general, but rather, at least according to one of the key claims of antipsychiatry, it is opposed to the Establishment of psychiatry or, if you will, to the vices of psychiatry. The chief vices of psychiatry, say its opponents from within, is the fact that it is built upon a general medical model. This model, the complaint continues, is employed in traditional psychopathology as much as in traditional physical medicine; yet in psychiatry it is entirely useless. The mere words — 'the medical model' — provoke endless anger and uncontrolled rage in some antipsychiatric circles.

It is hard to say what exactly is '*the* medical model' that the antipsychiatrists are so hostile to. Fortunately, we do not think we need spend much time describing it in any way, especially since we do not endorse the jaundiced view of the antipsychiatrists concerning traditional psychiatry — indeed, we consider the antipsychiatrist's criticism a dangerous means for the defence of the very ills of traditional psychiatry. Suffice it to report, then, that according to antipsychiatry 'the medical model', sometimes known as 'the contemporary medical model', is at serious fault because it artificially separates the sick from his sickness, the ill person from his illness, and views them as opposites: for the good of the sick, we must exterminate the sickness and do so by excessive physical means quite unrelated to the sick, such as drugs or any other chemotherapy. This is a fairly simplistic description of the chief complaint antipsychiatrists launch against the psychiatric Establishment. Regrettably, we consider antipsychiatry simplistic, be its complaint whatever it may.

The complaint against 'the contemporary medical model', at least as we have described it above, seems to us to be easily capable of broadening. Indeed, it is hardly new in medicine in general: indeed, it has been voiced as early as the 4th Century B.C. Thus it is also, of course, hardly peculiar to antipsychiatry. The first one to rise against the so-called 'medical model' was not a psychiatrist but a general physician, perhaps *the* general physician, namely Hippocrates, who himself had a different, but still a medical kind of model. And so, traditionally, at least two distinct medical models are perennial. The one is the already mentioned fairly mechanistic view that serves as the target of the antipsychiatrist's criticism; the other, which they hardly notice, and which is Hippocratic, medical and traditional, yet very much in accord with the views which antipsychiatrists think of as so novel.

Our sympathy, let us declare our hand at once, is decidedly not with '*the* medical model', wherever else it may lie. But we prefer, really, to class views in a way different than the naive antipsychiatrists follow. Nevertheless, we wish to start with an observation favourable to 'the medical model' before we attack it, or rather before we discard it in favour of a better model that we also intend to attack. Let us, then, describe the positive side of the model.

'*The* medical model', to repeat, is the separation of the ill from the illness. It is the concept of an illness with a known or suspected origin or aetiology, with a predictable course and hopefully with a rational treatment based on the etiology − all of which is fairly divorced from the persons suffering from it. This model has served medicine for quite some time, and remarkably well. Indeed, had it been more serviceable, this in itself would constitute an ideal situation. Were we able to ignore the patients and describe the aetiology, course, and rational treatment for all diseases, we would be very pleased. Were all treatment based upon removal or repair (adjustment) of the defective factor(s), regardless of the patient himself, then we would be pleased and want nothing better. Many important conditions in medicine are still a mystery to us: we do not know their causes; sometimes we are not familiar with their clinical course; often we search blindly and mostly in vain for any treatment, appropriate even if only mildly useful. Yet this is how medicine progresses − in fits and starts, and by paying attention to the illness, not to the patient.

So much for the defence of the model. It is a very strong defence, and we could elaborate on it to quite some length. But we leave this to the adherents of *the* model. We, instead, now move to the attack. But first the question: why, in the first place, should we blame the medical model, which (we admit) has served medicine so well in the past?

The charge against the medical model is that it is 1) an illusion, and 2) too mechanistic. First the illusion. The medical model makes us seek the description of an entity called the disease. We only see a suffering person and already we pronounce, 'there is a disease here, and we should find it'. But, 'a disease' is an abstraction; there is no such thing as 'a disease'; there are only sick people, and sick people are diseased; but to conclude from this that diseases exist, is like concluding that colours exist as distinct from objects which are coloured. The question, does redness exist? has occupied philosophy for thousands of years and is still not settled, yet even the most ardent defenders of the existence of the abstraction redness, do agree that no redness exists within the confines of space and time. Every medical student, upon finishing medical school, is struck by the fact, that often patients are diagnosed as having this or that 'disease' (the jargon even identifies the two, so that a doctor may all too often call an ulcer patient by the nickname 'ulcer', which is, indeed, equally unpalatable in physical medicine as in psychiatry). Now, first of all a disease is not a diagnosis, i.e. not a set of symptoms and signs. And, indeed, a patient 'diagnosed' as a disease X will seldom if ever have the list of signs and symptoms which characterise the disease. Often, more often than not, it is logically impossible for a disease to be identical with its diagnosis, since there are alternative possible diagnoses characterising almost any given disease.

Of course, this objection is well known. One need not be an expert in differential diagnosis to know that there is many a slip between the diagnosis of a patient as having the disease X, and his having the disease X. This is clearly expressed by the frequent correction of the diagnosis or even by its initial wording: not the patient has, or is, an X, but rather he is or has a typical, a classic, a characteristic, a textbook case of, a problematic or an unproblematic diagnosis of, X. Now diagnosis is at times − by far not always − precise enough. If the classic diagnosis of X is clearly − often people say it is clearly but do not check − a definite unique set of symptoms and signs, then, and only then, being a classical X or having a classical X, is logically equivalent to a given specific diagnosis of the disease in question.

The conscientious novice who may be disturbed by the confusion of a diagnosis with a disease and who may − it is not too difficult − work out all this for himself, would wish to check a classical case of X against the list of symptoms uniquely characterising the classical case of X. If he does this, he will discover, to his great disappointment, that the person described as a classical X, or as having a classical X, does not always conform to all the symptoms and signs of the so-called classical case of the disease. A 'classical' case is anyway rarely found, and the mere emphasis on the existence of such 'classical' cases, is evidence of their rarity. And, like many an illusion, this one is dangerous, since it leads to costly errors.

So much for the viewing of diseases as entities, and its resultant infelicity. Now, in addition to abstractness, the defect of *the* medical model which will be the running theme in the present study is its mechanistic character. Something foreign and external attacks the organism, enters it, and irritates it. Resistance ensues, forces conflict, and the disease emerges. This is a universal image of all diseases and obviously it is rather mechanistic.

The mechanistic bent of this model is best noted when one remembers that the foreign bodies able to attack the body and damage its health are bacteria and fungi, viruses and simple chemicals like toxines or solvents, simple physical objects like needles or silicon dust. There is no difference, from the viewpoint of the medical model, between a bug and a dust particle, but between a harmful bug, particle, etc., and a benign one. Indeed, a victim of a motor car accident can be proclaimed diseased due to hostile metal, or even due to high impetus, and burns are diseases due to the rapid transfer of energy, just as a victim of diphtheria is diseased due to the attack of the hostile toxin secreted by the otherwise benign klebsiella.

There is a lot of wisdom, and even far from obvious wisdom, in the medical model, if and when it properly and judiciously applies. It is far from obvious, for example, that diphtheria is no relative of tuberculosis, even though the diphtheria bacilus (klebsiella) is a cousin of the tuberculosis bacilus; that, rather, diphtheria is a cousin of certain food-poisoning, where the bug in the food creates a toxin similar to the one created by the diphtheria bug in the infant's throat. Similarly, exposure to radiation or to boiling water may cause the same burns in the patient.

But, the medical model seldom works that easily; the world simply fails to conform to so simplistic an image of disease.

We can see here the link between the two major objections to the medical model – that it is harmfully too abstract and too mechanistic. These two qualities are one and the same simplification which severly limits its application – even though at times it is nevertheless applicable, and then it is even admirably suitable: the simplest occasions even call for it. Of course, the defender of the medical model is now given an excellent occasion to retort: the model applies admirably suitably to cases which we understand, and not so to cases which we still find obscure. The obscurity is in the eye of the beholder and with the persistent attempt to apply the medical model to newer cases, we solve problems by the very success of applying the model to them suitably and accurately enough. There is no other way, the defender of the medical model will conclude.

We do not oppose the idea that the medical model may apply to innumerably many as yet unknown cases; we oppose the dogma that it must apply, in the last resort, to all cases. And certainly to say that there is no other way is to ignore the other tradition in the history of medicine which has now its success and which is antimechanistic. Indeed ever since Hippocrates rejected *the* medical model, the two models, or the two schools, kept alternating throughout the history of medicine.

Just as we do not deem the success of the medical model proof of its universality, so, we must in fairness admit, we cannot view failures to apply it as disproof. In other words, we think *the* medical model, just as its competitor, are not susceptible to empirical refutation or to empirical tests; rather, it serves as a conceptual framework for empirical studies. Nevertheless, we confess we consider a gigantic cul de sac one part of *the* medical model, namely psychopharmacology or psychochemotherapy. As we say, there may yet be a successful psychochemotherapy available, perhaps even in the near future. We feel, however, that too often trumpets were blown and drums were beaten in order to usher in new psychochemotherapeutic wonder drugs, which soon turned out to be great disappointments, and here we do blame the rather dogmatic adherence to *the* medical model − though not *the* model itself, of course − for the rather regrettable haste and incautiousness.

Thus far we only mentioned the Hippocratic opposition to '*the* current medical model'. It is now time for us to describe Hippocrates' own view. This, however, is a bit problematic, since the medical model as presented thus far, is, indeed, a current version of a more general approach. To cut things short let us ignore for a while '*the* current' model and present the two opposing conceptual frameworks as generally and as briefly as possible. We shall elaborate on them later on.

There are two easily discernible and entirely different pathological theories. On the one hand there is a theory which is a) vitalist, b) physiological, c) humoral, and d) totalist. This is a theory of synthetic pathology, relatively unconnected with the question whether a given disease is due to a foreign body or not. On the other hand there is a theory which is at one and the same time a) reductionist, b) anatomic, c) solidist, and d) atomistic. It is an analytic pathology applied to isolate 'entities' of 'diseases'. a) A vitalist theory, as opposed to a reductionist theory, admits biology its autonomy and its own legitimate place, rather than force it into the mold of physics. (This is not to say that all non-reductionists or vitalists endorse the élan vitale or the entelechy theory. To look for a simple component in a living system which distinguishes it from a non-living system, and to call it *the* lifeforce is by far too mechanistic.) b) A physiological theory, as opposed to an anatomical one, allows for function, rather than confines studies to forms. c) A humoral theory is a theory of harmony or balance or coordination, whereas a solidist tends to view the body's parts as replaceable, in principle, by spare-parts. (Note that blood transfusion, especially for babies with rhesus negative reaction, is a triumph for solidism:

the blood 'solids' are replaced: Yet as late as in 1972 H. Laborit has declared that many patients die because their physicians look, rather mechanically, into their intercellular situation and ignore their cellular situation.) Indeed, surgeons are the most obvious victims of naive solidism. d) The totalism of the one theory is opposed to the atomism of the other. Atomists will recommend replacing a damaged part: totalists will rather stress the functional substitution value of an organ, rather than the replaceability of an organ by an artificial part or by a transplant: if possible he will replace function rather than organ.

Now Hippocratism is presented as a standard and early target of ridicule in most histories of biology and of medicine. True. Hippocrates himself is there highly complemented, and for diverse reasons, but his most general views are regularly dismissed off-hand. In particular, his humoralism is dismissed on the poor ground that his doctrine of the four or five humors is obviously false. Now the old four humors theory is one thing, and humoralism quite another, just as any silly old and defunct mechanistic theory is one thing and mechanism quite another. Hippocrates offered both the humoralist conceptual framework and a specific humoral theory. The latter was overthrown, and as current prejudice has it, the former is defunct too. This is false both in principle (conceptual frameworks are seldom testable) and in fact (humoralism is as perennial as atomism).

The prevalence of the mechanistic bias or of *the* current medical model, and the resultant rejection of vitalism (as opposed to the mechanistic view, of course) is quite understandable. Yet the mechanistic disrespect for vitalism forces us to glance at the history of medicine before we can proceed with our business. Yet we must, again, remind the reader that this study is not intended to be historical. Even an attempt to present here an adequate historical background to the contemporary scene seems to us to be beyond our present ability, and a task requiring a volume all to itself. Yet we hope the reader indulges us if we devote a few amateurish pages to an isolated historical figure, and an ancient one at that.

2. HIPPOCRATES

One can say that what made modern medicine modern, i.e. qualitatively different from ancient medicine, is the discovery of preventive medicine (asepsis in medicine and in nutrition), the use of anaesthetics, and bacteriology.

Of course, the experimental method in medicine is always praised for whatever advances and breakthroughs medicine ever made, and for reasons too obvious to articulate. The obviousness of the reasons, however, suggests that the method itself is as old as the hills — only the sophisticated elaborations on it are not. Now many historians of science declare that the ancient and mediaevel scientists were opposed to experimentation. This is a myth which can be refuted by simple checking in the relevant literature. Certainly Hippocrates himself found it too tedious to advocate experiments and observations.

Admittedly, there were taboos against certain experiments and observations, in the Middle Ages, perhaps even in antiquity. They never stopped the curious; they only risked his life and reputation, and gave him in return a magical status to use or abuse. Indeed, Hippocrates most famous view, famous because favourably viewed by historians of all colours, is his dislike for the magical tinge of medicine as illustrated best, but not only, in his view that holy madness — usually viewed as epilepsy, but really mental illness in general — is in no way sacred and has no connection at all with any sanctity.

Historians of science and/or medicine at times notice that it is a bit funny to declare the great recent advances in medicine as due to so obvious an idea as that we should experiment, yet they are reluctant to ascribe success to anything else — not even to some specific experimental techniques (as opposed to the experimental method in general). They note that the desirability of experimentation was commonplace, even the desirability of proper experimentation, i.e. careful, quantitative, etc. Yet, they say, no one quite knew how to properly conduct an experiment before the Scientific Revolution took place. The Scientific Revolution added the idea that all experiment is worthless unless performed by an unprejudiced observer. And an observer is indeed prejudiced as long as he comes to the laboratory with his own preconceived opinions.

There is truth in this view, which incidentally was invented by Sir Francis Bacon early in the seventeenth century: we all know that a dogmatist will rather dismiss evidence which goes contrary to his principles than given them up. Yet, on the whole, we cannot believe either that anyone can be as utterly unprejudiced as Bacon required, or that everyone in medicine was so prejudiced before the nineteenth century that medicine had to lag so much behind physics and even biology.

We dismiss, therefore, the idea that experimentalism as such is new, and ascribe the novelty of the breakthroughs in modern medicine (not to experimentalism as such but) to specific ideas and techniques. We can say, then, quite generally and perhaps a bit too crudely, that doctors before the great breakthroughs, in Western Europe as elsewhere, could not do much more than doctors in Antiquity. Doctors in the times of Hippocrates possessed no such tools, as we normally associate with medicine today, no tools at all, except for applying poultices, bleeding, fasting and commanding rest. A few plants useful to medicine existed; but their usefulness was very limited. In such circumstances the doctor's trouble really was that he was unable to do anything. Disease was thus understood as something supernatural, caused by evil spirits. From this emerged the treatment, largely composed of magic and witchcraft, and/or healing in sacred places, such as temples. One tends to refer to this kind of medicine as irrational, in comparison to modern medicine, and enlist Hippocrates' help in a pointless campaign against it. Now we cannot dismiss offhand ancient medicine as an irrational mode of treatment. If one is a believer in magic, namely in the claim that certain effects can be achieved on application of certain specific acts of magic, then it is rational for him to act accordingly. Moreover, the belief in this or that magical effect may be rational to this or that degree, depending on many factors. No doubt, on the whole, the more one applies the method of empirical examination, the less prone one is to believe in magic. And, perhaps, magic as a general metaphysical system cannot be empirically tested at all, as argued by the anthropologists James J. Frazer and E.E. Evans-Pritchard or by the methodologists Michael Polanyi and K.R. Popper.

One might jump to the conclusion that any acceptance of an untestable metaphysical theory by a scientist is a crime of jumping to conclusions and prejudicing all one's future researches. This view we strongly resist. We admit that a cursory reading about Hippocrates in a traditional Baconian history of science offers the impression that he rejected magic as such, perhaps also magic as a framework, that he also rejected all frameworks as frameworks, and in the name of strict Baconian empiricism. But the point we are going to make in this section is precisely that Hippocrates did not reject all frameworks as such but rather exchanged one for another. And our peculiar interest here is precisely rooted in our claim that the framework Hippocrates endorsed, or perhaps originated, is generalism. (The *Corpus Hippocraticum* is notoriously not the work of one man but of a whole school of thought, they say; of course, clearly, it is not one but two schools! Therefore it is impossible to discover the background to Hippocrates' development[1].) And the generalist model or framework is the one that today antipsychiatrists are proud to have invented.

Back to magic. Our claim is that magic was popular among physicians all through the ages. Even when the externalist model or framework won in the

---

1.   Sir Karl Popper, in his classic 'Back to the Pre-Socratics', reprinted in his *Conjectures and Refutations*, notes that you cannot have a proper history of ideas before you have standards of explicit criticism that ousts surreptitious change. He says this à propos of Pythagoras, whose case is shrouded in myth; the case of Hippocrates is quite the same.

natural sciences, and by accretion (and through Sydenham's influence, see below), in physical medicine too, even then the magical attitude remained supreme in the mental department of medicine.

And so, as far as magic is concerned, there is no difference between ancient medicine and much of later medicine until fairly recently; let us repeat here that even after the concept of the disease as supernatural was discarded due to mechanism, medical opinion still regarded one part of the disease as supernatural, viz. mental illness. It was not until the Enlightenment and the French Revolution that mental illness was freed by some pioneers of its supernatural aura.

Indeed, the very debate we are summing up here, between mechanism or externalism and vitalism or generalism, was largely possible due to the survival of magic, though largely repressed because of the fear of magic. There is no doubt that externalism, which we oppose, is a decent important theory to be assessed on its merits and defects. Yet we must also observe that the appeal of externalism for many is just its remoteness from magic. That is to say, if externalism is true, then clearly magic is wider of the mark than if generalism is true. At least the previous sentence seems true and is admitted by many physicians of the externalist school. It is as if one tries to escape from magic as far as possible.

Now this is no argument for or against externalism, just as the possible similarity between generalism and magic is no argument for or against generalism. (The similarity, incidently, was repeatedly noted by certain philosophers who consider the concept of the whole mystical and so smacking of magic.) It may be amusing, however, to note that at least in one respect similarity goes the other way: 19th century externalism led naturally enough to the view that mental illness is physical brain damage or some such. This hypothesis attracted even its greatest detractor, Sigmund Freud, and was authoritatively advocated early in this century by Kraepelin − the great authority on psychosis to date. And, this hypothesis is nearer to the magical view of the madman as possessed by external force and so not his own (human) self.

But enough of that. We mention it so as to keep the hostility to magic out of the present study, or, if we cannot fully do so, at least do so partially. Also, a by-product of this discussion, we hope, is the elimination of the widespread and naive view that since Hippocrates was opposed to magic, he was an externalist: whether he was or not is a matter of further historical investigation, not of a deduction from the historical fact that Hippocrates claimed that epilespy is not divine, but caused by natural causes.[1.] Why he denied that a disease was supernatural in origin, still remains a mystery, but nevertheless he did (and in doing so he indeed became the pioneer of medicine). We can also conclude that he regarded all diseases as natural — since this is an obvious result of his theory that 'nature is curative' — referring to nature as causal. For, obviously, what supernatural causes do, nature herself is powerless to undo.

What did Hippocrates mean by the phrase 'nature is curative'? Or, we can also ask, how come that he discarded magic? (We mean in principle; we deny that he managed to exorcize all instances of magic from his medicine.) We do not know the answer, but the fact remains that he did discard magic (in principle). In so doing, we have seen, he lost a frame of reference, within which it was possible and quite customary to understand the disease (as is still customary in most societies except Western society). This frame of reference was replaced by another, namely the theory of humours. This theory of humours is a version of a more general theory — that of equilibrium; of inner equilibrium, that is. Thus, 'nature is curative' can be explained by the claim that equilibrium is natural, and subsequently that when nature is distorted, nature adjusts accordingly. It is not easy to see at a glance the difference that comes about when the switch is made from magic to generalism, or even from externalism to generalism for that matter. After all, whether a spirit invades our body or a bacterium, it is obvious that the invasion itself need not cause any malady — the spirit or the bacterium may well be benign. Hence, the invader causes a malady other than by his very invasion, and that is the distortion of the body's balance or harmony. What, then, is so special to generalism?

The answer is rooted in Hippocrates' slogan 'nature is curative' (and this is why we take him to be an arch generalist): in non-Hippocratic medicine, the disease was regarded as disturbed equilibrium, while for Hippocrates the disease was a combination of both the distortion and the attempt to restore the equilibrium.

That is to say, a disequilibrium itself need not be a disease, either in a case where the tendency towards equilibrium quickly overcomes it or where the tendency yields and instead of a patient we have a person with inferior balance — maimed, chronically ill, asthenic, constitutionally feeble, or even defective from birth. The disease is, then, the ill balance plus the battle to regain balance.

The maintenance of the balance or harmony or equilibrium, can be regarded as health, though, of course, different people may be in different

---

1. Hippocrates — i.e. the corpus — did not deny that nature itself is divine, of course, encompassing all illness. This seeming contradiction has aroused much pointless scholarly dispute. See in this connection the delightful small book by Erwin Schrödinger, *Nature and the Greeks*.

levels of balance and so in constant but different levels of health. This is one of the basic cornerstones of modern medicine. 'La fixité du milieu intérieur' was the apt phrase coined by Claude Bernard: 'the fixity of internal environment is the condition for free and independent life'. Modern works on homeostasis – on the maintenance of balance – as that of W.B. Cannon, the inventor of the term 'homeostasis', and that of H. Selye on stress, are natural extensions of Claude Bernard's theory of la fixité du milieu intérieur. We shall return to all that in greater detail when studying the modern part of the perennial debate between externalism and generalism.

In parenthesis, one could add that Hippocrates' concept of the humor is manifested in modern concepts not only in general, but also in details such as the buffer systems, hormones, intra tissular or inter cellular liquids. But these details are much less important than they seem. For, we are loathe to commend Hippocrates for and only for any agreement he has with the standard up-to-date medical textbook: these similarities may indeed be purely accidental, and worshipping them even though they may be accidental is rather silly. Alternatively they are linked with inner logic, but since most medicine since the days of Hippocrates is forgotten and extinct, there can be no logical connection between these modern details and any ancient ones, except through the general conceptual metaphysical perennial framework.

So much for theory. Still, in the day of Hippocrates, in practical matters there was little that could be done, as far as practical medicine was concerned. Of course from times immemorial to the days of the modern breakthroughs physicians were extremely active. They used poultices as well as cupping and leeches and other methods of bleeding; they fed patients with all sorts of horrid diets, usually emetic, purgatives, diuretic, and perspiratives. All these were usually harmless and at times, especially with bleeding and overdoses of potent herbs (such as digitalis), even harmful. They were seldom useful except for quinine, digitalis, etc. and perhaps also some vitamins. Except for these there was surgery, mostly bone settings and amputations (including the cutting of tumors), and tooth extractions. There were also adjacent activities – child delivery (including caesarean) the closing of wounds (including cauterizing), and last but not least, the handling of poisons and of antidotes which were administrated by all sorts of paramedicals.

The question, then, must be raised, was there a practical difference between magic and generalism? (We shall discuss the same question later regarding generalism and externalism, indeed we shall do so repeatedly.) The answer must still stay with Hippocrates' maxim 'nature is curative'. For, it says, do as little as you can, and when in doubt don't. This is closely linked with the Hippocratic maxim, primarily do no harm to your patients: the maxim is not meant to exclude intentional harm, of course, but quite unintentional, indeed one full of good intentions.

It was but as a derivative of Hippocrates' theory of nature as curative that he devised his own way of careful meticulous method of observation: it was his wish to study nature so as to imitate nature whereever possible. This is another realm where modern clinical medicine could still learn from Hippocrates. For, though we are all for experiments and observations, the externalist's empirical method differs from that of the generalist and there is room for fruitful debate here. Since Hippocrates' clinical observational methods were not closely followed by a larger sector of medicine, the question arises, why? We shall return to this later, when we shall describe the triumph of externalism, and then argue that there is room today also for Hippocratic generalism in empirical studies.[1.]

The reader may be dismayed by the fact that throughout the whole of this section we have made use of only three clear-cut specific historical details regarding Hippocrates. Of course, there is much more handed down to us as the *Corpus Hippocraticum.* How much of it is Hippocratic, how much of it is Hippocratic yet reluctantly so, we do not know. We do know that even much later, Hippocratists, such as Sydenham, Stahl and Boerhaave conceded to popular medicine and endorsed dubious medications and treatments. Indeed, it strikes us as odd that Sydenham who advocated the prescription of simple potions, himself prescribed very complex ones — though much simpler than common in his day. And so, it is really useless for us to cite Hippocrates unless we think the cited passage represents something peculiar to the man. We did not cite all we could, even in that direction.

For example, we think, contrary to the majority of historians of medicine who are externalists, that his advocacy of cleanliness is not an expression of an externalist fear of dirt (externalists do not fear the food or medicine or placeboes which they prescribe), much less something to be commended by the standard of the up-to-date-science-textbook-worshipper. Rather, we think it was a generalist view that here we can prevent something which may do harm and certainly can do no good.

Moreover, quite possibly, Hippocrates connected the internal balance with the balance of Man with the environment. This would explain both his epidemiological interest and his interest in broad environmental factors which

---

1.   Our bold speculative hypothesis is, in line with Popper's 'Back to the Pre-Socratics', that Western medicine begins not with externalism, as most historians suggest, nor even with generalism, which is more Oriental than Occidental, but with both.

may pertain to health and epidemics. But all this is frankly speculative. And so, we do not wish to impress the reader with a semblance of completeness or of finality. We are no historians and we have merely tried to present generalism on its lowest, least scientifically informed level; and we think that for this Hippocrates is the proper starting point. We hope historians of science will do a better job at examining our hypothesis that Hippocrates was indeed the first significant generalist. What we mean here can be explained in the following manner. The constants of each organism have their fixed values, or limits at which a certain level of health is maintained. The organism has a certain degree of leeway in which to adapt to external pressures or forces in its efforts to maintain health. When the organism is no longer able to adapt itself within the given limits, it falls prey to these external forces, and is harmed; it tries to recover and is then said to be diseased; this condition sets up new limits of its own, within which the organism has to fight for survival or at least to prevent the disease from spreading so as to maintain control. When this last and vital function fails, deterioration or death results. If the disease ends otherwise, a new level of balance is attained.

We should mention here, to complete the picture, the Hippocratic idea of crisis or turning point. Whereas most writers mention the crisis or turning point of a disease as an empirically observed fact, we deem it a highly theoretical construct, and one which generalism yields most naturally. Moreover, we explain the strange and obvious error of deeming the crisis an observed fact by the observation that, as the theoretical construct that the crisis obviously is, it has no place in externalism: once the crisis is obvious yet not theoretical, then, clearly it must be an empricial matter. That it is not empirical can be seen from the very impossibility of describing it as a general observation. That is, if health is a balance of factors, and ill health an ill balance plus a struggle to regain balance, then the turning point will be obviously noted as the point of return of balance or of an arrival at a new balance (possibly death). The empirical part of this generalist idea is that in some cases different outcomes result from stuggles which take the same course along a large portion of the way, and then differ and diverse dramatically, only at a very late point. Thus, case histories of recovery and of death may be at times, but only at times, very similar almost all the way through to the last day (or rather night) of the disease. As we shall see, this led the generalist Sydenham to study diseases as entities, a quaint idea that has a history of its own. (Incidentally, some historians of ideas treat certain ideas or themes as entities with lives of their own.)

3. SYDENHAM

Thomas Sydenham was 'the English Hippocrates', indeed the Hippocrates of the Scientific Revolution. For historians of medicine he is an embarrassment and a pain in the neck, as evidenced from the fact that they make so much of the fact that he advocated experiments. After all, in this he was preceeded by the greatest 17th century authority, and the greatest advocate of the experimental philosophy of the day, Robert Boyle, who many historians think was the father of the Royal Society of London. John Fulton, the famous 20th century Yale physiologist and biliophile has made it general knowledge, through his *Bibliography of Robert Boyle,* that Boyle was all his adult life engaged in medicine and experimented extensively with medications − much of it on his own body. To say that Sydenham's main contribution was the advocacy of experiment, is thus to say that he made no contribution.

The second attribution to Sydenham is of the maxime: Nature is curative; primarily do not harm the patient. This is Hippocratic, indeed, but it is hardly greatness to quote Hippocrates.

What, then, if anything, was great about Sydenham's teachings? H. Sigerist thinks that Sydenham's differentiation between symptomata essentialia and symptomata accidentalia, in the analysis of disease, is of importance. Sydenham, he said, 'distinguished two groups of symptoms: symptomata essentialia which means the symptoms caused by the lesion, and symptomata accidentalia which refer to the symptoms caused by the reaction to the lesion. When a finger is burnt, tissular parts are destroyed by the action of heat. We observe phenomena directly derived from the lesion. The atrophied tissularly parts play the part of a foreign body in the organism which reacts, eliminates them and replaces them by new cells. Thus we observe a whole syndrome which is the expression of this reaction. According to Syndenham's concept, the clinical picture of the burn is thus composed of some symptoms caused by the lesion, and others by the reaction. In numerous cases it is extremely difficult to say into which group one has to classify this or the other symptom.' So much for Sigerist.

Now, of course, the very distinction between essential and accidental qualities is Aristotelian. The distinction between primary and secondary symptoms is as old as differential diagnosis, and we can hardly believe that the ancients were unfamiliar with it, in specific examples as well as in general. What remains, in the above attribution by Sigerist to Sydenham specifically or originally Sydenham's, is the identification of the primary with the essential and the secondary with the accidental. It is hard to say much more on the topic because (Aristotelian) essentialism is notoriously obscure and was, indeed, attacked at great length as obscure, especially in medicine, by Robert Boyle. This, however, can be said: for disease to have essential qualities at all, it must have an essence of its own, and so be an entity. This quaint idea, is indeed, Sydenham's. Sigerist knew this, of course, but praised him not for the quaint idea but for its corollary that seemed to him more reasonable (though not as original).

For an externalist the disease appears to be something foreign to the organism (external), and as such is a trauma; a morbid condition caused by a wound; literally, a wound. For a generalist, like Sydenham, where the external and internal factors are reciprocal, the disease appears to be a process. It is of interest that Sydenham, in his drifting towards generalism, uses the analytical approach, and so, at least in part, can be viewed as an externalist; whether his externalism was consistent with his generalism or not is another question. Even in his already mentioned distinction between those symptoms which he considers essential and those he considered accidental, even in this respect he is an atomist, anatomist, and perhaps finally a reductionist, and so conspiciously an externalist. However, he continues to overhaul and revise his ideas and perhaps tried to reintegrate what he previously dissected into a totality. We shall not discuss how successful he was in the last resort in this process of reintegration – there is no last resort anyway. It is as though Sydenham employed two contrary modes – of first dividing, and then reassembling or reintegrating the data. If so, then he was acting very much according to the fashion of the period, which advocated resolution and composition or analysis and synthesis, a fashion current in all the sciences of the time. One would expect this fashion to be stronger in the life sciences than in physics. History, however, does not oblige. It seems that for the externalist only the first part of this movement is of importance, for the generalist the reintegration is more important since it comprises more than the (externalist's) idea of the assembly of parts into a mechanism.

Nowhere was the clash between generalism and externalism in the thought of Sydenham sharper than in the view of disease. On the one hand for him a disease, no matter 'how prejudicial soever its causes may be to the body, is no more than a vigorous effort of Nature to throw off the morbific matter'; on the other hand it is the same 'morbific matter' in the abstract. In viewing the disease as a perpetual interaction between external and internal forces, a generalist could conclude and even emphasise that health is, in parallel with disease, a satisfactory interaction between external and internal forces. It is as though when no harmful results are apparent we could speak of a state of health, and when an interaction of forces produces harm, we refer to the visible reaction as disease. Here the following concepts are employed: consider simultaneously the virulence of the external force − call it the micro-organisms if you must be up-to-date − and the degree of resistance of the organism, and again, as in the conceptual scheme of Hippocrates, you find yourself thinking in terms of equilibrium and harmony.

We have already hinted that perhaps Hippocrates himself viewed both health and disease in the same manner, thus being drawn into the consideration of healthy and unhealthy states of human communities in their environment. Sydenham, too, had epidemiological interests intertwined with recommendations of cleanliness. It is hard to judge how much this connects logically with his study of illness and of symptoms, especially since these are of the rather externalist ilk. Epidemiology is not easy to assess even regarding later and clearer thinkers. Take for example, Hughlings Jackson, who also differentiated two kinds of symptoms. He distinguished between the negative and the positive symptoms where the negative symptoms emanate from traumatic causes, i.e. are primary, and the positive are results of previously inhibited functions, i.e. are secondary. The disease itself, then, is a mixture of both negative and postive symptoms, since either kind can throw the body out of balance. Jackson's distinction is more modern than Sydenham's: it is historical, evolutionary, diachronic, whereas Sydenham's is synchronic. Yet for both thinkers some symptoms are compensatory parts of the process of healing, of fighting the primary symptoms, as being a part of the totality, which is the state of disease.

For, what may be ascribed to all generalists, whether Hippocrates, Sydenham, Jackson, or others, but is perhaps more of our understanding of their ideas than theirs, is the idea of compensation as a general idea of any kind of attempt at regaining equilibrium. Some compensation easily follows the generalist conception, e.g. one kidney overworks when the other is defective. Yet at times compensation is readjustment, perhaps to a new kind, or even a new (low) level, of equilibrium. This then, is a generalist antiexternalist conception. The regaining of equilibrium or the compensation may at times be more successful at times less, and the successful readjustment may be at a reasonably high level or at an unacceptably low one. Yet quite generally, regaining of balance may be a restoration of a prior state or a compensation for some lost part, or a readjustment of every small part of the whole. A simple example, indeed, is fever, understood by all generalists throughout history in the same broad manner, yet presented broadly as a general pattern of the diverse 'fevers' by Sydenham for the first time.

The principle of compensation, then, says that some seemingly morbid signs and symptoms result from beneficial or partly beneficial compensations for ills not restored to the original situation which give different or no signs and symptoms.

The generalist idea that health is an interaction of factors (in which the result is not harmful) is further enlarged upon by Claude Bernard. He speaks of the fixity of the internal environment. By this he means the constancy of the pH of the blood, the inner temperature, oxygen saturation, etc. − all the factors which Walter B. Cannon later considered parts of the homeostasis. Bernard says that the effort to keep constants constant is the whole business of life. 'The fixity of internal environment is the condition of free, independent life'. These constants are kept at an even level (constant) as a result of operating forces which direct the pH of the blood, body temperature, oxygen saturation, etc. to within their limits of fixed values. Outside of these limits of the fixed values, death results.

Now, we do not wish to read Cannon into Bernard or Bernard and Jackson into Sydenham. We only indicate that it is extremely easy to read successors into works of their true predecessors and that it is precisely when succeeding to avoid such reading that we find it easier to understand the predecessors. This peculiar situation is not specific to these thinkers. It is specific to any series of thinkers sharing a metaphysical framework. The later thinkers simply exhibit the framework more clearly and illustrate it with better details. It is the shared framework, then, usually the shared metaphysical framework, that links predecessors and successors. Hence, when avoiding reading modern generalists into Sydenham we gain insight into the generalist Sydenham at the cost of ignoring Sydenham the externalist.

In conclusion, we hope we can repeat the same apology we have offered in the case of Hippocrates. We have not attempted here a historical study of Sydenham, but used a few scraps of his to illustrate a line of a generalist development. In doing so, we have managed, we hope, to raise afresh and more poignantly the reader's doubts as to the significance, or even validity, of our generalist-externalist distinction. Not only do we find the generalist Sydenham doing clearly externalist pieces of work, but we show that the very idea of homeostasis, now a paradigm of externalism, was developed by a tradition of generalists, culminating with the generalist Cannon. More on this soon.

4. CLAUDE BERNARD AND PASTEUR

Our historical sketch is both very scanty and very fragmented. We chose to speak of Hippocrates in order to illustrate the antiquity of generalism and its most basic tenets. We next chose Sydenham as one who reviewed and began to elaborate on generalism. Others followed suit, such as Stahl, Boerhaave, Cullen, Brown, Laënnec, and their disciples. We shall not dwell on them. We hasten to open a discussion of modern generalism by discussing a towering, explicit, detailed unquestioned generalist. We chose Claude Bernard. He turns out to be problematic: is he an externalist or is he a generalist? Since so much of modern new research goes back to his 1856 *Introduction to Experimental Medicine,* this is no idle question.

The reader may think it finicky to ask in an introductory historical sketchy fragment, such an exegetic question as, was Claude Bernard − or anyone else for that matter − an externalist or a generalist. Let us assure him that this question is a very general and important one. The division into generalist versus externalist in the whole of medical history, or in the most contemporary of today's medical researches, is indeed elusive and problematic. We shall have repeatedly on our hands the question, who, if anyone, is a generalist?

On viewing Claude Bernard at first glance, one may gain the impression that he obviously is an externalist: he unites biological phenomena by reducing them to physico-chemical reactions. For example, he reduces both vegetables and animals to the same mode of respiration; this way he assimilates animal heat to combustion better than his predecessors. Indeed, the title of his famous work *Phénomèns communs* speaks volumes.[1] As he says there, 'the discoveries of physics and of biochemistry established that an intimate accord, a perfect harmony, exists between the vital activity and the intensity of physico-chemical phenomena.'

But a more profound view of Claud Bernard's work, indeed of the very passage just quoted, may yield the insight of him as possibly a generalist. Indeed, while there are some vital phenomena which one should reduce to the physico-chemical realm, there is an additional dimension in the physico-chemical world, which is not physico-chemical: this is the organization principle. He says, 'life is organization in action'. He quotes Lamarck to say, 'the state of affairs of life is organization'. To these Bernard adds: 'The

---

1.   *Lecons sur les phénomèns de la vie communs aux animaux et aux végétaux,* Paris, 1885. All translations are ours.

structure is not a property of the physico-chemic realm. ... it supposes a cause of itself'. One can only characterize living organizations by comparing them to brute or inert matter. And this comparison yields seven characteristics of living matter which differentiate it from inert matter, all of which are of a distinct generalistic flavour. These are: organization, generation, nutrition, evolution, caducity (= fleeting nature; literally, ability to fall off), disease, and mortality. They all have to do with the physico-chemical realm, but possess that special additonal characteristic, which stems from the principle of organized matter (la matière organisée): 'Organization results from a melange of complex substances that gives birth to the properties of life.' It is a very special and very complex arrangement, 'but one which nonetheless obeys the general laws of chemistry of the grouping of matter. The vital properties are in reality but the physico-chemical properties of organized matter.' So far for organization.

The second characteristic of living bodies is their capacity of reproduction; it is generation, or evolution; this 'is perhaphs the most remarkable trait of living organisms, and consequently of life'. 'The organized living being has a tendency to reestablish itself in its form, to repair its mutilations, to cauterise its wounds, to have its unity proven thus, its morphological individuality.' 'This tendency to realise and to repair a kind of an individual architectural plan,' 'kind of a small world in the big one' is what gives the organized creature a characteristic of being a harmonious totality. Here we have the Hippocratic view of nature as curative as well as the mystic doctrine of Man as microcosmos, so favoured by all generalists up to Cannon and beyond.

The third characteristic of life, according to Claude Bernard, is nutrition. While he did reduce nutrition to a physico-chemical process, namely combustion, he still saw it as a phenomenon of the formal permanence of the living being. 'Nutrition is the continuous mutation of the particles which constitute the living being. The organic edifice is the site of a perpetual nutritional movement which incessantly works upon each part.'

But while Claude Bernard sees nutrition as that special characteristic of life, which indeed can be added to the physico-chemical realm, he nonetheless emphasizes the importance of the latter, without which life cannot even begin to exist. 'One cannot 'capture' this interior vital principle, isolate it, or act upon it. One sees, on the contrary, that the vital functions constantly have physico-chemical circumstances as conditions which are external and perfectly determined'. Here, thus, is the final conclusion: 'The vital whirlpool is not a unique manifestation of a quid intus, nor the only effect of external physico-chemical conditions. Life will not, in consequence, be exclusively characterized by the only vitalist conception theory, nor by the only materialist one.'

Bernard distinguishes, thus, two orders of phenomena, the exterior physico-chemical one, and the interior, the vital one. One has to view life as consisting of these two elements: first, the phenomena of vital creativity or organized synthesis; second, the phenomena of death, or organic destruction. The first cannot be compared to anything else, nor can it be reduced to anything else, the evolutionary synthesis is the ultimate vitality: 'Life is creation.' The second, the vital destruction, is of physico-chemical origin; it is the result of combustion, a fermentation, a putrefaction. It is these phenomena which we observe, and therefore, when speaking of the phenomena of life, we indicate in reality the phenomena of death. We are never struck by the phenomena of life. The organizational synthesis is interior, silent, hidden, under its phenomenal expression — we only see directly the phenomena of organization.

It is as if between both these distinguished planes, the vital one and the physico-chemical one, that 'all creatures, animals and vegetables, maintain themselves. Both orders of action are necessary and inseparable.' In other words, 'the vital force directs phenomena which it does not produce. The physical agents produce phenomena which they do not direct.'

Bernard deduces his own views on vitalism and on materialism from the above. For him, both these conceptions are illusions. Vitalism considers life as a kind of special force. Materialism considers life as the result of the interplay of the general forces of nature. 'Science does not pronounce a verdict for the one or for the other.' Science rejects both of these hypotheses. For the vitalist, there is a 'superior and immaterial principle'. For the materialist, there is no such intervention, 'the living being goes by itself, and is moved only by the structure, arrangement and activity of universal matter'.

Just as his unification of botany and zoology as well as his reduction of vital functions to physicochemical processes seem so obviously externalist, so the above quotes seem so obviously Hippocratic. Nature cures. But just because these quotes are so obviously generalistic, it is possible to understand Bernard to be merely using some universally accepted generalistic expressions as mere modes of speech. After all, what does he say?

He says he rejects both current metaphysical systems, the materialistic or mechanistic — which is the traditional classical form of externalism — and the vitalistic — which is usually deemed the late 19th century variant of generalism but which we consider mechanistic as well. Not only that. Bernard quite generally rejects all metaphysics on general, methodological empiricist grounds. No doubt, as a citizen and as a nineteenth century man of culture, he had many opinions which he never hid, including opinions on metaphysical matters. Yet in experimental physiology, he insisted, there was no room for speculation. We must admit then that he would not have liked to be deemed a generalist.

Nevertheless, a generalist he does seem to us. For, what were his seven criteria demarcating living systems from inert matter if not generalist principles, if not regulative ideas guiding his specific research projects? It is impossible to give a unique answer to this question. We, the authors of the present study, will unhesitatingly agree: we do think these are, or can serve as, metaphysical guiding principles. Not so Bernard himself. He met the question squarely, and gave his clear though unconvincing negative reply. His seven principles he declared, were not a priori, but based a posteriori on experience. That's all there is to it, he thought.[1.] Indeed, we may view with little effort Bernard's seven principles as a mode of reduction and so present him as an externalist par excellence.

We will not engage in exegesis in the present study. Rather, we shall skip the exegetic problem, if not leave it as an exercise to the curious and well-disposed reader, and go straight to the most forceful evidence, which is Bernard's own attitude to history's most conspicuous externalist, namely Louis Pasteur. (But was Pasteur really an externalist?)

Pasteur discovered around the middle of the century that a broken crystal heals while it grows – when put in its natural habitat of course. Pasteur explicitly took this, obviously externalist case – there can be no better externalist paradigm – as the model for the healing of wounds proper.

And Bernard agreed. Who, if not Pasteur is to be viewed as an externalist par excellence? After all, he was the founder of bacteriology, of the germ theory of disease. And, the germ theory of disease says that there is no disease without an external factor operating (adversely) upon the body. At first the external factor was the microbe and one could formulate the germ theory of disease to say that there is no disease without a microbe producing it. Yet what is to be done, in this case, with rabies, which is after all caused not by microbe, but by a virus? The fact that the virus responsible for rabies can easily be substituted for the microbes without causing any harm to the theory, shows that the germ theory is not a specific case – every disease is produced by a microbe – but a much wider, more general idea: every disease is produced by an external factor, perhaps with the rider that the only or the main external factor are microbes, especially bacteria. The same applies to diphtheria where the responsible external factor is not a bacterium nor a virus, but a special toxin

---

1.   In this section we made use of Raymond Bayer's *Epistémologie et logique* (Paris, 1954).

(which, admittedly is produced by bacteria, but the toxin is of the same kind as produced by food poisoning outside the body by similar bacteria). One sees how easily one can substitute a virus for bacterium, and toxin for virus or bacteria. In short, any external factor could be held responsible for the disease consistently with that theory, including all sorts of wounding and poisoning, etc.

A closer examination of Pasteur's germ theory, however, reveals that the above, 'every disease caused by an external factor', was not always seen by Pasteur as 'every disease caused only by an external factor'. Pasteur introduces another factor, not lesser than the external one, into the germ theory; the factor which he called constitution, or predisposition; the background of the individual upon which the external factor operates. The reason for this is all too obvious even for the most rabid externalists (thus illustrating again the difficulty we face of distinguishing externalist from generalist): There are germs that harm no-one, there are those that harm everyone of those who are afflicted with them, and there are those that harm some but not all of them. Clearly, this amounts to saying that internal constitution is a major factor in health and in disease even though disease is caused by outside factors. It seems that this internal factor is, in a way, perhaps even more important than the external one. Pasteur even asks himself if it is not truer to say that the external factor found in a special case is not the outcome, a symptom, of the disease, rather than its cause! Indeed, if a feeble constitution, predisposition,and background are necessary conditions for the external factor to operate, then and only then, it becomes an essential cause; and it is perhaps more essential than any external factor since external factors may be interchangeable!

This is no idle discussion. Many chronic illnesses are hard to diagnose because they only weaken their victims' constitutions so that the victims often fall prey to other illnesses and are then, presumably, misdiagnosed. In the histopathology of chronic inflammations there are even differences between the chronically afflicted cells and those hit by the outburst of an inflammation. Any diagnostic description of such cases must be couched in a consistent generalist or alternatively externalist language in order to be clear, yet this seldom happens.

What Pasteur calls constitution, predisposition, and background, can all too easily be translated into generalist terms. More than that: constitution, etc. is also applicable, according to Pasteur, to the process of healing. He states that the physician's role is to assist the organism in its effort to regain enough strength to fight the harmful external factors. In this he reminds us of Hippocrates' 'nature cures'.

It is undebatable that during Pasteur's life-time, and also to date, he was always regarded as an externalist. More attention by far was given his seemingly externalist views and much less to his seemingly generalist views. It was René Dubos, himself a known bacteriologist and virologist, as well as a writer of some reknown, a generalist in his views of bacteria and diseases, who alone among scholars stressed the generalism of Pasteur's views. Indeed he took the trouble to write a book on Pasteur as a generalist.

Historically, one can ask oneself, does it matter? After all, how does this relate to the contribution of a scientist to science? Is his contribution the same as his views? Which views should we ascribe to a thinker, the views he really held, or what his contemporaries − sometimes even mistakenly − understood him to have held? Obviously it is important for historians to know what a given scientist's views really were; also historians cannot easily dismiss the views professional public opinion attributes to that given scientist, even if they differ from the ones he really held. It may even be highly interesting to notice the fact − if it is a fact − that Pasteur was indeed a generalist, living in a period where externalism was dominant, and that he expressed his ideas in a language conducive to externalism thereby permitting his peers to misconstrue his ideas. But surely, what counts is his contribution, his great discoveries acknowledged as great by all parties involved. Can we, then, not leave the historical question, was Pasteur a generalist or an externalist?

Now, admittedly, one's contribution should be independent of one's views. Yet we may wish to study the generalism of one's contributions; we may hold the view that a scientist's views in general influence his specific work and so wish to find out whether he held this or that general view. And so, without going too much into exegesis we may profit from examining the question, was Pasteur an externalist or a generalist?

One difficulty is rooted in the ambiguity of the situation. A generalist may well allow certain externalist characteristics as good enough approximations of the truth. If we take even a work meant to propagate generalism, from its title to the very end, such as Charles S. Sherrington's *The Integrative Action of the Nervous System*, 1906, as an obvious example to the legitimate use of opposite ideas. He says towards the end of that celebrated volume, that 'with the nervous system intact, the reactions of the various parts of the system, the 'simple reflexes', are ever combined into great unitary harmonies, actions which in their sequence, one upon another constitute in their continuity what may be termed the 'behavior' (Lloyd Morgan) of the individual as a whole ... Our part of the problem is a humbler one. In the analysis of the animal's life as a machine in action there can be split off from its total behavior fractional pieces which may be treated conveniently, though artificially, apart ...' That is, when the animal is in good health, some of its reflexes may be artifically considered as separate from the whole, and so treated as an externalist would treat them.

But this is not all. After all, Pasteur's example of the self-healing crystal is, no doubt, congenial to the externalist. But it is only an example, a metaphor, perhaps an attempt to say that nature cures in the very externalist way. It is hard to say. Some philosophers have even questioned whether there ever can be a generalist example, properly speaking: some say the very opposite. That is to say, some externalists think that, though it is permissible to lapse on occasion into a generalist language, especially when the working of a very complex piece of machinery is involved, and more especially when we are in the dark about the details, nevertheless, strictly speaking there is no 'system', man or machine, to speak of, only parts working together or not so together as the case may be. The extreme generalist, on the contrary, say even the simplest machine, is a harmony. Sir Karl Popper goes so far (*The Poverty of Historicism,* 1957) as to say flatly that even a heap of things is a generality, an entity not reducible to its parts, as it has gradients of pressure and contours of equal pressure, etc., etc.

It is no surprise, then, that it is very difficult to pin down the externalist and the generalist, or even to identify him, even before we come to examine a particular author, such as Pasteur.

At this stage the reader will rebel, we hope, and ask, is the game worth the candle? Does it all matter who, if anybody, was what, if anything? Is it not better to let these elusive matters ride?

We must face this issue squarely. It is not our concern here, we confess, that in historical fact these elusive matters have caused much puzzlement and agony. Nor is it our concern here, we confess to much worse, to ease difficulties of students of nature, since the great students we cite are, after all, long dead and buried. Even the better and still practical relevant and live issue, how did the great students of the past harness their vague ideas to the tangible wagon of scientific and medical progress, even that issue is not quite our concern here. If it were, then this chapter would not be a historical sketch but an introduction to an ambitious case-work in history proper. Rather, throughout the present humble historical sketch we wish to heighten the reader's sensibility to the elusiveness of both externalism and generalism, and help him try and pin down some fraction of an idea as rather generalist or as rather externalist in character. This is the best sort of preliminary training we know of to any study of the very current main issue in contemporary psychiatry, namely, can we treat a patient's complaint or only the-patient-as-a-whole? But we are not quite there yet. We must now briefly speak of the rise of contemporary homeostatic theory before we can get where we aim to stay for a while. At least we hope that before we start we can tell the reader, without surprising him overmuch, that homeostasis is the strongest stronghold of externalism, yet that it was invented by generalists specifically in order to illustrate their own generalism and in sharp opposition to externalism.

The current issue, in medicine in general or in psychotherapy in particular, is often put thus: is there an illness or is there only a patient, a sick person? What is a person, physiologically and psychologically speaking? Is a person a whole or a collection of strongly interacting parts? Are these two alternatives really different? After all, it is very frustrating to be told that there is no such thing as typhoid, only the patient and the typhoid agent — salmonella typhi — and their battle: we all know that typhoid is a state, a pattern, a condition, a set of signs and symptoms which sends its host to the doctor. Why does it matter whether we talk of the patient or of the disease if all we want is his welfare? The person who first faced this tricky and frustrating question, the hero of the present study, was one John Hughlings Jackson.

5. JOHN HUGHLINGS JACKSON

Let us begin with the difference — if it at all exists — between a person as a system and a person as a collection. We already made amply clear, we hope, that each view has advantages uncontested by its opposition. Everybody agrees to this. Take the atomistic point of view of Man as a collection. A defective part of the body can at times be eliminated with obvious benefit; more so, if it can, and at times it certainly can, be replaced by an artifact or by a part removed from its natural place where its absence is less adversely felt than its presence in its new place is felt favorably. Examples are the elimination of a part of a gut which is ulcerous, and the transplant of a piece of a bone from a leg to the back of a person suffering, say, from a slipped disc; even turning a big toe to a substitute thumb. It may be deemed irrelevant to consider skingraft here, as its use is often only cosmetic. Yet a cosmetic treatment may be — at times is — just what the psychiatrist orders. Now, all this is very atomistic or externalist, as everyone will concede, and even the most ardent generalist will here use not only the externalist's terminology, but even his very way of thinking. Surprisingly, in the same vein practitioners in depth psychiatry may on occasion send a patient to a practitioner of behavior therapy.

To regain partial balance, look the other way: externalists, if they are good, are not too reluctant to use at times some generalistic ideas, approaches, and terminology. The most externalist physician who wants his drug-addict patient off drugs, will speak generally about the patient's need for general well being and relaxing surroundings, as well as for a general optimism and an aim in life. When anemia is at stake and its diagnosis not very obvious, exactly the same may happen. Indeed, sometimes the generalistic prescription for drug addicts and for anemics may be verbatim the same, and at times dished out with regularity by eminent level-headed and sincere externalists. As we have said, ignorance is the only real excuse for generalist talk accepted by the externalists, at least the extremists among them.

That much is ground-work. The debate goes on because we want to gain more ground. Where do we go from here? We tell the patient the best we know, but we know too little. The real work begins when the patient is not present and when we plan research − so as to understand better what is amiss and/or so as to help future patients better.

John Hughlings Jackson, a nineteenth-century English neurologist of the higest repute, was a disciple of the philosopher and sociologist Herbert Spencer. When speaking of his ideas on health and disease (of the central nervous system), Jackson always stressed and emphasized his personal indebtedness to Spencer for these ideas. Being a lonely generalist in a very externalist scientific-oriented society, doomed him to isolation, and his contributions were almost unnoticed at the time. They were meant to serve as important guiding or regulative principles for research in neurophysiology and in clinical neurology no less; and they were meant to be − how successfully they were, must remain an open question − generalist principles par excellence. As we have repeatedly indicated, health is for the generalist, from times immemorial, the harmonious, well-functioning state of the organism; illness is the attempt of the organism to regain harmony; and defectiveness, not illness, is but the organism's willingness to settle for a lower level of functioning, and thus, all the same, of functioning in some sort of equilibrium. Jackson went further and spoke of these levels of organization as given elements or aspects within the system, in any of these states. Briefly, he saw life as a hierarchy of levels of organization. And this aspect of his view is by now outmoded. It so happens, however, that without this aspect his theory is much improved, and for the following reason.

Jackson's chief and innovative idea was that levels are not some mystic entities imposed by observers on complex networks of self-consistent parts, but geneuine characteristics of the complex system no less real than the parts that go into it. Once we commit the cardinal philosophical sin − by the philosophical canons of the externalist or the atomist, of course − and reify or hypostatize such things as balances or !evels of organization or degrees of harmony, once we willingly commit what Whitehead called the fallacy of misplaced concreteness, and Jackson's idea is easy to grasp. Indeed, in these days of cybernetics it is quite commonplace. But as long as we are afraid of committing this sin, even tentatively and only in thought, then he becomes hopelessly obscure.

Well, then, if levels are things − and, contrary to his view they need not be hierarchically ordered − then they do not vanish. Whatever happens, then, to one level when it is overtaken by another? Of course, the one is called low and the other high, but the ordering is only local or partial and so the terms should be used gingerly. Of course, the higher level is the one which, when in conflict, inhibits the lower level. Now, if the higher level is damaged, i.e. wounded or maimed, or if it is eliminated or killed, then the lower level is released. The terms 'inhibit' and 'release' are used here very specifically, in a very highly context-dependent technical sense; they are Jackson's innovation.

Now, so far so good; we have presented a defective system that is not sick but in a low level equilibrium. We have thereby gained one or two new insights. The first is this: the new level of equilibrium which a defective individual organism settles for may be an atavism, an old level in that organism's ontogenesis or phylogenesis. This does not mean that the defective individual organism in question is always, exactly and generally, on the old level, because bits and pieces of the higher level of equilibrium may still be serviceable even if the higher level itself is demolished as a whole and because the low level is transformed and for many other possible reasons. (The view of the lower level as both ontogenetically and phylogenetically older is another peculiarity of Jackson, now superseded, rooted in 19th century evolutionism in general and, more particularly, in the 19th century view that ontogeny recapitulates phylogeny.)

Nevertheless, the idea is useful, that when a system slips, i.e. slips back, it possibly slips to a pre-existing lower niche − unless this niche is damaged too, or unless this niche is greatly altered anyway − and so the system must slip a peg further. Of course, we still can ask, what are these pre-existing niches. We do not know. Jackson tells us that they exist and enjoins us to look for them. His idea, we have said, is a regulative principle for research.

Second, and much more exciting, is this. If the higher level of equilibrium is demolished, we have a defective organism on some lower level of equilibrium. If, however, the higher level is not demolished but merely damaged, then, we remember, the organism or the system does not settle for the lower level but is struggling to regain the higher level. Where is the system, equilibrium-wise, when ill? Of course, the question is illegitimate: illness is defined as a lack of balance plus a struggle for regaining it. Yet, we can say, while the struggle goes on, the system is in a quasi-balance: its disorganisation has a lower bound and perhaps also a (moveable) center of action. Where is the center of action which directs the struggle? How is the balance of the struggle itself maintained? What happens to the normal functioning of the body while it fights?

Before we address these questions we must notice that we have slipped: we no longer speak a purely generalist language, but have taken recourse to an externalist artificial device of splitting the functions of the damaged organism or system to two: normal and fighting. Yet we can proceed, at least pro-tem, on this fiction, and say this. The normal functions of a sick system may stay in a stable equilibrium on a low level of organization, they may unstably stay on a higher level, and, finally, the struggle that goes on between the system's curative forces and the pathogenic forces (internal or external) is with no equilibrium and no stability.

Our question is, and remains, are Jackson's principles essentially generalist? After all, we admit that a generalist may endorse some externalist ideas, and so it may similarly happen that an externalist would endorse a generalist idea. Would he, then, also endorse Jackson's principles?

Before discussing this question, we must notice that the principles are limited, that seemingly they are false. Jackson himself noted that there exist situations − he cites epilepsy as an example − where a lower center is damaged yet the damage is transmitted to a higher center, quite contrary to his principles of the containment of the damage as far as possible, and by reorganization if need be. Even if we give up the idea of hierarchy, in epilepsy the idea of containment is violated too; and giving it up Jacksonism is so impoverished as to be worthless.

The Jacksonian answer is obvious: a seeming refutation of Jackson's principles would hint at a way to rectify the fault and so to make a new discovery. In our example, the case of an epilepsy of the lower centers, where the sub-cortical centers discharge electricity, the principles tell us that the sub-cortical damage is possibly prceded by a cortical one; in that case the epilepsy is, indeed, a grand mal. Moreover, presumably the epileptic fit is an attempt of the system to regain control. Perhaps, then, the first step in the epileptic fit was to relegate the damage from a higher to a lower center, from the cortex to a sub-cortical tissue, and that step was either unsuccessful or one which backfired. These, of course, are very general considerations that ought to be further specified and empirically checked.

Viewed thus, as guidelines for research, Jackson's principles reveal their generalist nature very well. Yet, they also thus reveal the way an externalist may very well endorse them, as means of exploration; for an externalist may, in principle, endorse any generalist picture as a crude first approximation − even while insisting that this way Jacksonism helps him understand a grand mal without showing any ability to cope with other cases — be they some forms of epilepsy or perhaps merely global fits, however mild or severe (including fits which may accompany high fever in children).

More specifically, if we can reverse a counter- example and make it conform to Jackson's principles, we may just as well insist on the counter-example and declare the principle false. Even after the principle is rectified to the generalist's own satisfaction, the externalist need not accept the rectification as a rectification — indeed he will declare all talk about levels of organization a mere façon de parler. Another example, which we prefer, is this. In the course of a trauma of the spinal column there is a paralysis of the members innervate by the higher level of neuronal activity, namely voluntary movement. Simultaneously, a reflex reappears, which was present till the age of 3, and afterwards inhibited. It is called 'Babinski's sign', and implies that the high, pyramidal system is damaged. Now this sign, Babinski's sign, was not known before Jackson and could not be used before him as a sign, though it could be simply 'empirically' associated with the damage if anyone was lucky enough to notice by accident that all people with damaged pyramids show Babinski's peculiarity. Now the importance of the point at stake is this. When we notice, say 'empirically', a peculiarity as associated with a damage, we may consider it as a part of the damage or as a corollary to it. What Jackson says is that one important corollary of a damage is the system's attempt at regaining its balance. And, these very attempts and what goes with them need not be treated and are better left to themselves: they serve the system well while released and are inhibited as soon as their services are no longer required. Here is a striking example of a modern spelling out of the ancient Hippocratic saying, 'nature is curative'. And in three ways. First, when the high level equilibrium is inoperative, at least the lower level is released; and second, when the higher level is regained it inhibits the lower level. Third, and most important, signs and symptoms may be part-and-parcel of the self-cure: do not suppress fevers, inflammations, and similar bodily hyper-activities unless they do harm and endanger the patient's life.

Of course it is quite possible that discovering a released control and identifying it properly may have no medical function at all. Clearly, however, a priori it may have both diagnostic value and value for research: it is most important for research to know which new phenomenon is which.

6. CANNON

It was Henri Laborit, a French naval surgeon, who introduced the concept of physiological surgery into medicine[1] as late as the late forties of this century. He argued that every surgical procedure is in actual fact an act of aggression against an organism. It is, he said, as if we add injury – the operation – to the initial wound. He thus introduced an operational procedure which he technically termed, artificial hibernation. This is an expression of his physiological approach. He reasoned as follows. The most important and dangerous event for a patient undergoing surgery, we know, is the actual loss of blood. The main art of surgery is traditionally from times immemorial, the prevention of injury to the bloodvessels, particularly to the arteries. Now, says Laborit, suppose the patient is placed in a situation where the bloodflow is reduced and slowed down then the loss of blood will also be likely to be reduced. Moreover, this mechanism functions and reduces the loss of blood in the event of any unforeseen injury to a bloodvessel caused by the surgeon during operation. He compared such a physiological state in which the bloodflow is reduced and slowed down, to animals in a state of hibernation. During hibernation all physiological functions are indeed slowed down, and without any apparent injury to the animal. From this observation emerged his suggestion: produce artificially in a patient requiring operative surgery a state similar to hibernation by applying appropriate drugs. In principle, artificial hibernation is an example of a physiological approach to surgery. The first one, incidentially, to reason in this manner – physiologically in surgery, or indeed, in medicine in general – was the famous French surgeon, René Leriche, in the inter-war period, whose *Philosophie de la Chirugie* appeared in the form of a book in 1951. Laborit considers himself a disciple of Leriche. Those very views of Leriche and Laborit were enthusiastically accepted by many surgeons, and equally rejected by others. The reason for this polarization is fairly obvious: their method is none other than application of the Hippocratic 'nature cures', that is to say, a generalist method; not surprisingly it was in fact opposed by the externalists. Most surgeons fall into this category. Laborit publishes a journal especially devoted to the attempt to extend the knowledge of biological and physiological processes to general medicine and particularly in surgery. Ironically, he calls his journal *Agressologie*.

Laborit's methods strongly remind us of Cannon, who is an extreme example of generalism. For Cannon the point of departure – referred to in his

---

1.   H. Laborit, *Physiologie et biologie du système nérveux végétatif au service de la chirurgie.* Paris, Doin, 1950.

1932 classic *The Wisdom of the Body* — is the concept of equilibrium. He speaks of the maintenance of equilibrium in the body, and its (equilibrium) relation to the external world. Here we must make a correction. If an equilibrium was to exist between the body and the external world, death would have been the result — complete equilibrium and tranquility. However, what really exists is the exact opposite — a disequilibrium between the two extremes. Thus what Cannon really meant when he spoke of equilibrium is the maintenance of a constant, in this instance, the disequilibrium — in short, life. It is this very constancy which he refers to as homeostasis (a word he coined in 1929). For Cannon, stable homeostasis is health. We usually explain homeostasis today with the use of the concept — not available to Cannon — of the feedback and of the feedback mechanism. A feedback occurs whenever some of the output of a productive system goes back to the system itself. An example is the engine which, among other things cools itself, as a motor-car engine does, or the shoe factory that also provides shoes to its workers. However, the feedback that concerns us here is that part of the output that goes back to the productive system which is used as information. Quality control is the best example; when the quality goes down the quality controller contacts the production management and requires changes in the output. This is a case fundamentally different from the case of an energy producing machine, say, which consumes part of its energy in order to get going.

Now, the feed-back mechanism is that which uses the information attained from the part of the output fed back into the system in order to control the system. The control can be towards stability or away from it. If an energy generator uses a fixed portion of its output for increasing its production, it is explosive; if it uses it to maintain balance it is a homeostat. The simplest example is a mechanism which accelerates production when the feedback gives information of slackening and vice versa. The simplest homeostat known today are the myriads of sorts of thermostats: they raise the heat-flow when cold and reduce it when hot. The very fact that the thermostat is heated by the oven it controls makes its heating a feed-back of information which helps the system keep its stable temperature. The thermostat, then, is a part of the system. And the stability is in the smallness of the fluctuations of temperature above and below the prescribed point of stability. Cannon viewed the human organism, including its normal temperature control, blood pressure, blood sugar level control, etc. as homeostats.

Applying Jackson's principle we can at once conclude that Cannon's concept of homeostasis is of interest not only in the case of health, but also in the case of disease. It would be more accurate to say that there is a constant in the case of the inner equilibrium of the organism, namely in the case of health, and that there is a certain deviation from this constant, appropriate to cases of disease, but still within the limits of life. Beyond the outer limits of deviation (disease) death comes into focus. Exactly in the same way as the constancy of the inner equilibrium constitutes health, so every degree of deviation therefrom − disease − has its own level in the order of constants. We thus revert here to Claude Bernard's theory of the 'constancy of the internal environment'. Cannon's main contribution to the elaboration of Bernard's theory lies in the following: Bernard spoke of the constancy of the internal environment, but could illustrate only few of the mechanisms of maintenance of that inner equilibrium, e.g., the cycle of sugar in the body. Cannon, on the other hand, began the systematic study of many of the currently known regulating and self-regulating mechanisms keeping equilibrium in the internal environment. He was also able to study mechanisms for the maintenance of the equilibrium in the event of disease, trying to specify the regulating mechanism of every disease and its specific level of equilibrium.

Cannon began his revolutionary work while he was still a medical student. It is told that one day he saw a machine tucked away in a corner of the hospital, apparently unused. Upon being told that this was X-ray equipment, he proceeded to experiment with it, in studying the behavior of a cat. He thus observed, that a cat upon being fed, showed increased visceral activity, which coincided with a simultaneous decrease in the activity of the lungs and heart. The story is suspect, since the involved item of knowledge is not in the least new. Yet it may be true of Cannon that he was personally so stimulated. Anyway, he went on working. Gradually the theory of the sympathetic versus the parasympathetic system in the body then emerged.

The nervous system is, traditionally, considered as a network of two parts, the volitional one and the autonomous one, commanding for example the arm's muscles and the heart's muscles respectively. The autonomous nervous system was further divided by J.N. Langley around the turn of the century, to the sympathetic and the parasympathetic parts. His division was anatomic: nerves of the sympathetic part emerge from spinal ganglions, follow blood vessels up to the heart and intestines; those of the parasympathetic part emerge from ganglions placed near the heart, lung, and intestines. Soon afterwards Cannon developed his theory of the function of these systems, which is, that the sympathetic system relates to the external stimuli and the parasympathetic one controls the activity of the visceral organs.

In the beginning of his research, Cannon assumed the two systems to be antagonistic to each other. Later on he learned to view them as complementary.

Before concluding our presentation of Cannon's concept of homeostasis and his theory of its function, we must contrast them with Claude Bernard's concept of internal environment and his theory of its function. The medical literature traditionally identifies Bernard's and Cannon's concepts and theories. Indeed, the legitimation of this identification was given by none other than Cannon himself during a celebrated lecture series in Paris in the 1930's. Yet, Cannon's generosity aside, it is important to distinguish the two, similar and related though they surely are. Bernard's concept − of internal environment − signifies the sum-total of vital variables including variables essential for life, namely, the degree of blood acidity (pH level), its temperature, and its level of oxidation. His theory is of the constancy of these variables, to wit, in order to stay alive the organism must keep these variables within specific narrow ranges.

Comparing cold blooded animals and hot blooded animals, Bernard observed a paradoxical situation: when the range is wider the adjustability of the organism to external conditions is smaller. Bernard called the effect of a narrow range of these variables 'free, independent life' meaning to emphasize that when the organism controls its vital functions internally it has a great freedom to choose its external environment.

Now, Cannon's concept of homeostasis parallels Bernard's concept of the fixity of the internal environment, though it is broader. It is broader in that it relates to fluctuations from the narrow compass and that it relates not only to vital functions. As to Bernard's theory of free independent life, Cannon is reticent about it or even about any comparison between different kinds of organism, such as cold blooded and warm blooded animals. His theory of homeostasis is that each organism is a homeostat. He further illustrated this general theory by many specific theories of specific homeostatic actions. But he did no comparative physiology and so never related to Bernard's theory.

Parts of Cannon's theory relate to general bodily functions, to blood pressure and to shock, to sugar level, etc.; other parts relate to some specific ones, buffer systems of enzymes in particular. Our concern here, regarding the generalist versus the externalist debate, relates directly to all this. Whereas Bernard's idea of balance as essential to independent ways of life is overtly generalist and relates only to some very general factors, Cannon's is different: he only examined mechanisms of balance. His very idea of the wisdom of the body is admittedly generalist, of course, and using this expression as the title of his magnum opus he clearly indicated his generalist preference. So are, also, his general homeostats; yet since his theory may apply both generally and specifically it is all too obviously given to an extreme externalist interpretation. This is so much so that today homeostasis is the bastion of externalism and people are surprised to learn of the generalist ancestry of homeostasis itself.

7. CONCLUSION

We have centered, throughout this chapter, on the controversy between generalists and externalists, be they known by any name, banner, or color, and be their adherents conscious or not, clear or not, explicit or not, critically-minded or not, about the issue at hand. Now, no doubt, many medical topics contribute to the controversy, though they center on different problems altogether, and most of them we have left untouched. Some of the topics left untouched look so technical that their very relevance to the controversy may seem highly questionable, yet a closer scrutiny will show how deeply related they are to the controversy at hand. We shall mention only one such topic, just in order to emphasize the extreme narrowness and unsatisfactoriness of the present sketchy study.

We have already met, in the beginning of the last section René Leriche, the famous surgeon, who attempted to develop a physiological approach to surgery. It is very surprising to see how lonely he was in this attempt and how few have taken up his challenge in the last fifty years or so. Now Leriche has observed, what is pretty obvious once you stop to think about it, that the onset of any bodily disease is not, as people repeatedly and thoughtlessly assert, the appearance of the first bodily lesion, not the first clinical occurance (overt or latent) of some physical damage or pathology; rather, says Leriche, the onset of the disease is an etiological event, whatever it is, not its anatomico-pathological later consequence. Leriche further asserts that the route between the first etiological event, known or unknown, diagnosable or not, the route between it and the lesion, the route or course between cause and effect, is a process that takes the body out of its internal equilibrium. The disease, in his opinion, cannot be identified properly, either with its cause or with it effect; rather it is identifiable as the state of disequilibrium; or the process away from equilibrium, if you wish.

The Jacksonian character of Leriche's view is all too obvious. The point at issue, however, is not generalism, rather it is the technical determination of the moment when the body should be declared diseased. And thus, what is so very technical a point, is very quickly seen to be a point of principle, and very relevant to the one on which the present study centers.

To be more to the point, the present study relates to mental illness. And so, the question is, when is a person sick, what are the earlier factors of mental illness in terms of the clinical equivalents to either lesions or etiology – or the process of reaching disequilibrium. Now the clinical mental equivalent to lesion is the psychotic episode, the etiological factor equivalent to infection should be either trauma or faulty conditioning or arrested emotions on the way to atrophy of what-have-you, and the process towards (or away from) disequilibrium is utterly absent in the literature. Not only that, but, much worse, mostly the etiological literature is neurotic and the diagnostic literature is psychotic. This should not be surprising in view of what has just been observed: since the clinical equivalent of lesion is the psychotic episode, psychiatric diagnosis has to be psychotic, just as since the etiological equivalent of infection is trauma psychiatric etiology has to be neurotic. Thus, it is not surprising that a practitioner who diagnoses a case as a psychosis, when he moves to etiology he finds himself having unwittingly reduced his diagnosis to a case of neurosis. To bridge over this inconsistency he will glibly declare neurosis and psychosis essentially the same and merely a matter of degree.

We shall not elaborate on this. We have done so in a separate volume. We mention it here, just in order to show how intricate matters can be and how much beyond our reach. The fact is that questions deeply involved in psychiatry deeply relate to technical questions such as when has the disease begun and these deeply relate to the issue of the present study.

Now, what we have attempted to argue, throughout the present chapter, was a very simple point. The controversy looks both very straight-forward and simple and at the same time very elusive and confused. This is irritating and discouraging and frustrating. We therefore sought to put some order into the situation.

We contend the following as a general historical hypothesis concerning the leading participants in the dispute, throughout the ages, and in all fields of medicine and biology and psychology and so on. We contend that the dispute is clear but that participants are not sufficiently clearly committed to one side or another. Let us expand these two points and conclude this chapter. We shall first say clearly what the dispute is and then clearly again, we hope, how unclear people can be as to what party they belong to.

The disagreement itself is clear. The externalist view of disease is, all diseases are in principle etiologically discernable. The generalist view is, diseases are not very discernable either by etiology or by pathology, since they constitute the struggle of an organism to regain equilibrium. So much for the controversy which is crystal clear. Even arguments against this view or that are amply clear. In an attempt to refute generalism externalists might argue that it is too wide a view of illness: equilibrium is at times sought after in the changing environment; healthy organisms enter and leave states of equilibrium repeatedly without ever getting sick; growing organisms seek equilibria that normally they reach only in maturity, yet growth is no recuperation and infancy is no disease. Externalists may also argue that the generalist view of illness is too narrow, since medicine may well attempt to shift an organism from one level of equilibrium to another. Generalists, in their turn, will attack their opponents by showing the same etiology leading by different routes to different pathologies, different etiologies leading by converging routes to the same pathology, similar defects in disequilibrium generally viewed as illness but in the state of equilibrium generally viewed as scars, defects, atrophies, and such. Whether these lines of attack are commendable or not, they are clearly directed from one school against the other.

So much for clarity, which relates to positions and to attacks on them. The trouble starts with defense. Attempts to defend either generalism or externalism soon land us in confusion. For, it is very easy to answer objections unless one takes care not to use arguments from one's opponent's arsenal. For example, the externalist under attack launched by the generalist will naturally find himself defending his view by reference to a patient's constitution, oblivious of constitution being the generalist stronghold. Let us take a specific case. One third of the male population is naturally immune to syphilis, or, to be precise, to its agent, treponema pallidum. Of those infected, about one half — data are not good on this — are liable to show all pathological consequences of the infection. Why? Here, where the view of the disease is almost universally externalist, the answer to our specific question is generalist: the differential factor, whatever it is, and it is still unknown, is universally taken to be constitutional.

Now, on the face of it, constitution seems to be a generalist not an externalist factor. And so, it seems, even such an externalist diagnosis as that of syphilis does contain a clearly generalist factor. But this need not be so. The question can be raised concerning the constitutional difference between those given to paralysis progressiva, the last and severest clinical and pathological stage of syphilis, and those not given to this terrible condition: can this difference be externally explained? Externalists naturally hope that it can. This is why most physicians who, as we keep reporting, are externalists believe the difference to be immunological. Immunology is obviously a science with strong externalist biases: take an organism, leave it almost as you have found it, except for a minute alteration of its haemoglobulines, et voilà! it is immune to a disease. Not only that; the change is so minute that it cannot be the factor that prevents disease. Rather, when the disease enters the body from the outside, or, as the generalist will insist, when the agent of the disease will enter from the outside, it will activate the generation of more and new immune bodies, the antibodies so-called.

The generalist will see matters very differently, especially when looking at such natural or inborn immunity as to syphilis.

What all this shows is, we think, clear enough: an argument may look externalist or generalist and it may be convertible to a generalist or an externalist argument. And an argument may, indeed, switch sides with varying degrees of success. This makes the two doctrines quite metaphysical and irrefutable. We can cite instances conforming to each of them, and we can cite very forceful arguments against each of them; but we cannot construe a crucial experiment between them. Their significance, however, is exactly here: an externalist will allow himself at times to be generalist in order to serve his externalism, while promising to later convert or reduce his generalist hypothesis to an externalist one. This is to say, he will declare, ad hoc and as an excuse, that it is possible to effect such a reduction. And, later on, he will try to effect the reduction so as not to be in need of an ad hoc excuse. All in all, both schools resort to the same strategies, and both repeatedly cover newer grounds. The new ground covered is a new theory conforming to my metaphysics, or a theory initially conforming to yours which I have reduced to one conforming to mine.

We wish to get rid of one philosophical red herring here. Traditionally there is a feeling, but only a feeling, though at times it has been articulated by an aggressive (young) participant in the perennial dispute, which we suggest is neither here nor there. Externalists are prone at times to view themselves as empiricists, especially when their search of a bug to blame for a disease is crowned with notable success; and they view the generalists as mystifiers who refuse to admit the obvious empirical facts, or at least as bound to some a priori metaphysics.

Now, first of all, each party to a dispute has instances conforming to his metaphysics: just as bugs conform to externalism so the congenital resistance to bugs and the functional diseases conform to generalism. Moreover, there is no doubt whatsoever that a generalist factor can be found even in the instance best conforming to externalism, and vice versa! And therefore one misses the point when one claims that one party must be more or less orthodox than the other — regardless of whether orthodoxy requires clarity, empirical character, open-mindedness, force of evidence, or any quality not central to the dispute itself. That some participants in the dispute were friendlier, some more fanatic, that some were more enlightened, others more narrow etc., etc. including the claim that some were plainly obscurantists, all this goes without saying. We insist, however, that all these qualities, good or bad, are shared by some members of this party and by some of that. If anything specific tilts the balance it is the distribution of wit: when one school is dominant, then some of the subtlest minds belong to the opposite school, as if to keep the dispute going. But this is, of course, a mere illusion. We should particularly stress the openness and dynamic character of the ongoing dispute, especially in view of our tremendous ignorance of everything concerning disease, or even symptoms, such as their function, course, etc.

In psychiatry the case we have mentioned, of paralysis progressiva, has played a special role. It used to be highly problematic, until the middle of the last century – for, in 1822 A.L.J. Bayle found in post-mortem examinations of paralytics some physical damages in brain-structures, thus permitting the correlation between the paralysis and syphilis. Later this was fully confirmed by the discovery of the treponema in the diseased brain. It came, thus, to be the externalists triumph and paradigm of both externalism and organicism, i.e., of the externalist view of all psychopathology.

We hope we need not reiterate that an externalist triumph indeed it was, but silence the generalist it could not. Nor did it. And, as we shall now see, the greatest externalists of them all has become the father of the new generalist school in the profession. We mean Sigmund Freud.

II. CONTEMPORARY SCHOOLS OF PSYCHOPATHOLOGY

1. INTRODUCTION

What is psychopathology? Etymologically the answer is quite simple. It means: the science of the suffering of the mind. But if one goes further from the mere translation of the word, then things immediately become complex and some elaboration on the subject is indeed required.

Is medicine a science, as most people think, or is it an applied science, as all physicians know? The sciences on which medicine is based, the sciences of which medicine is the application, are anatomy, physiology and pathology. Anatomy is the science of structures, physiology is the science of the functioning of these structures and pathology is the science of morbid changes in these structures and/or in their functioning. We should here like to distinguish between a science on the one hand and an applied science and a technology on the other. By science we mean the study of the corresponding fields for the sake of study, not necessarily application. One studies 'pure' science when one studies in order to feed one's curiosity − one studies for the sake of knowing, not necessarily for the sake of using the knowledge attained. One begins to study and one follows the steps which are laid before one, as it were, along the way wherever it leads one. One does not stop a 'pure' study in order to use it or because it becomes inapplicable. The usefulness of 'pure' science is a by-product; it is completely of secondary importance in the process of 'pure' study. The moment one stops studying and looks for applications, one has moved into the field of applied science. Thus physics is the science of which engineering is one possible application; botany is the study of which farming or gardening is an application. Physiology is the science of which medicine is the main application (other applications may exist as well, such as kalesthenics). Pathology is another science, the application of which is medicine. There are, of course, other sciences and other applications, such as pharmacology and toxicology. We shall not discuss them here, as we are concerned with psychopathology right now. Psychopathology is the 'pure' science whose applied science and associated technique belong to psychiatry, literally the curing of the mind, by a physician − by a iatros. Now both 'psychiatry' and 'psychotherapy' mean the healing of the mind. Yet, for historical reasons they have different references. Some healers of the mind, the psychiatrists, have medical training and medical degrees; others, the psychotherapists, do not. Moreover, some treatments of mental patients are restricted by law to healers with medical degrees, i.e., to psychiatrists e.g., the dispensing of drugs; some treatments are not so restricted, e.g., the listening to lengthy complaints. Further, some mental patients go straight to mental healers without medical degrees, to psychotherapists, some go to those with, some go to general practitioners who channel them hither or thither depending on many factors, not yet fully investigated.

And so, mind healers with medical degrees are more often called psychiatrists than psychotherapists, and the others are called psychotherapists. Also, more often than not, in professional circles psychiatry is viewed as more professional and so both more responsible and more prestigious – and also more externalist in orientation; consequently the practice of psychiatry is often distinguished in professional circles as the art of careful diagnosis and scientific, i.e., externalist, treatment: drugs and shocks today; cold showers and hot baths a mere couple of generations ago. Psychotherapy is more often Freudian and dispensed by lay analysts, i.e., by professionals with no medical degree proper. This too, is a local matter: some Freudian societies oppose lay analysis contrary to the Master's explicit injunction. One might tolerate diverse psycho-therapeutic methods but contend that, of necessity, since psychopathology is the science, there exists only one psychopathology. In point of fact, however, there are several schools of psychopathology: the Freudian, the Adlerian, the Pavlovian and Skinnerian, the existentialistic and the Ey-ian. Each school provides a theory, a scheme of references within the frame of which psychopathology is considered: there are several psychiatries (applied sciences) and psychotherapies based on these several psychopathologies.

Since psychopathology is not one monolithic science but indeed a group of schools and theories – each applying its own frame of references, its own spectacles, to psychopathology – it is our duty to examine these theories one by one. And one better remember that indeed not more (but also not less) than theories they are: though they all see the same known and accepted facts, all see them in different ways, through their particular spectacles. And therefore, when one speaks of psychopathology, one has always to specify what psychopathological theory one refers to.

It seems to us that, quite generally, the distinction between theory and practice is clear enough. We have dwelled on it for some time because all too often arguments are confused, because rather than hold tenaciously to a theoretical position in a theoretical debate even when under fire so as to find out whether one can survive the onslaught or not, parties often tend to take refuge in irrelevant pragmatic arguments. We also find that when practical values of techniques are questioned, their defenders tend to take refuge in theory. This will not do. To secure avoidance of such malpractices, we have devoted the present chapter to theory and the next to practice.

A general philosophic point may help us conclude this introduction. Often in human history, one course is taken at a junction to which one later returns in order to seek an alternative. This is a very plain matter. There was, for the simplest instance, the choice of looms with woven material placed horizontally or vertically; the vertical choice seemed preferable, yet with further progress the horizontal choice won. In more abstract matters, we come back to the junction and admire those who proposed the option that now looks better. For example, Einstein gave up Newtonianism and reverted to Leibnizianism. How come Leibniz lost to Newton? asked Einstein. And he answered: Newton won on technicalities: he had the tools and he delivered the goods. This is a special case of mechanism winning against holism. And in psychiatry, too, we can go back and be amazed at the insights of generalists — but only in retrospect. Here is a passage from an essay on Sydenham and hysteria, by Jeffrey Boss (*Psych. Med.*, 9, 1979, 232), in which the author uses a most up-to-date language to characterize ideas of 17th century Sydenham. How accurate is his characterization of Sydenham we cannot judge, but it certainly is a proper characterization of Henri Ey's views on the matter — hysteria in this case: 'It is a shift neither from one organ to another [even to the brain] but from organs to person. It is a shift in the level of organization taken as the central field of consideration.'

2. FREUD

The nineteenth century concept of psychopathology before Freud was quite simple. Psychopathology was one; there was only one school of thought governing the field: the organicist school. The saying was, 'no psychosis without neurosis', where 'psychosis' meant mental suffering and 'neurosis' meant organic damage to the central nervous system. Causes of damage could be considered external or internal depending on the views of the thinker making the consideration, but the organic nature of the damage was not put to doubt, not even where all efforts to locate the cause failed. Kraepelin, for example, declared that sooner or later the cause must be found, and Kraepelin was and still is the leading figure in psychiatry, ever since the eighteen-nineties. Eugen Bleuler too, of the same generation as Kraepelin and Freud, who for some time even was a follower of Freud, even he could not discover any organic cause for the schizophrenias, but was convinced that some such cause did exist, and that one day it would be revealed. Yet there were exceptions. In particular, the case of Freud's teacher, Charcot, should not be forgotten. Though Charcot believed hysteria to be a disease, comparable to any other organic condition, he also knew that he could evoke or strike out any hysterical symptoms by mere psychological means, particularly by hypnosis.

Now Charcot was an organicist as everybody else was at the time. Yet he still was an exception, and a very important one. Perhaps in this respect he was much more of a predecessor to Freud, and much more of a profound influence on him, than in his mere remark, cited in gratitude by Freud, 'it's all sex'. For, organicist though he surely was, he could work while letting organicism recede into the background. If he could induce psychological symptoms purely psychologically, then perhaps he could also cure them purely psychologically. Now organicists might object and say, purely psychological treatment may help but has to leave the true (organic) cause of the trouble untouched. So be it, one may answer for Charcot; if I can relieve a patient of his symptoms for a few decades whereas you can only hope to find a cure for his disease, then my service is better than thine.

It should be noted that the opposition to Freud from the organicist camp was largely justifiable even from Freud's own viewpoint. For, hardly before Freud came onto the scene, the mentalists harped on the guilt of their patients, and the organicists used their theory in order to justify a more compassionate, seemingly morally neutral attitude towards their patients. And they rightly feared that Freud was reverting to an outdated view (clinging to an old fashioned view). His saying that we all feel guilty, that we are all sexually obsessed at heart, even though we repress the fact, all this only made some thinkers feel the risk all the more. It is, indeed, lucky that a reactionary variant of some Freudian theory was never a strong social force. After all, St. Augustine's *Confessions* comes closely to just such a view.

All this, need one say, is of a supreme importance for the understanding of Freud's conversion in practice from organicism to a mentalism of his own brand, a conversion that perhaps was never whole-hearted, and even as a half-hearted conversion he accepted it only in his old age; in his youth he saw it as a mere stop-gap operation. For, he noticed, not only can the therapist effect a relief of the symptoms by mere psychological means; he soon believed that even a full cure was possible by such means (and even attained, at least in some cases of neuroses and psychoneuroses). Of course, this raises the question, how can one stick to organicism while assuming the possibility of a purely psychological cure? We shall return to this question soon. We wish to say now no more than that we owe it – this very question – to Charcot. And this was Charcot's great contribution to psychopathology.

We must remember that Freud visited Charcot for only a few months, yet these were decisive. Hysteria before Charcot – like all psychopathology – was entirely organic, not in the least psychological in etiology, and the young Freud had been trained as a neurologist, not in the least as a psychologist. And while researchers were putting so much effort to transfer mental illness to the physical brain, here came Charcot and did the very opposite: he transferred the obviously physical cases, convulsions, paralyses, and the like, into the mental field – at the very least in the sense that he could achieve certain improvements by the use of no surgery and no drugs and no other physical tempering with his patients, but by mere psychological means.

Freud was troubled by all this. He wrote a paper on hysteria, which occupied him for a few years and was finally published in France and in French. In it he offers a clinical differentiation of hysteria, so very much in the spirit of Charcot, as the organic disturbance not complying with the theoretical requirements of the anatomical and neurological and muscular structure of the human body [unless the patient is an expert in the field!]. The distinction – Freud's but pre-Freudian – is sill diagnostically accepted today.

Parenthetically, we may contrast this pre-Freudian idea of hysteria, as not conforming to physiology, with Freud's later and very Freudian view of hysteria as caused by a conversion of cathexis, i.e. of mental energy, to a bodily manifestation. This idea is aetiological and metaphysical (not to say pseudo-scientific) and nowadays hardly accepted even by the most ardent Freudians, much less by the non-Freudian clinicians; yet all of them still accept his diagnostic (clinical) differentiation as a matter of fact. Moreover, in his very same early paper where he offers his diagnostic differentiation, he also offers the theory of the symbolic meaning of the specific form of hysteria of a given patient, a theory much later rediscovered by Thomas S. Szasz, who offers this discovery as an argument against Freudianism: if hysteria is a symbolic expression, says Szasz, then it is a communication, perhaps a defective communication, but not a state of health, poor or otherwise. Moreover, we should notice, it is exactly Freud's differential diagnosis of hysteria that differentiates it from all somatic illness, psycho-somatic no less than any other: psychosomatic illness is somatic – physical – and in no conflict with anatomy and physiology; only its origin or etiology is presumed psychological. As we have indicated, all this does not conform to the organicist program, to the mode of behavior expected of organicism, but it is still an open question whether it can be reconciled with organicism. Let us mention that just at the time when Freud learned from Charcot that he could remain faithful to organicism while seemingly violating it, a young assistant of Charcot, known to Freud or not, we are unclear about the facts of the matter, by the name of Pierre Janet, went much further and began to postulate psychological etiologies and treatments for psychological ills. We shall discuss his pioneering work later on.

Freud's concept of psychopathology was de facto psychological and this effected a real revolution in psychiatric thinking. Though one can say that Freud held the most externalist view of organicism amongst psychoanalysts — in his emphasis of the special importance of the constitution in the making of the disease (and we shall later discuss his twist of the generalist concept of 'constitution' into a part of an externalist theory) — he is nonetheless the father of the most mentalist, or psychogenetic, approach in psychopathology: all his theories are of mental causes of mental sufferings and of mental cures to them. One can accept or deny Freud's own views in psychopathology, but there is no doubt that psychopathology has not been the same since Freud: only under his influence is the etiology of mental diseases nowadays ascribed to psychological factors.

Thus far, we spoke of organicism versus mentalism and declared Freud an organicist in metaphysics, yet one whose theories are all mentalistic pro tem. The major issue of the present volume is the externalist-generalistcontroversy. And, of course, these two dichotomies are different so that we have four possibilities.

But, needless to say, first of all, most externalists are naturally organicists, because both externalism in medicine in general and organicism in psychology derive their rationale from the same metaphysics, to wit mechanism. It is a bit hard on the reader to call mechanism organicism, when in other contexts, such as theoretical biology, organicism is the negation of mechanism. But these are rather insignificant traditional terminologies that should not trouble us too much.

The purpose of our present study is to draw attention to a peculiar traditional inadequacy that goes deeper. In the tradition of Western philosophy the debate about the soul has a special importance due to the religious — or anti-religious — background of all thinking until fairly recently. And so, the debate between the organicists and mentalists loomed large. But the debate between the generalists and externalists, we think, was of much greater import, though it was less in the limelight.[1]

Moreover, we do not wish to conceal our prejudices; in our own view a serious attempt should be made to dispense with both organicism and mentalism: the dichotomy between them is an error, we think. This view is fairly common these days, whether in its general-systems guise, or in any other. For our own part, we prefer the guise initially given it by Hughlings Jackson.

This is not to force Jackson into a discussion of Freud, even though Freud himself was Jacksonian while he was a neurologist. What Freud did with Jackson's hierarchies was to mentalize them as he mentalized hysteria, for example. The result, however, was less felicitous, as we shall soon explain. And so, Freud's studies in hysteria became an arrowhead to further conquests, whereas his inverted Jacksonianism simply atrophied. Let us examine it for a while nonetheless, because it affords us an insight into Freud's externalism or his distance from generalism, and raises the questions, how did he manage to contribute so much to generalism nonetheless?

Hughlings Jackson was a generalist; apparently Freud followed him; at least Freud, like Jackson, used terms which imply hierarchical layers of organization of behavior. Freud's contrast between primary and secondary processes of thinking, as well as his theory of the barest drives which may be transformed into higher ones through processes of sublimation, both involve hierarchies, or levels, of organization. Moreover, Freud's very personal view of psychoanalysis was that this theory contributes to the understanding of life as a set-up full of perpetual conflicts between drives and reality, between drives and superego, as well as between the various drives themselves; indeed, in the profession, psychoanalysis is sometimes labelled 'a dynamic theory' (if not '*the* dynamic theory'), precisely because Freud viewed life as conflict-ridden. Now, all this seems to fall in line with the generalist's view of disease as a conflict, or as a struggle to regain equilibrium, and thus one may want to label Freud a generalist. And considering Freud's view of psychopathology as displaying levels of organization, he may perhaps be considered a Jacksonian or a

---

1.   Materialists deny the existence of the soul as an object, but only if they are mechanists do they have to deny that it at all exists; if they are generalists they may (and usually do) say that it exists as a harmony. Mechanists deny the existence of a harmony, but only if they are materialists will they deny the existence of the soul: anti-materialistic mechanists can postulate the existence of the soul as the non-material part of Man. Thus, materialists who assume that souls exist must be generalists to stay consistent, whereas mechanists are, of course, externalists; but others can choose between generalism and externalism; in particular, materialists who deny that souls exist may be generalists but are usually externalists and even mechanists. Thus, organicism in psychopathology ('no psychosis without neurosis') is usually materialist.

neo-Jacksonian of sorts. But a closer examination of Freud's terms will reveal that they are not only dissimilar to those of Jackson but even their opposite.

Let us briefly recapitulate: Jackson distinguishes between clinical manifestations which are primary in nature and those which are secondary in nature. Primary, he says, are those clinical manifestations of neurological defects which appear when a higher level of organization is affected; and, due to the absence of a higher level of integrative organization, there is a release of an integrative principle of a lower level of organization, and it is the latter which Jackson refers to as secondary.

As is known, Freud also makes a distinction between primary and secondary manifestations. Freud refers to primary and secondary processes of thinking; but by processes of thinking he actually means more than mere thinking (reasoning, etc.); he really means modes of cognitive organization (aperception). Primary, says Freud, are the clinical manifestations which result from the atavistic drives, those which constitute the lower level of psychic organization; and the higher elaboration of these drives, the well organized and harmonized facets of the psyche, result from the secondary process of organizations.

For the sake of clarity two remarks should be made. First, as to the terms used; second as to their content. As for the terms used, one has to notice that Freud calls primary precisely what Jackson would call secondary, and vice versa. What Freud refers to as secondary is this integrative behavior, whose absence itself causes symptoms called by Jackson primary.

So far for the difference in terminology. As for content, the difference becomes a real contradiction. For Freud, the source of mental pathology is in its point of origin, and this origin is to be found in the drives that are at a lower level of organization, definitely not as a result of a defect at a higher level of organization. For Freud, the drives — which are of the lowest level — invade and destroy the psychic organization of the highest level. The primary (low) process of thinking takes over from the secondary (high) processes: and mental illness is the result of a lower level activity when this invades the higher level and takes over its function and perhaps even destroys it. In short, for Freud, the disease is a disorganization of the higher level caused by lower levels, whereas for Jackson, the disorganization of a higher processes opens the way to, and thus results in, a reorganization on a lower level. It is a strange fact that such a reorganization was observed by Freud in his clinical studies on aphasia, yet it is completely absent in Freud's psychological theory.[1]

We may be understating our case. For, at least in one prominet essay of his Freud speaks of the analyst's task thus. The task is the reconstruction of the patient's once integrated system, prior to his becoming a patient, as of an archeological task. It is important to notice that the material Freud says the analyst seeks is not only to be dug out of the subconscious (where it was repressed) but also that the analyst has to construct it, or rather reconstruct it — or rather help the patient reconstruct himself. This is highly Jacksonian, since, as Freud himself notices, both archeologist and analyst dig up destroyed objects, and for the analyst it is precisely the destruction of the psychologically significant objects that matters, i.e., that is the root of the trouble ('Constructions in Analysis' *S.E.*, Vol. 23). So much for Freud the de facto Jacksonian; let us now briefly explain why we consider him a de jure anti-Jacksonian.

Whereas Jackson spoke of a physiological hierarchy, Freud spoke of a mental one. It looks, then, as if Jackson was an organicist and Freud a mentalist. But, of course, it is precisely here that we see the organicist-mentalist dichotomy crumble. At the very least we can be assured that Freud was no mentalist. Indeed, his viewing of drives, of low drives, as primary, was rooted in his reductionist bias, in his hope to explain one day all mental phenomena as purely physiological. And so, what matters is not what we call primary, but how we view a disturbance: Jackson stressed that it is not just the damage that should be the focus of our attention, but the effort of the whole system to regain its prior state, which involves the reactivation of centers lower than the damaged one. Freud said the opposite, since otherwise sublimation would be utterly impossible. For, in sublimation higher centers are both damaged by lower ones and activated in a new way.

To conclude, if we regard the generalist as one who sees in the disease a struggle for regaining equilibrium, it is clear that Freud was not a generalist. For him the disease is a real defect in patterns of behavior, a disequilibrium and not an equilibrium, even not an equilibrium of a lower level of organization, as a generalist would claim. (Only the neurosis of the adjusted citizen was thus viewed by Freud.)

This is no accident. Indeed, when Freud had to express himself on the subject of equilibrium, he was quite explicit; for him equilibrium was not the result of a play of forces, but something quite different. It is somewhat difficult

---

1. The omission of Freud's interesting neurological works from Freud's English language Standard Edition is justified by the title, *S.E. of S. Freud's Psychological Works,* which, however, is a veil of a technical excuse for the omission of the unpalatable pre-Freudian phase of the Master's progress. After all, the gain due to this omission is negligible.

to believe that the so called 'dynamic' Freud could hold this view, but it is nevertheless the case: Freud expressed himself on the matter not casually, but when dealing with a fundamental issue of his theory, the theory of drives. These are his views: drives and instincts, says Freud, are innate forces which act in order to achieve satisfaction, disappear and only reappear when a new state of disequilibrium manifests itself. Whether it is hunger, or the sex-drive, and there is no other basic drive, it activates a whole chain of reactions, which press until they exhaust themselves, usually until they achieve a sort of 'null' equilibrium. (This is the Schopenhauerian element in Freud's philosophy: rest is best and all desire is mere pain, a nuisance at best. Here libido and death-wish unite.)

We have compared Freud's views on levels of organized behavior with Jackson's. Let us now compare Freud's view on equilibrium with that of Cannon (who is on this point a generalist). Cannon views the maintenance of equilibrium as a result of constant conflicting forces, 'fighting' as it were against one another, in order to uphold a steady state. For Freud, a state of 'rest' is a state where all drives are static, in other words, sated, and therefore result in equilibrium. (For Freud conflicting opposite and equal forces need not keep the system at rest in equilibrium.)

To sum up, the difference between Freud and Cannon is, in a nutshell, this: (following Schopenhauer) Freud identifies the 'null' equilibrium with the death instinct; Cannon, in direct opposition, defines the fight of forces to maintain equilibrium as life itself. So far for instinct. As for disease, we shall add, in our view, when a disequilibrium of the homeostat occurs, there is always still an equilibrium à la Jackson, on a lower level, and it is this state which may maintain the system as a defective but still functioning one; or, it may even function while struggling to regain its higher level equilibrium; and it is this very struggle which, we think, constitutes disease. Except that the word 'equilibrium' here is vague and at times entirely metaphorical and merely stands for continued maintenance.

Before going to Adler, we have to cast a broad glance at the background of the Freud-Adler rift: externalism versus generalism. For the externalist, like Freud, looks for the etiology, the root cause of the ill, and seeks ways to get rid of it. The generalist element in externalism was discovered by thinkers late in the last century and crystallized by Freud: getting rid of the foreign hostile cause restores balance: homeostasis was Cannon's new word for stable balance, and it describes Freud's view perfectly. The generalist pushes the idea further in two ways: first there is an inner cause that makes the foreign factor hostile rather than immaterial, second, therefore we may strive for improved balance that handles the foreign factor better. The biologist's (C.H.

Waddington's actually) word for improved homeostasis is homeorhesis, which is something akin to what economists designate as dynamic equilibrium and Alfred Adler viewed as a desirable style of life.

Yet, clearly, Freud, more than any other contributor to the field, is known for his method of mental healing. He was not the first mental healer, and he even observed that his own method of healing is practiced unbeknown by father-confessors of all sorts. Yet he is the one who invented the method of systematic free-association, the couch, the digging out of the subconscious all that needs mending. When all his views are put into doubt, his uncritical defenders triumphantly point at the couch.

We have no objection to the couch as such, since it is the means the patient uses to put distance between himself and his analyst, and the patient may need such means in order to overcome initial anxiety: any means for the reduction of initial and surface anxiety is useful means to open a dialogue between healer and patient so as to reduce deeper and malignant anxiety. Yet Freud and his sycophants are in error when they defend the couch as the only legitimate means of diagnosis and the means with which to prevent all dialogue on diagnosis for fear of healer influencing patient. Here Adler has shown that the healer's diagnostic background-knowledge may be put to better use when the couch is dispensed with and patient and healer converse freely and honestly. That Freud has made some diagnosis very easy is a fact: Freudian psychoanalysts, Skinnerian behavior therapists, and healers of other schools will all tend to examine the adolescent with an obsessively trembling hand for guilt-feelings about masturbation. But the Freudian will elicit the diagnosis — be it the initial one or an alternative to it — from the patient; the behavior-therapist will ignore it or pretend to ignore it even when he finds it useful in his treatment. The Adlerian therapist will frankly air his suspicion with the patient. And, indeed, all therapists will applaud the Adlerian if he can cure the youngster fast. Yet they will deny that this is a paradigm-case: even though the Freudians will deem the diagnosis a paradigm-case, they will deem the treatment shoddy. Let us see, then, what made Adler insist on dialogue with patients in all cases, and why Freud frowned at Adler in all cases.

3. ADLER

The major shift from Freud to Adler is the replacement of the Oedipus complex with the inferiority complex. There is more there than meets the eye. First, the sex drive is now replaced with the social drive. This requires an explanation. No doubt, both Freud and Adler observed people motivated both by sexual desire and by the desire to excel and dominate and be recognized. What Freud insisted on, however, is the primariness of the sexual drive. For him all social activity comes to further either sexual ends or ends which replace sex by the process of sublimation, and thus essentially still sexual ones. It is hard to see why, if a person replaces the forbidden fruits of sex with the permitted pleasures of the arts and sciences and religious activities, why these should be viewed as essentially sex. Here we meet again the weakness of Freud's organicism which even he may have relaxed towards the end of his life. Be it as it may, surely Freud viewed social motives as disguised sex-drive. Adler, in contradistinction, viewed social motives, whether the wish to dominate or the wish to be adored, as quite autonomous. Freud found this very unphilosophical as it assumes the autonomy of sociology. Adler conceded this point, but insisted that sociology is, indeed, autonomous.

It might be permitted, we hope, to deviate for a moment and remark that all externalists must of necessity deny the autonomy of any social science, except perhaps psychology, and demand that all social science be reduced to psychology. Usually externalists also wish to see psychology reduced further — to neuro-physiology and beyond. Generalists, however, may remain skeptical as to the advisibility or possibility of such a reduction.

Historically, Freud's psychologism — his demand to reduce all sociology to psychology — conflicted with the Marxist view of the primacy of society, with Marx's sociologism. And so Adler looked more progressive in political circles, even though Freud looked more progressive in philosophical circles. When, under the influence of Marxism, or of socialism in general, some Freudians felt that the philosophic foundation of Freudianism needed some revision so as to enable them to introduce the sociological component independently of the psychological one, they found their views uncomfortably Adlerian. But for the organizational problems created by the expulsion of Adler from the Freudian galaxy and his subsequent creation of his own galaxy, the story might have come to a happy ending.

Another fundamental difference between Adler and Freud, so it seems, is the shift of the center of gravity of the cause and origin of mental pathology from the individual (Freud) to society (Adler). The question here is, who is to blame, really, individual or society? This is a rather well-known, not to say banal, question; it is surprisingly far more profound than seen at first glance. Its close examination provides us with some unsuspected insights into the nature of generalism and externalism in psychoanalysis. Furthermore, the well-known controversy between Freud and Adler is in itself enriched with a flavor, previously unsuspected, of an existentialist trait in Adler's psychology.

So let us first examine Freud's view of the cause and origin of psychopathology, which we consider to be essentially externalist. This we conclude both from Freud's view of the importance of traumata in all psychopathology, and from his view of the role played by the internal constitution of the individual — the instincts (drives). As for traumata, they are the paradigm of external causes. As for constitution, one could say, since constitution is that which is within the individual, it might be a generalist concept. Not so for Freud, for whom the most significant part of the individual constitution is the given and fixed instinct and for whom its total inner set-up is an accumulation of external entities — objects (people) or norms — internalized. For, this is the only way by which, according to psychoanalysis, Ego and Superego are cumulatively constructed. We see here how Freud's famous bias towards 'constitution' is really of a strong externalist flavor.[1]

Freud's view of the internal organization of the individual constitution is not a generalistic view either (though, not externalist either; indeed we do not know how to name it). According to his theory, all drives converge — in the final account — to a common pathway, namely satiation. And here Freud links together all instincts which, in his veiw, 'tend to satiate themselves'. This, then is the final end of all instincts — satiation. This satiation is ultimately death; and so all instincts are finally the death instinct. Where, then, is there room for the pleasure principle? Perhaps the latter is a version of the former[2] — much in accord with the philsophy of Schopenhauer which, as is well known, Freud much admired. For, in Schopenhauer's view (as in Hinduism and Buddhism) the highest pleasure is no pain and no desire.

From a generalist point of view, which is dominated by the concepts of equilibrium and disequilibrium, and more so by the concept of the re-establishment of equilibrium — including the equilibrium between individual and the external world — Freud's concepts of equilibrium and disequilibrium and their interplay are severely limited. They have nothing to do with the external world; in Freud the dramas of conflicts and their resolutions are completely and totally in the mind. Now, one would say that if there is no relation between inner drives and the outer world, Freud is not an externalist, but an internalist of sorts and hence a generalist. This is an error. Freud is an externalist, and this can be concluded from the very picture he gives of inner psychic life. To repeat, Freud allots a very central place to traumata. But an external event becomes a trauma only if it gains some psychological

---

1.   To complicate matters still further, constitution is at times, for Freud, all that is not psychological in the living being. This does not get Freud off the hook, however.

2.   One subtle variant of this is the idea that when the death instinct is realized to the full it annihilates all, itself included, thereby giving birth to the possibility of life=Eros=libido. No comments.

significance from the individual's inner life. An event by itself is neutral. So that an event becomes a trauma only on the background (matrix) of the individual psychic inner set-up. But according to Freud what is the inner set-up, if not an accumulation of external people, internalized? How is the inner set-up built? How are the ego and superego constructed, if not by the continuous encounter with external meaningful objects (people)? We see here, as already mentioned before, that Freud's famous bias towards 'constitution' is really of an externalist conception.

It is also here that Freud and Adler are opposite poles. For Adler the inner set-up is, from the beginning, not passively dependent on external figures, it is — from the onset — struggling with these figures: the inferiority and superiority feelings are the expression of a struggle for 'domineering'.

Thus we have a 'paradox' on our hands. Freud, in spite of his 'internalist' view of the individual, is an externalist. Adler, because of his view of the importance of external social figures — is not an externalist but a generalist.

What is Adler's view on external social figures and the individual? An individual has, according to Adler, a life style, a goal in life, which is the result of a combination of his own view of himself and of what society expects from him. How one is seen by others is not only extremely important in one's life, says Adler, indeed it is essential to the understanding of all human behavior. Now, the theory that my seeing myself — my self-image — is the same as my seeing what others see in me is a Sartrian theory (this makes Sartre an externalist); that my seeing myself is a complex of both what others expect me to be, and of my own view of myself, is an Adlerian theory (and it is the conflict, interrelationship, and moves between equilibria and disequilibria of these two poles of existence — my view of myself and of others' view of me — which makes Adler a generalist). It is interesting to see in Adler a precursor of the dialogists in psychotherapy (and perhaps of R.D. Laing).

4. PAVLOV

When we began to write this book we did not know in advance where our studies would lead us. Moreover — as we have extensively explained — we did not even know whom to view as a generalist and whom to view as an externalist (that is why we took a quasi-historical course). But one thing was clear to us from the start, namely that at least two great figures, Freud and Pavlov, should most certainly be our prototypes of the most extreme of the externalists. Freud, since for him both the origin of mental disease was the trauma, and since the very rationale of cure was its removal; what the psychoanalytic treatment is supposed to do is, in essence, to remove the cause of the disease exactly as the surgeon removes a harmful foreign body; with the catharsis, the flush, as the scalpel. (Indeed, in somatic medicine flushing out a foreign body is common enough.) We have already explained in the two preceding sections that this formulation which might seem simplistic at first glance seems to us nonetheless correct, and that indeed we do view Freud as an even more sweeping and more profound an externalist than we had originally thought.

Equally, we said, Pavlov should be deemed an externalist: if all behavior is either reflex or conditioned reflex, i.e. determined or conditionally determined, if his disciple Watson could have said: 'give me a free hand in the conditioning of a baby, and I'll determine what he'll be', then surely Pavlov should be deemed the extreme of externalism. Well, then, much to our surprise, we found that regarding Pavlov, we were completely in error. We found, even by not too careful a study of Pavlov, that he was the very opposite of externalism: he was profoundly a generalist. Indeed, a comparison of Pavlov with Freud is strikingly instructive in this respect. We shall attempt such a comparison now; before that, let us add, it is no accident that (a) Pavlov's physiology was expressly generalist and was renown as such and led to his celebrated (psychological) researches on conditioned reflex and (b) Pavlovian psychology got bogged down just here: from the start the opponents of Pavlovism asked, what is conditioning? and, finally, the arch-Pavlovian, B.F. Skinner, said in response, anything − perhaps everything? − that has preceeded the response. As long, said Skinner, as I can modify response patterns by series of conditions, I need not know what is a stimulus. Behaviorism − Pavlov's, Watson's, and Skinner's − is so pervasive, that the organism appears to the behaviorist as a black box; so complex and baffling as to be virtually unapproachable and unanalyzable. (Skinner at times sounds as if he is an externalist, and perhaps he is; nonetheless, considering the facts of conditioning he comes up with the most extremist generalist reply. Also, it is well-known, Pavlov had some strong reservations regarding his American disciples. He deemed them not generalist enough, we tend to surmise.) Thus, the critique of behaviorism takes it to be externalist and is therefore misplaced: Skinner answers it off-hand by viewing behaviorism as a version of extreme generalism.

So much for generalities. Let us now backtrack.

Both for Freud and for Pavlov, the origin of neurosis is conflict. For Freud, things are simple. Two antagonistic forces produce a conflict; and in given conditions, which we shall discuss further, a conflict gives rise to a neurosis. For Pavlov, there are two points of cleavage where conflict (and neurosis) can begin, both have to do with his theory of the conditioned reflexes

– and of stimulation and inhibition – and must be examined on this background.

It is important to notice that whereas for Freud no problem arises unless and until a conflict of interests arises within one and the same person, Pavlov totally ignores all Freud-like conflicts. He does not explicitly say they cannot exist, but he comes as close as possible to saying that if they exist they are utterly of no importance. It is well-known that Pavlov drove his dogs out of their wits by making them have conflicting expectations. But the expectations were purely of external events, having no roots in any sort of conflicting wishes, desires, wants, motives, drives, or forces.

No doubt, the Pavlovian organism is internally motivated: the Pavlovian organism is active. But, taking the activity of the organism as given, the Pavlovian psychologist – experimentor in this chapter and psychotherapist in the next but one – has nothing to do with it, and only grafts on it everything else, whether a normal conditioning or conflicting ones, that may but need not drive the organism to destruction.

One may, then, view Pavlov and his followers, including all behavior-modification psychotherapists, as externalists who lay primary emphasis on external factors, albeit behavioral rather than chemical or physical as in the case of somatotherapy. Indeed, for behaviorists what distinguishes psychopathology and psychotherapy from somatopathology and somatotherapy is precisely the fact – alleged fact, need we add – that the psychological trauma is behavioral. Now unbelievable as this sounds, we have already ascribed this very view to Sigmund Freud in our previous section. We hasten to add that this unbelievable discovery is common knowledge.

If, on the contrary, one lays emphasis on the fact that the grafted conflict cannot take – still according to behaviorism – unless it is forcefully grafted (by association or by conditioning or by any other means) on the organism's given innate structure (of instincts or of reflexes or of anything else), then one may indeed view behaviorism as somewhat intrapsychic but falling short of generalism. For, as we have stressed above (in our section 2 to this chapter), generalism includes the view of illness as located in the pattern of interaction between the organism and its environment; and so externalism is only the counterpart of 'internalism', both of which together fail to constitute generalism. This point has caused much confusion and grief, since the trauma, Freudian as well as Pavlovian, indeed any wound, psychic or physical, is of the organism, and in the organism, yet prima facie it follows the pattern of the externalist philosophy, not of generalism. Indeed, generalists refuse to view any wound as any damaged tissue; rather they will call in their generalist philosophy in order to distinguish between a wound proper and other damage

− an open wound and a scar, not to mention the distinction between a healing open wound on its way to becoming a scar and an open cancer.

And so, the fact that Freud or Pavlov, or anyone else, has a theory of trauma makes him a prima facie externalist. He, or anyone else, would become a generalist if and to the extent that he views trauma as a part of a whole system − stretched over a time-span − or as the organism-environment-interaction. Here, to repeat, Pavlov looks externalist and yet he is a generalist. We shall now illustrate this in the details of a study of Pavlov on neurosis.

The first area, as far as the origin of a neurosis can be pinned down, is the area of ambiguity of the conditioning stimuli. The observed fact is as follows: a dog is conditioned to salivate whenever a circle of, say, 10cm of diameter is presented to him. He is conditioned to inhibit his salivation whenever an ellipse of say, 15cm of larger axis is presented to him. A neurotic behavior appears when an ellipse of just over 10cm of larger axis is presented to the dog. A conflict, says Pavlov, exists bvetween stimulation and inhibition; the reason for the conflict is not inherent to the primary reflex (salivation); it is not an inherent conflict between drives or between a drive and a higher inhibiting function (such will be a Freudian's formulation); the origin of the conflict lies in the ambiguity of the conditioning signals which are combined with the primary reflexes.

Incidently, the view of a neurosis as originated from a conflict between stimulation and inhibition, is somewhat simplistic. It is as if there is only one way of behavior for the animal: either by stimulation or by inhibition. But it is a simplistic on purpose: a simplistic theory is probably mistaken, and if it is, then, perhaps its very simplistic nature may help us eliminate it fast with the help of some simple pieces of evidence (C.S. Peirce and K.R. Popper).

Pavlov's second area of origin of neurosis is not in the ambiguity of the conditioning stimulus, but is, indeed, a conflict between two primary responses. Yet the conflict is aroused out of a peculiar set of a conditioning of these responses. The conditioning is as follows: a dog is conditioned to salivate through one signal: whenever that signal appears the dog gets food. Then it is conditioned to run away whenever another signal is presented, such as an electric shock. Then the two signals are experimentally associated to the dog. The conflict is then, between two primary responses − incidently two antagonistic ones, namely, a primary reflex of nutrition (pleasure?) and a primary reflex of self defence (pain?). A question may be raised: do any two primary reflexes which became antagonistic through conditioning produce neurosis? or is there a hierarchy of primary reflexes, such as the reflexes of nutrition vs. defence − i.e., reflexes which are naturally antagonistic ones −

are more important in the production of a neurosis than two otherwise not naturally antagonistic reflexes? We shall explore this further later on.

It is interesting to know that in Freud's theory only a certain type of external events, events which are affectively 'charged', which have symbolic meaning, etc., are responsible for the beginning of a neurosis, namely produce neurosis, even if they are affectively not in the least 'charged', i.e. even if they are biologically neutral. Therefore Freud's theory can not account for the 'experimental neurosis' of Pavlov, where two neutral antagonistic stimuli are brought into interaction. On the other hand, Pavlov's theory can account, and seemingly easily so, even for such a highly 'charged' (and in addition so very complicated) happening as an Oedipal situation. Thus, for example, a given stimulus such as 'my mother's figure' signals an inhibition on my sex drive, while any other female figure signals a stimulus to that drive. However, if a female figure appears, and it is similar to my mother's, a neurotic situation is at hand. The resolution of this situation, indeed, be marrying a woman of very different ethnic and physical characteristics than one's mother's, instead of visiting a psychoanalyst. The psychoanalyst for his part may claim that one who avoids a conflict by marrying a foreigner is not thereby cured; but he will also have to explain the success of marrying a foreigner. Indeed he will say that one who may solve one's problem by marrying a foreigner is initially less sick than one who, say, becomes a woman-hater or a man-hater. Here, incidentially, we see, as usual, that members of two schools cope with all the facts; yet, clearly, some facts prima facie are more Pavlov-like, i.e. all cases where the ambiguity is sucessfully removed, and some, clearly, prima facie more Freud-like, i.e. all cases where the neurosis re-emerges when symbolic meaning sharpens, such as when the removal of the object of anxiety merely leads the patient to project anxiety to another object. Clearly, for Pavlov no tools exist by which to create such thing as projection.

All this, however, does not close the issue. The Pavlovian will have to translate all relevant symbolic meaning − including projection, introjection, etc. − to plain conditioning. But, still on the prima facie level, the Pavlovian will have to recognize the existence of meaningful signals which he should then translate into his conditioning system. Indeed, Pavlov himself already took care of this and postulated the existence of a whole meaning system; the 'secondary system of signalisation' he called it. And once postulated, secondary signals, i.e. meanings, could be found everywhere. To begin with, the sight of food was primary and the sound of the bell secondary. But, certainly, the taste of the food, however defined (the touch of the food in a point on the pharynx which activates the swallowing reflex, they say), is primary, not the sight of food; this is merely secondary sign, i.e. means to designate food proper. (But perhaps it is the sense of a full stomach? who knows?)

Now, since Pavlov saw 'meanings', however behavioristically or even physiologically (allegedly) explicable, it is easy to lose sight of the difference between Pavlov and Freud. For, we remember, Freud, too, hoped to reduce meaning to physiology. No matter; whereas for Pavlov the conflict is grafted on a simple system and one which is on the whole integrated, for Freud the system struggled to integrate but suffers from inner strife. Whereas Pavlovian psychotherapy – on which more in our fourth chapter below – calls the environment to emit clear signals, for Freudians signals are usually taken to be clear enough but they only enhance already existing inner conflicts and therapy should put better order inside the organism, not in its environment! For example, for Pavlovians homosexual tendencies are explained by similarities between members of opposite sexes of the species, for Freud the same tendencies are the outgrowth of our conflicting feelings towards our parental authority. Konrad Lorenz finds here the greatest weakness of Freud, and though anti-Pavlovian in general, here he sides with Pavlov.

We do not wish to end upon a Freudian note. It sounds very profound for the Freudians to shrug their shoulder and say, as they regularly do, alright; let the behaviorists treat the superficial cases where symptomatic relief will do, and they should leave to us the deep analysis of the highly disturbed cases. The question still is, can Freudians explain the superficial but effective success of the behaviorists? Is it not possible that this success is inexplicable by Freudians, that this is a flaw in Freudian theory, and that compounding it will lead us further and further away? Or are there two types of neurosis so that both Freudianism and Pavlovism is false but, as Bertrand Russel has suggested, their synthesis is true? We leave matters at that for a while.

4. EXISTENTIALISM

Existentialism, or more generally, the phenomenological school of which existentialism is a sub-school, was always concerned with psychopathology. Karl Jaspers, the famous philosopher, who is often considered a phenomenologist and/or an existentialist, wrote a classic thick and extensive monograph on general psychopathology in three editions. Jean-Paul Sartre wrote much about psychopathology, even in his most philosophic, major, *Being and Nothingness*. On the whole the new school of antipsychiatry is largely associated with existentialism and, in particular, R.D. Laing professes to be a disciple of Satre.

Nevertheless, there is a vast lacuna.

What is psychopathology, according to existentialism, is hard to know. Indeed, no existentialist in his writings ever suggested any theory of psychopathology. Is it an accident? We do not believe so. Those psychiatrists who try to systematize the schools of thought in psychiatry, and deplore the absence of existentialist psychopathology, do not know that in principle an existentialist, indeed any phenomenologist, cannot provide any such theory. For phenomenology is, in essence, based upon the immediate subjective experience, and thus upon the uniqueness of Man and his actions in the world; hence, no general rule, i.e. no rule of universal validity, is ever possible. Incidently, this inevitably leads any consistent existentialist to the paradoxes and the problematics of mental illness considered as a disease. If truth is validated by the immediate subjective experience, then on what grounds may I claim that my truth is better than thine? − J.J. Lopez-Ibor, a famous Spanish psychiatrist, an existentialist, and a very wise man, ends his *Schizophrenia As A Style of Life,* thus: "What is madness?' asked Don Quixote...'

Still, existentialists have something to say about psychopathology. First, by condemning all existing traditional theories of psychopathology. Second, by implying what a valid theory of psychopathology should be.

However, the same objections existentialists present against traditional theories of psychopathology should be checked against their own implied theory of psychopathology. Indeed, some existentialists have attempted such a self-critique.

Here a remark should be inserted. While the rejection of traditional theory of psychopathology is based upon phenomenological grounds, the 'true' theory, suggested instead of the rejected one, is based upon an existentialist approach. Obviously, phenomenology and existentialism are not quite the same. An existentialist must necessarily be a phenomenologist, but the reverse is not the case. This is so, perhaps, because phenomenology will correspond to epistemology (theory of knowledge) and existentialism to epistemology plus ethics (theory of morality). And so, an existentialist's ethic must be based on phenomenology as corresponding to its epistemological basis; a phenomenological theory akin to epistemology does not necessarily lead to an existentialist ethics. Now, since the existentialist's claim against traditional theories of psychopathology is a phenomenological argument, the claim is not a specific one − against some psychopathological theory − but a general one: against traditional science as such − and perhaps, more precisely, against any science of Man that approaches its subject from the 'outside'. What is the source of our knowledge? What is the origin from which we draw our criterion for validity? What can we know? What is truth? The phenomenologists' answer is: our experience,[1] when properly comprehended, is our only sure and sound source of knowledge. So, if Man's immediate subjective experience is the source of knowledge, then the question, what is Man? might replace the question, what is truth? Now, to follow this line of reasoning into the moral dimension, and on the view of Man as that of Man as freedom, is to become an existentialist; yet on the view of Man – of his moral quality – as different from the one of Man as freedom, then one is still a phenomenologist, but not an existentialist. In this context, the question must be raised: Was Descartes an existentialist? For the archphenomenologist Edmund Husserl, and also for the arch-existentialist Jean-Paul Sartre, Descartes was a pioneer of phenomenology. Also, for Sartre, he is a pioneer of the theory of freedom. And if so, he might be regarded as a precursor of existentialism. Now Kant was a pioneer of the theory of freedom no less. Indeed, many regard Sartre's ethics – not his epistemology though – as simply Kantian.

Pioneers or not, however, clearly Descartes and Kant were not plainly phenomenologists. Both Descartes and Kant began their epistemologies with their own immediate subjective experience of themselves as being the only source of this very special experience which is precisely the immediate subjective experience of themselves.

This very experience, just described, is indeed at the heart of phenomenology. How is it, and why, that Descartes and Kant felt it necessary to pass from the immediate subjective experience to look for an objective source of subjective experience, i.e. to look for a support from the 'outside' world? And why does the phenomenologist deem this an unnecessary move?

We cannot go into all this here. Briefly the facts seem to be these. Husserl criticized Descartes' move from the phenomenological to the objective: the move failed and its failure led people to idealism, i.e. to the denial of the very existence of any objective reality, of an outside world. Husserl himself was intent on avoiding this denial – which he thought could be achieved by the avoidance of that move. Yet Descartes felt, as Kant did, that unless we expressly assert the existence of objective reality, anything goes and your conclusions are as good as mine, no matter how crazy they look to me, or mine to you. And this point still haunts phenomenologists.

Thus, no psychopathology is possible for a phenomenologist since there is no absolute model of mental health or of anything else human; each case

---

1. The German Erlebnis and Erfahrung are both rendered experience in English, thereby making the English-speaking reader less open to existentialism; a point English-writing existentialists keep complaining about.

should be examined in the context of which it is both a part and a constituent. Each case should be studied on its own, each case is unique. The problem remains, can we pass from the subjective to the objective? from the unique to the universal? if not, how can we give the validity of the absolute to the completely subjective event? we confess that we do not know the answer to that obstinate question. Incidently, following the same lines, no pathology in the medical sense will be possible for a phenomenologist, either. Since physicians have generally no interest in philosophical issues of this kind, no somatic physician (to our knowledge) has dealt with the problem of how is pathology – or disease – at all possible? There is only one phenomenological medical book by a physician, J. Heaton, on *The Phenomenology Of The Eye* (London, 1968).

And nevertheless phenomenologists do suggest a psychopathology. The most obvious thing to do here is to generalize the ungeralizability of all psychopathology and conclude that no one, not even the best diagnostician, can tell you whether or not your are sick: only you can.

Now, this will not do. For, no psychotic will just come forth and say, with the same ease and grief as a malaria patient would, I am sick. And so, instead of the previous generalization, we can take this very fact. Existentialism sees its moral ancestry in the writings – moral, not philosophical – of the celebrated 19th century Dane, Søren Kieskegaard, who wrote about conformism as a sickness – a moral sickness, a conceit. Sartre, using Freud, altered Kierkegaard's ideas, and saw in conformism a moral and psychological sickness – an expression of anxiety and self-deception combined, as not conceit but shakiness. Sartre invented a major philosophical term – bad faith – to designate selfdeception plus anxiety plus lack of moral fibre. Bad faith, incidentally, adds an Adlerian dimension to Freudianism, since the neurosis or illness or what-have-you is now conformism and conformism involving the individual's image of the public's image of himself – as a part of his own self-image.[1.]

Is, then, the patient the judge, or is the diagnostician? If the disease is bad faith, if the sick is sick because of his poor credibility, or in his poor credibility, who is to judge this? The answer will not come. Indeed, exciting as existentialist psychiatry is, in the final resort it is but an elaborate evasion of this question. In brief, we say, the refusal of existentialist psychiatry to admit that the central question it poses is unanswerable, this refusal amounts to bad faith.

---

1.   Self-image is not ego-ideal. The latter is a part of the super-ego and repressed; the self-image is a part of the individual's coordination mechanism and so of the ego; Freud overlooked it, but his disciples added the self (or self-identity or identity) to the ego, and in the self resides the self-image and the non-regressed coordinating part of the super-ego, which is tacitly Adlerian. Of course, to be coordinative it has to be fairly conflict-free.

Let us go into detail. We begin with the already mentioned Karl Jaspers, whose most famous work on psychopathology (1913; English translation, 1963) came well before Sartre's. Not being able, by the nature of things, to present a comprehensive psychopathology — and Jaspers honestly admits this shortcoming — he felt that at least some presuppositions could be useful. For our purpose, i.e. for the examination of psychopathology from the point of view of the controversy between externalism and generalism, one important thing is clear: it is that phenomenologists are necessarily generalists. The enormous gulf between 'inside' and 'outside', as well as the requirement that the individual's make-up is involved with his own (conscious) involvement with his environment — these are part and parcel of the very foundations of phenomenology.

Skipping over much intricate material, we move from Jaspers to Sartre's work of 1939 and 1943.

It seems that Sartre was preoccupied by the problem of 'the essence of Man' both as a philosopher and as a psychologist. As a philosopher he felt he could tackle the problem; as a psychologist, he felt he could not. In his 1939, *Esquisse, The Emotions: An Outline of a Theory,* he explains why psychology is an empirical science (or, as he says, a positive science) using the inductive method, and therefore, by the nature of things (or 'by definition', as he then put it) psychology can deal only with contingencies (and not with necessity), with the accidental (and not essential) with disorder (and not with order). Thus, traditional psychology is not able to give an 'absolute' answer to the question, 'what is the essence of Man?' This view of psychology, clearly a Watsonian-behavioristic one, was Sartre's understanding of what psychology was; this behavioristic, anti-introspectionistic view, was then the dominant view of psychology in France. Sartre felt, however, that another psychology is possible. Perhaps, he said, we could profit from psychoanalysis, which was then a 'new adventure' in psychology, slowly penetrating the scene in France. A psychology should be created which will deal with significances (in the existentialistic sense), with essences and not with mere events and contingencies. He proposed that with the help of psychoanalysis a new kind of phenomenological psychology could be created. Sartre attempted himself to build such a (phenomenological) psychology, a psychology which in the last resort will provide the answer to the question which Sartre considered the most important one for humanity for generations, i.e. the answer to the question, 'what is Man?'

It was Sartre who had to lay down the foundations for such a psychology. After the attempt to schematize an appropriate theory of the emotions, he went deeper into an attempt to synthetize psychoanalysis both with traditional (positivistic) psychology and the phenomenological approach is developed in his *Being in Nothingness* (1943). At the close of that very study Sartre himself doubted whether he succeeded in making sufficient progress in his attempt. He says explicitly: 'But the question whether this [existentialistic psychoanalysis] now exists is of a minor importance. What is important is, that it is possible'; i.e. the project seemed to him feasible though his execution of it could be wanting. The heart of the matter for Sartre, anyway, is the problem of freedom. And, a distinction should be made between freedom as a mode of existence, and freedom as the very essence of Man. In many studies the distinction is not made clear. Many people confuse Man's mode of existence and the essence of Man; according to Sartre the essence of Man is the project of becoming God. 'Every human existence is a strife, since its projection is to annihilate itself...in order to establish...that which religion calls God...But the concept of God involves a contradiction and we annihilate ourselves purposelessly. Man is an absurd strife.' (So ends the book before the concluding chapter.) Here is the crunch: according to Sartre, freedom is the ability of the individual to choose, to wit, the existence of some contingent alternatives given to the individual human being at a given time and place; yet we attempt to be perfect, even though in perfection there is no contingency and so no possible choice – in addition to the very impossibility of perfection. Thus, in Sartre's view, the nature of Man is the choice of self-destruction through excessive ambition. And psychology dwells between this freedom, and this nature. The individual, who is the subject-matter of psychology, is free to realize Man's essence, which is the subject-matter of philosophy. Here, it is very important to stress that whereas human nature is given, that whereas mankind does have a given essence, the case of the individual is different: his existence precedes his essence; he can mold himself; he thus is morally responsible for what he is (and can't blame anyone for what he is – his parents, environment, or complexes). But, since only the individual is free while the nature of essence of Man is given, the individual's freedom is bound to express itself in the striving towards Man's essence, i.e. progress (paradoxically towards destruction). Now, this looks as if the freedom just granted the individual has been taken away. This is not so, since the individual can shirk his obligation by bad faith. Bad faith, thus, equals psychopathology yet it also is the guarantor of freedom.

All existentialist psychiatrists who we know of, in their daily practice, disregard Sartre's view of the essence of Man as absurd, and put the main emphasis on the view of Man as freedom. This may not be orthodox Sartrian, yet it does accord with Sartre's own appraisal of himself: his intended contribution to psychology in general and to psychopathology in particular should have been the abolition of the traditional incompatibility between contingency and the abidance by the law. Sartre began his task by asking how can contingency (which is the subject-matter of empirical psychology) become law (which is the aim of any scientific generalization)? All he could say on this he put at the end of his *Being and Nothingness:* contingency is indeed the law, provided that we view freedom as the law, since 'the contingency of choice is the other face of freedom'.

This – to us obscure – assertion may be somewhat a result of a forced game of words. But for many psychiatrists it is still a useful formulation, at least intuitively. Be it philosophically what it may, at least psychologically there is no doubt that the immediate spontaneous experience that there is freedom is an important empirical fact. Even if freedom is in the last resort but an illusion (incidently, this is ironically Sartre's own claim), this illusion is grasped abstractly, intellectually, as a fact on the deepest level of reality, whereas what is grasped intuitively, experientially, is both the burden and the marvel of freedom, and these in fact are here with us. It should be surprising that non-phenomenologists should find it necessary to remind existentialists, that phenomenologically freedom is an uncontested fact, and that morally freedom is a marvel of a delight and a burden. Yet all too often existentialists are so tangled as to forget this very essence of their own message.

And so, we see, the question against which Sartre's system seems to collapse is, repeatedly, who says who is sick? Just as easily as Sartre will say of his anti-hero Roquentin that he is crazy, Roquentin can say the same of Sartre. Indeed, he will see the whole system of existentialism as nothing but an expression of Sartre's private neurosis in an attempt to evade it. And, were Roquentin a bit better informed, he could quote Sartre's own autobiographic *The Words* to confess to just this sin.

Sartre's own confession, his cavalier dismissal of his own philosophy as rather phony, of course came to confuse the heathens, and so was dismissed by the heathens as a mere ploy. And so it is not clear whether Sartre is still to count as an existentialist. Likewise it is not at all clear whether he is to count as a Marxist, nor is it clear whether existentialism, Marxism, or existentialist Marxism, really (in essence) rejects all theory of the essence of Man or only dismisses them all in order to clear the ground for a new, existentialist theory of what is the essence of Man. It has to do with Man, facing himself as freedom, anxiety, guilt, death etc... In any case, the same objection that existentialists have against traditional philosophy, may be turned against them. To say that 'the essence of Man is X', is to use scholastic language. What is its validity? The question of alienation which is so basic both for existential thinking and psychiatry, becomes very relevant here. If Marx viewed the true essence of

Man as optimistic, a nature which strives towards social harmony, then this true nature of Man will realize itself in the new classless society, where alienation will be abolished, and if anyone will refuse to realize Man's true nature in classless society, we shall presumably compell him to do so. Yet consider that person, unreasonably alienated, for a moment. Here we are facing again the alienation of Man from himself, and thereby facing an individual as he really is. Political philosophers, from Rousseau to date, could not reconcile themselves to his very existence. And so commit him to jail (Rousseau) or to the psychiatric ward (Soviet Russia). This absurd is condemned by the existentialists on the ground that we all jailed and committed anyhow. The only consistent existentialist, then, is R.D. Laing, for whom madness is freedom and thus, by the existentialist canons, the very birthright of Man.

6. LAING

Before we can present Laing's view, we must locate the source of the trouble with his existentialist antecedents, mainly with Sartre. The statement that madness is the true nature of Man is a logical conclusion from Laing's work. However, it is not certain that this statement is correct, though it was logically deduced; nor is it certain that Laing himself will subscribe to it. Neither do we. A logically deduced conclusion is not necessarily also a true statement; for this it has to be deduced from true premises. In our case the deduction is perfect, yet the conslusion is false: and so the premises are false. Let us consider madness as a special case of the irrational: is the irrational as such the whole of the true nature of man? Even classic advocates of the value of the irrational, like Nietzsche, did not claim this. The irrational is important, yes. It is as powerful as Nietzsche claimed, yes; it is not only of the nature of Man, it is of his true nature. But it is not the whole nature of Man; not by any means. Others, for example the surrealist intellectuals, concur. The irrational part of surrealism is not a mere game: it is of the true nature of Man; but it is not his whole nature, and so, when a surrealist claims to be drawing the whole picture of man, he is in a serious error. The same for madness: it is of the true nature of man, but it is not his whole nature: of necessity we are all a bit mad; each of us is also at times mad, and at moments even utterly insane; but we are definitely not all mad all the time.

What is madness, then, for a phenomenologist, for an existentialist? It is a situation or a condition — not in true medical sense of a disease, but in the existentialists's sense in which he speaks of the human condition, i.e., an inescapable aspect of being human. Let us assume Sartre and his followers describe madness correctly as bad faith in accord with the discussion in our previous section, even though they incorrectly see it as prevalent. Assume with Laing, that it is utterly prevalent. This change alone, we say, will move us from Sartre to Laing. (We shall later see both the Marxian character of the move and the failure of Laing to rescue Sartre with the aid of this move.)

What, then, is the situation or condition of madness? To begin with, madness is not incomprehensible, even though, we remember, not generalizable either. Indeed, the paradox of madness viewed as incomprehensible is just here: people try to generalize the ungenerizable, fail, and then blame the facts. But viewed from within, madness is as understandable a human situation as any other — and as equally ungeneralizable. It is a behavior understandable on the ground of (in the context of) a given individual 'in his world'. No less and no more. It is thus neither better nor worse a situation than any other. It just is. You may call any given item of behavior madness if you wish, but this will be just a name; you may consider it as an illness, and say that madness is a mental disease, but then again this is a name, just as you may call our need to die sooner or later a disease. Anyway, any disease is considered by the phenomenologist as a situation understandable in its own context, and not as 'the thing in itself'. Thus when Jaspers speaks of 'psychopathology', he really speaks of situations, not diseases in the traditional sense, and he is aware of this even though he is not very happy about it and offers no arguments for his views and no prescription. Laing drops the concept of disease altogether, seeing it as unnecessary and even harmful. Indeed, the social function of the terminology of psychopathology is merely to stigmatize some deviants and thus to penalize them for their deviance. Hence it is a social evil.

And thus the problem is solved. In essence perhaps everyone is mad, perhaps no one — as you wish. In the social context, however, mad is the one labelled mad, usually the deviant, and thereby socially discriminated against, usually as a social sanction.

This sounds refreshing, but it is glib. It will not do. It is clear that society does not call everyone mad, not even every deviant; nor does it arbitrarily select scapegoats amongst them so as to brand them mad. And so Laing adds a further qualification that earns the deviant his stigmatizing label.

As Nietzsche said, the mad man is he who goes around carrying a lantern and seeking God. Hence, as Kierkegaard said, the really sick is the conformist. The independent individual who is still seeking his way, says Laing, is branded mad because he does not conform. Not all deviants, then, but the true deviants, the free spirits, are those branded madmen.

This too will not do. We know that madmen suffer and Laing himself tells us he tries to help them. But he only tries to help them after they go mad – he will not try to prevent madness; indeed, in his most famous and most moving cri de coeur he says he would induce madness in everyone if he only knew how.

In brief, the story is this. We all suffer from bad faith. Some of us can take it no longer and take a journey into inner space. The journey is risky, as the traveller is utterly without a map and utterly alone, alienated in the deepest sense of the word. Nor is this all. In addition to his inescapable suffering there is the stupid malicious frosting society adds to his condition by the very label of madness. The traveller into inner space has also to endure the persecution by the conformists who will not let him be (because of too much bad faith, of course, envy, of course, etc.).

We said in the beginning of this section that it is difficult to know what according to existentialism should count as psychopathology. Now we see that it is indeed difficult, but only in the frame of the traditional terminology. Once that terminology is eliminated the existentialist's understanding of what is traditionally called psychopathology becomes clear. There are human situations, and human situations only. Each is in its own right (each stands for itself), but some are more painful than others and must be endured by anyone who wants to be someone of consequence; both inner pain and outer persecution are just about as inevitable as the fact that so many can take it no longer and consequently become conformists.

Here, we see, existentialism – especially in Laing's variant – adopts a complete reversal of traditional psychopathology. Traditional psychopathology is characterized by two features: first it is a comparative science, comparing behaviors to a model of absolute health and condemning whatever does not measure up to standard. Secondly it is a science of causal explanations. Existentialism first eliminated absolute models and thus all deviations; further it replaced cause by meaning.

Of models and uniqueness we already spoke at length. We can now concentrate, then, on meaning. Let us consider the meaning of psychopathology. What is the meaning of psychopathology according to the existentialist? (To be precise, one has to ask: what is the meaning of those human situations, usually called psychopathological, according to the existentialist?) We saw that Laing presents psychopathology as the freedom to face alienation in the Marxist, social sense of the word (and psychotherapy as the encouragement and sustenance of the alienated free); but this is not the view of all existentialists. There are many existentialists who will argue just the contrary. Still, at least in the realm of freedom they will all concede that disease limits freedom, or even that extreme disease altogether prevents freedom from taking place. Will madness too count as disease? Perhaps it will. Such will be

Ey's position. (This difference of views between Laing and Ey has its point of origin perhaps in the difference between Laing's Marxist antecedence and Ey's Bergsonism.)

In short, the problem of freedom is given the highest priority by the existentialist, be it a limitation of freedom or a realization of it; hence, psychopathology is inconceivable for the existentialist psychiatrist, unless it is couched in the language of freedom. To this we subscribe: we do not yet know whether madness is a limitation of freedom or its realization (in a way it may be/a combination of both, the nature of which should be precisely demarcated) but madness is unconceivable without consideration of freedom. This is perhaps the most important contribution of existentialism to our subject-matter (both in Laing's and more so in Ey's variant).

Having gone so far as to agree with the existentialists, mainly Laing, we must also, for the sake of clarity, express our serious qualification. We do think that meaning is important, but we shall not give up the study of cause. Moreover, we think it is obvious, that some things cause meaning to be important. It is an empirical fact that great stress makes people seek meaning everywhere, at times to the point of making them find meaning everywhere, and with ease. We do not wish to say that stress alone is the cause of this finding of meaning everywhere; but we do say, and categorically, that psychiatrists will not fail to declare this condition psychotic. Of course, the meaning found (as opposed to meaning sought, and not found) may be general, i.e. existentialist, or particular, e.g. persecutionist, and for good or for bad reasons. Nevertheless, the ease with which the meaning may be found everywhere is usually analyzed as psychotic.

We do not mean to endorse this diagnosis. In a previous study of ours we have said tht this diagnosis does not differentiate the psychotic from the mere crank. But psychotic or crank, one finds meanings more easily than normal, or even looks for meanings more than normal. Perhaps he seeks meanings because he is troubled by a philosophical problem and tries to solve it in a manner that will brand his solution existentialist; perhaps he suffers (patient=sufferer). Even were Laing right and the philosopher and the sufferer were forever one and the same, even then meaning need not displace cause.

Laing may not want to agree, but, as he neither explains nor argues we cannot but reiterate a commonly endorsed sentiment: he who wants to help has to study causes. All that Laing can present by the way of causal connection is the connection between the social pressure to conform and the patient's troubles. This is not enough for a cause as Laing himself concedes. It is therefore the severest criticism of Laing to observe that some conformists and some non-confirmists are mad and some are sane.

We respect Laing's Kierkegaardian emphasis on the pathological aspect of conformism ('sickness unto death' was the Kierkegaard's expression) and his bringing it to bear on psychopathology: schizophrenics are, indeed, people struggling against the easy conformist way out of their distress. Also, the generalism of his position appeals to us, except that it is excessive to the point of making psychiatry not medicine at all. Perhaps were medicine, especially psychiatry as medicine, more anthropocentric (as proposed here) Laing would change his colors. The reader may notice the absence of our standard topic in the whole of our discussion of the existenialists in general and Laing in particular, the absence, that is, of the standard topic of the present volume, the generalist-externalist dispute in medicine and its projection to psychiatry. This absence is required by the rejection of those people of the very idea of psychiatry as medicine. The existentialist who endorsed this idea is Henri Ey.

7. EY

Henri Ey, the leading French phenomenologist- existentialist psychiatrist, stands at the cross-roads of psychiatry and medicine. Though psychiatry is obviously 'part of medicine', so they say, there is a sleight of hand here. When one claims that psychoanalysis is or is not medicine, one meets the violent response that it is not or that it surely is. In hospitals and in clinics proper psychiatry is the practice based on psychology, indeed psychoanalytic psychology plus the occasional prescription of medication, plus odds and ends. Once in psychoanalysis, whether as a practitioner, a patient or a theoretician, one is not in hospital anymore, indeed, not in medicine any more − not in any of these medically integrated roles. The psychiatric clinic is not a medical institution at all in some contexts, and is in other. Popular views, it is true, may confuse psychoanalysis with some sort of medicine. This is however not the case. Psychoanalysis is even no psychology. It is a discipline in its own rights, one amongst others amongst the diverse sciences. The academic world has not yet ascribed to psychoanalysis the proper status of a scientific discipline on its own (there is almost no university with a chair of psychoanalysis even though some chairs or even departments of psychology are surreptitiously devoted to psychoanalysis); it was Freud's own view of psychoanalysis as a special discipline and it was his personal desire that it so be recognized. It is Ey's claim for merit to have attempted to integrate psychoanalysis into medicine; and of course many psychoanalysts do not like it. What was the reason for Ey's move? It is that he could not accept the psychoanalytic way of explaining psychopathology which is so different from the medical sense of explaining.

Psychoanalysis can explain the content of a neurosis (or a psychosis), not its formation. Medically speaking, in order for psychopathology to take place, there must be first a defect, a disturbance in the psychic organization; and only then the specific neurosis (or psychosis) can occur as the outcome of the disturbance. This is a medical point of view. Indeed Freud took a bow to this very point of view when he developed his theory of the trauma, the (mental) wound. But for Ey the connection between the trauma and the ensuing neurosis remains obscure. And Freud's added claim that the neurosis is caused by a conflict simply makes the trauma superfluous. Ey's view is different on this point. It is not the conflict that produced the neurosis, he says; the conflict is an aspect of the neurosis − it is the (higher) organizational defect in the mental apparatus that makes possible the appearance of the conflict. One sees here the connection Ey makes between psychoanalysis and medicine. In medicine one can look upon pathogenesis in two different ways. Either one sees the germs 'invade' the organism; which invasion or presence of foreign bodies, to be precise, one considers the disease; or one sees the organism's struggle against the germs as failed, and consider that failure or the continued struggle against the persistent presence of the germs, to be precise, as the disease. That is to say, any chronic condition, however unsatisfactory, is not a disease but a defect. We have here, in a nutshell, the externalist versus the generalist versions. Since psychopathology is these days either Freudian or Pavlovian, and since behaviorism is taken to be externalist par excellence, all psychopathology is traditionally externalist. Ey is a rebel and a generalist. Since Ey thinks that psychoanalysis is of imporance, he does not dismiss it. Rather, he translates it so as to be able to incorporate it within a generalist view. Now his mode of translation is that of relating the trauma etiologically to the ensuing neurosis: the trauma turns into a systematic defect. This of course pushes the analogy between psychopathology and somatopathology a step further and gives it content, exactly in line with his effort to bring psychiatry back to medicine.

Now, to the heart of the matter. Will Freud deny that the trauma causes neurosis by causing a permanent damage in the mind? We do not think so. Indeed, Freud even says, in places, what we may construe in his view of the damage. The trauma is met by the young person by some effort to understand the situation or cope with it emotionally or intellectually. This alters his makeup. The alteration is done by a young person under pressure and is thus not the best. And, indeed, later in life he may go over the same grounds and make further alterations as he becomes an adult person. Yet, due to the painful memory the whole incident, including the emotional-cum-intellectual change, gets repressed and so fixed and thus it becomes neurotic.

This will not do: nothing is said in the previous paragraph about conflict;

nothing about the effect of the local fixation of the mental mechanism as a whole; nothing about which trauma is healed in adolescence and which turns into sickness. At best Freud's theory is incomplete.

Freud himself took a bow to all this when he said, if we can remedy the situation it is not neurotic; he said not every fixation is neurotic; he admitted for the trauma to become neurosis it somehow has to become constitutive.

This will not do. We have now two or three problems on our hand: (1) how is the neurosis thus caused? (2) how does it integrate both into conflicts and into the mental apparatus as a whole? and (3) what is the role of conflict in this integration? Ey's answer to these questions may be true and it may be false. Our concern here is to present his views as an answer to these very questions. That answering these questions make Ey a generalist is all too obvious: they are the very expression of the generalist bias; they are the search for the way to translate Freud's externalist and fragmented theory into a comprehensive view integrated within the generalist system. All we wish to add in conclusion to this introduction to Ey is that what has been thus far presented is no interpretation; it is straight from the horse's mouth. Ey dreamt of writing a treatise on the natural history of madness. Only its first volume appeared and only posthumously: *Naissance de la Médicine,* Masson, 1981. Ey begins with placing madness in the context of psychiatry, psychiatry in the context of medicine, and medicine in the scientific attitude as traceable to original duality of nature versus magic. Moreover, Ey has changed details of his views a few times; not, however, what we have thus far ascribed to him.

Here it is perhaps the place to add another dimension to the strictly medical one. For Ey, this dimension will mark the difference between neurology and psychology. The dimension is a moral one, i.e. that of meaning or significance (in the existentialist sense). Here medicine and morals join. In neurology the presence of a disease has no significance to the 'liberation of lower hierarchies' in the human sense and at times not even in the physiological sense – when one may view the disease as a local affliction. In psychology disease is total, leads to the 'liberation of lower hierarchies', and has a human significance. For example, epilepsy is a disease due to an affliction of a total kind or a systemic disease; thus, simultaneously with a 'liberation' of some neural lower function there is a human sort of 'liberation', there is a spcial kind of human existence; there is Homo Epilepticus; it is for that reason that Ey will consider epilepsy as a psychological condition and not a merely neurological one! Here we see that for Ey, and for that matter for all organo-dynamic thinkers (Charcot, Bleuler), a psychic disease will be viewed as simultaneously of a global nature and of human significance no matter what its etiology is. Here Ey will substitute the traditional appelations of 'neurology' and 'psychology', to 'organic' and 'psychological'. The organic origins can be the cause of a psychological condition. Thus, Ey views epilepsy not as a mere neurological disease but as psychological, even though organically caused. The same applies to paralysis progressiva which is a psychological condition, organically caused by syphilis (luetic) infection. Hence, all diseases – somatic or psychic – are organically caused in their very deficit: were there no global organizational deficit, no psychological 'liberation' will manifest itself. By saying 'organically caused', Ey does not mean 'organic' in the sense of a physical, material cause; he views the highest organization of man as 'organic', and calls it 'the mind-Body' ('le corps psychique'). At any rate, psychological causes do not create the disease, they can only liberate it.

The problem at hand: what is the demarcation between neurology and psychology? At first glance, no problem exists at all: neurology deals with neurological diseases and psychiatry with psychic ones. But this kind of answer to our problem only pushes it further, but does not answer it. Indeed, what demarcates the neurological from the psychiatric disease? We shall further see that the question is even more complex than meets the eye, since to the demarcation between the two kinds of disease runs in parallel with the demarcation between professions; and it will immediately be seen that some neurological diseases are treated by the neurologist but also some by the psychiatrist; and vice versa. This, moreover, is not unique. Thus, some neurological diseases are treated by the internist, e.g., polyneuritis which, caused by malnutrition or virus, i.e. by general or external cause, being diffuse, i.e. inflammation of the nervous system as a whole, is for the generalist. Similarly some internal diseases are treated by a neurologist, e.g. embolism, which has a spot of coagulated blood as the external enemy to abolish by the specialist, even though its effect, once it reaches the brain, is a general paralysis. This is confusing, quite apart from the fact that either or both may be relegated to the gerontologist or to the psychiatrist.

What, then, is a neurological disease? Of course, it is a disease of the peripheral or of the central nervous system (or of both). Yet we start with symptoms, not with diseases. If a patient comes and presents such a complaint as paralysis of a limb, he is considered prima facia a neurological patient. Now, such a complaint may be due to three (for the sake of argument three will suffice) different conditions. The first is a purely neurological one: a lesion of the pyramidal tract (the tract responsible for the voluntary movements), say due to a degenerative disease of the central nervous system. The second, a psychological one: the patient exhibits conversion hysteria. The third condition which may produce a paralysis is a stroke in the brain, say due to an internal condition such as an arteriosclerotic hypertensive cardiovascular disease. Now, even the first condition, the 'purely neurological' one, is most probably due to an enzymatic aberration, i.e. it is etiologically speaking a biochemical disease. What, then, is left for the neurologist? Only the clinical manifestations of the disease are neurological. Either the neurologist should be an expert in psychology, internal medicine and biochemistry, at least as far as they affect the nervous system, or else he should refer his patients to such experts. This is no flight of the imagination. Today, with the advance of our knowledge, mainly in biochemistry and in immunology, even such a respectable discipline as pediatrics begins to lose its independence. Many pediatric diseases are known today to be of an enzymatic nature, and the traditional pediatrician tends to disappear, replaced as he is, by the biochemist-pediatrician and other pediatric sub-specialists. One is tempted to imagine, what will be the face of internal medicine, since it will inevitably follow the change in pediatrics. To conclude, the significance of and benefit from medical specialization highly depends on flexibility, which flexibility can be maintained and checked only if high standards of diagnostics are maintained in a systematic and broad interdisciplinary fashion. Once diagnosis is clear, treatment is clearly prescribed, yet staying within a specialism insures systematic misdiagnosis.

Ey wants psychiatry to parallel medicine. What, then, is the psychiatric parallel to all this somatoiatric splitting? The psychiatrst's patients display psychological complaints (symptoms) and present morbid signs of a psychological nature. Now paralysis progressiva is a disease characterised anatomopathologically by changes in the brain, due to syphilis (treponema pallidum). Is it a psychiatric or a neurological disease? Is it a neurological or an internal diease? An infectious disease? What is its rule? The reader can see the complexity of the problem. The complexity lies in medicine having different though closely linked aspects, clinical (the nature of the symptoms and the signs, the course of the disease in time), pathological (the site of the lesion) and etiological (the cause of the disease); all three aspects of medicine are intermingled and thus present a complex. For example, a patient is sent to the emergency room of a hospital, because of severe pain in the right hypochondrium. He is suspected of having an 'acute abdomen' as the jargon has it. This is the surgeon's bread. Now an X-ray examination of the chest reveals pneumonia, it means that the site of the pathology is in the lungs, not the abdomen, (the pain of the hypochondrium was a 'referred pain') and the patient is transferred to the internal medicine department (medical ward). Now, it happens that the pneumonia is caused by a bacterium or a virus, and thus it is of the competence of the bacteriologist or virologist.

Let us go back to psychiatry. We mentioned the problematic aspect of paralysis progressiva. Another psychiatric 'classical' condition is dementia senilis. The psychological symptoms are well-known. The patient complains of loss of (immediate) memory, difficulties in his orientation in space and time, diminishing mental concentration, etc. He also displays signs of emotional instability, etc. Now dementia senilis may be due to a normal process of aging, or to an arteriosclerotic disease of the brain, or to a degenerative disease of the nervous system (itself due to an enzymatic aberration perhaps). Now, does dementia senilis belong to the psychiatrist, neurologist, or the internist? or should it belong to the geriatrist, who in turn, should draw from psychiatry, neurology and internal medicine?

Let us continue this discussion. Child psychiatry is diagnostically of the psychiatric domain. The patients display particular psychological well-known behavior patterns. Many are the possible causes of mental retardation: genetic, congenital, biochemical − or one of the psychological causes. One may say similar things of childhood autism. Who should treat these children? the psychiatrist? and what remains of his psychiatry if he becomes an expert of heredity (genetics), immunology, endocrinology, and biochemistry? Is psychiatry based on theory which is a part of biology or part of the theory of human conduct?

It is not difficult to understand why those psychiatrists, who are interested in human behavior and psychology, so easily turn to psychoanalysis. Most psychiatrists neglect the mentally deficient, the old, the organic psychotics; they turn to the neuroses and to the study of their possible psychological causes and psychological modes of treatment. A minority of psychiatrists occupy themselves with the psychoses, trying psychological treatments (psychoanalytical or other). Another minority of the psychiatrists study drug therapy, mostly on a trial-and-error basis. Now those who turn to psychoanalysis obviously abandon psychiatry. Those who turn to other psychological treatments likewise abandon psychiatry: they become a sort of psychologist. Those who play with drugs are empirical pharmacologists. What remains of psychiatry? Where did it evaporate?

This explains the neglect Ey's ideas suffered in his lifetime. For, Ey's attempt to rebuild psychiatry by bringing it back into medicine has, therefore, the characteristic of a radical move. Ey's organo-dynamism is not just another theory amongst others. It is the expression of a profoundly dissenting view of medicine, and of the place of psychiatry in it − even though many of its basic tenets are hardly controversial. Such is the claim that there is no harm in one discipline borrowing and using knowledge from any discipline in the sciences. One may draw from biochemistry or from psychology; it does not matter, since both disciplines may contribute to the living issues. The aim is not to prevent the 'evaporation of psychiatry'; it is, on the contrary, to integrate this knowledge — any knowledge — into a medical over-view, a medical frame of reference, a medical model proper.

And already we are in the middle of the debate. What is a medical over-view, a medical model proper? Were this the simple matter of dismissing the current medical model, Ey would not be so important a dissident: not only a small group of anti-psychiatrists inside psychiatry express their dissent from the current medical model; such a dissent is expressed no less vigorously outside psychiatry by many important social scientists and philosophers.

We think they make things easy for themselves. They may argue against an externalist model — they do not know that a generalist model exists since Hippocrates; they may argue against reductionism, which indeed is popular enough in medicine — they do not know of Claude Bernard; they may argue against deterministic tendencies in psychiatry with the all too obvious advantage that, metaphysics aside, all the sciences of Man admit the phenomenon of human choice and so of human freedom (even in mental disease). To see Ey's significance let us look again at the general situation in the field. There are models and they belong to two categories: the generalist and the externalist. But this is our own bias. There are other possibilities of grouping models: intrapsychic (Freud) and interpersonal (Adler, Sullivan); diachronic (historical, developmental) and synchronic (structuralist); constitutional (genetic) and environmental (infectious). One can cut the cake as one likes. What Ey suggests is a program which will embrace both externalist and generalist views with both hierarchical and structuralistic theories, synthesizing all divisions known and spreading before us a more synoptic view of the problem at hand. What in general is a disease? Given this, what is a mental disease? This way of posing the question is an expression of a revolutionary and unique move of implementing a generalist bias in a field where progress was externalist.

How, then, should one best view disease?

Here it is the place, perhaps, to recapitulate our first chapter, in which we tried to examine the concpet of disease, following the history of its evolution in medicine. There is no disease, says Hippocrates, there are only sick people. There is such an abstract entity as 'a disease', said his opponents. In any way, both schools will agree upon the reality of a given person, be he sick or be a victim of a disease. This reality was approached by physicians throughout the history of medicine from different points of view, generally always from one and exclusively one point of view, either generalist or externalist, either constitutional or environmental, either historical or structuralistic, etc. Sometimes the boundaries were not sharp; sometimes a generalist had some externalist traits and vice versa, but, on the whole, each theory when it was applied, was exclusively applied as such. The beginning of an integration of points of view was suggested by Jackson. It is a generalized Jacksonian theory that we present here, following Ey's ideas. This generalized theory is itself ancient holism, and may be expressed thus: each element in a structure is responsible for the whole structure, as well as the whole structure is responsible for each element; each structure is responsible for all the hierarchies it participates in, as well as all the hierarchies are dependent on each structure. The newer element of holism considers the contributions of parts to wholes and vice versa as negligible or significant, and significant particularly as contributing to the stability and perhaps also the equilibrium of the whole or as contributing to instability or disequilibrium.

It is clear that in such a view, the concepts of equilibrium and disequilibrium play an important role. In such a view the mere attempts to characterize the equilibrium and the disequilibrium of a given system become crucial. So it is, for a given system in equilibrium or disequilibrium to examine how does it switch from one state to another? For, disequilibrium can be more easily characterized relatively to a state of equilibrium already characterized. Moreover, since the state of a given system is not usually very rapidly alterable, it may be viewed as quasi-equilibrium, as in equilibrium of sorts stable at a given moment, and to varying degrees of accuracy. Moreover, even equilibrium is not equilibrium proper, not too permanent, since no living system is in a permanent state. Thus, in a way, disequilibrium and equilibrium are matters of degree. Following this line of reasoning, the characterization of equilibrium emerges on the surface as well. If a disequilibrium is understood as a more than momentary equilibrium of the system, how shall we differentiate it from equilibrium? Not only is total equilibrium death and violent disequilibrium dying, the sort of equilibrium that is health is hardly different from the quasi-equilibrium that is clearly a state of chronic or prolonged illness. And, since we have characterized illness as any attempt to restore equilibrium, the questions we ask now (what is equilibrium? and the like) make our characterization of illness most questionable.

The relevance of this discussion to a possible understanding of psychopathology is obvious. The mere terms 'incoherence' and 'dissociation', which in the traditional view denote the patient's state of mind are metaphors for disequilibrium and/or for dissolution. Though this is highly problematic it may already be taken not to preclude the state of a mind having an inner coherence, a momentary equilibrium, and even dissolution as such may in the short range become an integration of sorts at the precarious circumstances. This removes much of the paradoxical in the description of mental illness.

This highly complex organizational approach to disease, is thus strangely close to the phenomenological and existentialist approach, but it presents matter as problematic and does not dismiss this problematic character of the approach on the grounds of deep meaning. It is also reminiscent of the general systems approach, except that it is a variant of general systems which sees problems where that approach has variants which exhibit only solutions. Indeed, thus far our approach − which is adumbrated by Ey − has produced almost nothing but problems. (The other factor just mentioned is the clarification of the situation to clear it of some uninteresting paradoxes. Yet we have argued elsewhere, in our *Paranoia: A Study in Diagnosis,* that an attempt to apply the strict canons of medical diagnosis to mental patients is of value.)

Henri Ey tried to understand psychiatry in terms of viewing psychopathology, on a broad pattern of a theory of disease, and the theory of disease, as a process of both as a dissolution and an integration. In his *Etudes Psychiatriques* he rewrote the whole of psychiatry, reviewing for each disease the traditional concepts − both the organiscistic one and the psychoanalytical one − and adding his own way of understanding the disease. We do not claim that he succeeded in his attempt, but that he attempted to develop Jackson's way − the only known promising avenue of understanding disease, somatic as well as mental.

8. THE BUBERIANS

Freud centered on the individual. The most he conceded was that society entered the individual's make-up, that society may be different for different individuals but that they all have it enter their minds the same way − by guilt and by internalization. The individual's super-ego is the code of his social environment which steers his ego when it coordinates his actions. But when Adler saw neurosis as social maladjustment Freud chafed: he did not deny that the inferiority complex exists, but he demanded to reduce all sociology to psychology and thus all Adlerian psychopathology to Freudian.

But Freud was in error here even on his own terms. He said, quite repeatedly and consistently, that neurosis is a mode of adjustment and that only the maladjusted or the poorly adjusted needs therapy. Now, of course, maladjustment is decided by both the ability of the individual to adjust and the level of adjustment required by his society. At times, the social requirements may be very specific, and force one to be a pilot rather than a monk, from whom a higher level of adjustment is socially required. This can be generalized. Freud saw neurosis as the mode by which individuals adjust. Hence, adjustment and neurosis are not the same, though they are closely linked. How they link may depend on many social factors which determine the final outcome: is the individual reasonably functional or does he need treatment?

Strangely, the move that Adler initiated in the social direction, was not conspicuously the leading one, even though its underground influences may have been significant. The leading influences were of Buber and of Harry Stack Sullivan. We doubt that any two of the three, Adler, Buber or Sullivan, ever interacted.

We start with Buber. We start with him not on account of his psychopathology, but on account of his philosophic innovation of interpersonalism. (He seems to have taken the idea of society as inter-personal interactions from Georg Simmel's idea of the web of group-affiliation and Gustav Landauer's anarchistic version of communalism; but this is another mater altogether.) The interpersonal is neither the classical individualism, though classical individualistic psychology always postulated the need that one person has for the company and affection of others, nor the classical sociologism, even though classical collectivism did assume the existence of interpersonal relations (more of a master and slave than of equals, by the way) and their importance for the well-being of both individual and collective.

Philosophically, Buber took interpersonality to be prior to both indviduality and communality; we can have no individual without interpersonal relations, and no community either. Individuals come into being through interpersonal relations, he said, and networks of such relations build communities, societies, civilizations.

The shift from the 'I' to the 'I-thou' is a shift from one universe of discourse to another. The traditional universe of discourse in psychiatry sees the 'I' as the source of all knowledge, experience, and the center of events. The intra-psychic life is the arena where life's happenings take significance. That is not to say that the 'thou' does not exist. It does. But the 'thou' in that universe of discourse is merely another 'I'. By contrast, in the Buberian dialogical universe of discourse it is not the 'I' — or the 'thou' — which is of importance. The real arena of life, the arena where life takes its very significance, is that zone between the 'I' and the 'thou'. 'Because I say 'thou', I am', said Buber. All manifestations of human life, which are not saturated with the significance of the relationships between 'I' and 'thou', are events of relations between 'I' and 'it'; they are not of the essence. What makes a man what he is, is the dialogue he conducts. It is clear that for a Buberian, life which is not dialogic is pathological. Buber did not provide us with any specific theory as for a specific mental disease. He never discussed in psychological terms when, why and how one individual realizes a dialogical life, and another does not, since for Buber this question is not of the psychological realm at all. It is perhaps a theological one. Man can become dialogical by the grace of God. Yet Buber stresses here one important fact, be it psychological, philosophical, or theological: to engage in dialogue – in any specific dialogue or in dialogue in general – is a matter of the individual's choice.

Can we dismiss Buber's theory as irrelevant to human life because it is theological and not psychological? We do not think so: the grace of God is a reality which cannot be dismissed off hand even by non-believers, such as we profess to be. In our view one need not be a believer in any religious sense in order to consider grace to be an important factor in human life. We are not the only ones who see things in this way. R.D. Laing, who has strong Marxist and Sarterian-aetheists antecedents, called his *Divided Self* not in allusion to any psychopathological division of the self in the traditional psychiatric sense. He so titled his book after the name of Lecture 8 of William James's *Varieties of Religious Experience* – 'The Divided Self and the Process of its Unification [in God].' What some people call the 'psychedelic experience' referring to Laing's views of psychotic episodes, is not only a misleading name, but a profound misunderstanding of Laing (and in our view, also of the psychotic experience). In Laing's view the psychotic breakdown is much closer to a religious-mystical experience than to anything else.

Though it is not clear how the dialogical universe of discourse and psychopathology are related, if at all, there is no doubt that in present day psychotherapy the dialogists have the upper hand – for better or for worse. If there was a break-through in the psychotherapy of schizophrenia, then it was achieved by the Sullivanians (or by the most famous of them, Frieda Fromm-Reichmann), and achieved by their dialogical approach even though they did not use this term.

Admittedly the alleged breakthrough did not bring about a clearly articulable method for treatment leading to cure. Yet it has changed the scene so radically that today it is hard to consider the severity of the Freudian injunction not to treat psychotics and the enormous authority and social pressure on all sorts of psychiatrists that went along with this injuction until very recently (if it is not still extant in orthodox circles). Sullivan himself treated psychotics already in the early century, but he was known only to a small circle of devoted disciples and never published any comprehensive work. It was in the 40's that his disciple Frieda Fromm-Reichmann published; her *Principles of Intensive Psychotherapy* appeared only in 1951 and was an immediate best-seller (1.5 million copies). We mention her because it is a strange characteristic of all members of the heterogenous groups that they have a wide popular appeal though they have but a smattering of some sort of Buberian philosophy and hardly any psychopathology to speak of. (Yet they did speak of the site of the pathology which they did not claim to have an etiology of; and what they focused on is not any individual but the interpersonal relations, or perhaps the individual's unsated need for them.) The idea they share − with Fromm-Reichmann too − is that both therapist and patient are ignorant and should study the patient together through shared intensive experiences − indeed they both must be together very deeply and totally immersed. Obviously, this severely clashes with the concept of Freudian therapy, with the therapist hiding behind the patient's back, lips tightly closed in the name of objectivity. Even Adlerians who demand therapist-patient interaction, propose to keep the interaction on a professional and intellectual decent respectable level. Clearly, also, once we say the total immersion is obligatory both because every patient is a law unto himself and because therapist must be committed to his promise to try to cure him, then − by the very act of committing themselves − the Buberians become existentialists. Indeed, almost all Buberians and almost all Sullivanians, not to mention Carl Rogers, Rollo May, Victor Frankl, and Fritz Perls, perhaps even Abraham Maslow, they all repeatedly flirted with existentialism but refused to commit themselves to existentialism wholly (as Laing does) because they are committed to cure, whereas existentialists are not necessarily so committed. (Existentialism only demands commitment, not commitment to anything particular.)

   This chapter was devoted to psychopathology, yet the schools we are discussing in this section do not claim to have any pathology, only therapy. Before coming to therapy proper, however, we better clarify a few more points which we found foggy not only in the public mind but also in our own minds. In particular, we shall speak of scientific psychotherapy in the next chapter, thus preparing the ground for the continuation of the discussion begun in this section. Also, we shall say then more, and speak more favorably, about these people when discussing their treatment of psychosis (Chapter IV, 8).

III. THE RISE OF SCIENTIFIC PSYCHOTHERAPY

1. FIRST INTRODUCTION: FRAMEWORKS, HYPOTHESES, FACTS

Without going again into general considerations, we now try to present our view of scientific hypotheses as intermediary hypotheses — intermediary between general facts and metaphysics frameworks: the scientific hypotheses ideally explain general facts and conform to adopted metaphysics. And they should be empirically testable. For example, Newtonian hypotheses should all conform to Newton's framework of forces acting at a distance within Euclidean space along a universal time scale; and they should explain all the known general facts of the physical world. The frameworks in medicine are, as we repeatedly say, generalist holism and externalist mechanism. The trouble with scientific medicine, we contend, is in the paucity of its explanatory hypotheses — regardless of their conforming or not conforming to either frame.

Having presented two general frameworks, one concerning general medicine, and presenting generalism and externalism as its two major schools, and the other concerning general psychopathologies, showing them as belonging to these two schools, we should now move, finally, to the topic of this volume, namely therapy. Yet we propose to tread softly: what are the relations between metaphysics, science, and practice? and is psychotherapy a branch of therapy? is mental health a legitimate department of medicine? is mental illness illness proper? For, we contend, most of the fog in the literature — and the literature is notoriously foggy — centers on these questions.

Ideally, general theories should incorporate specific theories and these should lead to direct prescriptions — in all kinds of human thought and action. We have had ample occasion to show that it is hard to say who is a generalist and who is an externalist, what theory is generalist, what theory is externalist, what pathology follows what theoretical lines. In addition to all these ambiguities there is the question of the theoretical basis of any treatment.Historically, no doubt, many practices could be founded on many ideas, specific or general, yet always controversially and always to a controversial extent. How much was humoralism responsible for bleeding, cupping, and so on? We do not know, and can elicit diverse answers from different historical figures and from different historians. In particular, we may consider suspect all specfic theoretical foundations to general practices. Was bleeding restricted to the west where humoralism was popular, for example? We do not quite know.

Yet, quite generally, certain commonsense methods, such as prescribing of a change of air, exercises and baths, diets, rest, and so on, all these were common to many medical traditions over centuries, and when psychiatry came into being, it used the same kind of commonsense prescriptions. And so we would not be surprised if the reader shows impatience here and calls for some less vague, metaphysical or commonsense ideas, and for more specific, sophisticated theories and means of treatment. This is understandable and easily satisfiable, yet with very disappointing results.

The reason is very simple and obvious: the specific theories and the specific treatments do not mix at all. For example, brain waves are as specific and sophisticated as they come, and can help diagnose epilepsy, but not psychosis. Epilepsy and Parkinsonism are chemically controllable, but precious little is known about how or why. To take a different kind of example, electric shocks and lobotomy are very specific and sophisticated treatments in the sense that last century no one thought about them, yet they are most nonspecific sorts of butchery, where the treatment is that of putting a bull in a china shop and waiting to see what effect it will have a week later. Another disappointing example: the Oedipus complex is a very sophisticated piece of psychological construction. Does it lead anyone, even the Freudians, to any practical conclusion? Is behavior modification, likewise, linked to Skinner's variant of behaviorism, not to mention his variant of operationalism, or is it a mere systematization of most ancient and most traditional learning theory?

These and similar questions seem to us too difficult to handle without first carefully contriving a frame within which to orderly conduct the present discussion. Yet we have by now enough of a frame within which to start with the most specific treatments available: we can describe and relate them to generalism and to externalism. It will soon transpire that the specific treatments obviously link to general theories but not to specific theories. Now, this being so, the reader should not be surprised to learn that such treatments, however specific, do not force the hands of opponents: when a specific treatment rests on a specific theory, it is the theory that challenges; yet when the treatment rests on a philosophy, however obviously and straightforwardly, the holders of the opposite philosophy may see the facts differently, and with little effort. It is easier, in other words, to reinterpret facts than explanatory hypotheses so as to make them conform to a given intellectual framework. And it is hardest to offer a competing explanation, especially in conformity to a given framework.

The matter is really foggy from the very start as long as we have only general theories and no intermediate explanatory ones. What causes mental illness? Generalists say, general strain; externalists say, some external factor, such as poison, which may enter the brain. What can be simpler and more straightforward? Yet, it is not. In our first chapter we argued that even if, for example, administering vitamins to a mental patient will restore his mental health this will not be a decisive externalist victory, as we may still speak of restoring the general balance of his system in accord with generalism; but this example is too sophisticated for our present purposes. Here we shall offer two devastating criticisms of the dispute and with them conclude this introduction and go into detail.

First, regarding illness. No externalist will deny that strain is of the essence; no generalist will deny that strain is causally related − both ways − to body chemistry. No one since Cannon will dare deny either claim; the evidence is considered by all to be plainly overwhelming. We now know for sure − as sure as empirical physiology permits, that is − that cerebral arteriosclerosis may cause suspicion that may be, and at times is, diagnosed as paranoid. But does the defect cause persecutionism or an organic deterioration that brings about mental deterioration including suspicion? We do not know. Does hashish cause persecutionism and not universal love? Was the psychosis triggered by LSD a psychosis that already was there or was it created by the drug? What does the question signify if every living being has to cope both with a delicate chemical balance and with a delicate mental one? We do not know. Were we heartless, tough-and-no-nonsense analysts, we would analyze the problem away as too foggy and the two contending schools as merely stressing each a different part of the picture rather than denying each other's views. But we do not wish to go that far.

Second, regarding treatment. The hard facts, if they at all exist, signify that all therapists use both mental and chemical cures, that some borderline cases are solved by one or the other of the two components but most cases are treated in both ways simultaneously − usually with too little success for comfort.

For all we know the success rate of any possible treatment or combination of treatments is the same.

This is why our present study is a survey of the situation: we have too little to offer and the little we have is too confused. There is a need, we propose, for more careful a study of what we have at hand before better ideas can be offered.

So much for the introduction. We shall now examine, first, the chemotherapeutic techniques now in use, then the psychotherapeutic ones, and then trace them to the beginnings of psychotherapy in the days of Pinel.

2. SECOND INTRODUCTION: THE PSEUDO-SCIENTIFIC CHARACTER OF CHEMOPSYCHOTHERAPY

In medicine the custom is that the term rationale (or therapeutic rationale), the very technical term so dear to practicing physicians (a term, incidently, which is, of course, far from being merely technical), is used as follows: the normal question routinely and frequently heard, usually put by a consultant to a young resident, is about the rationale for treatment practised or prescribed. In the case where no rationale exists for a given treatment, a practicing physician may say, all I know is, it works. God knows, this answer is all too frequently given. So, if no rationale exists, at least an empirical backing is necessary. In short, whatever you do in medicine, your action could not pass without some sort of other justification or validation.

Let us be brutally frank with ourselves. Whatever a person connected with medical practice in any way whatsoever, be he a physician, a historian, a sociologist, or a researcher, whenever he hears about wild claims of backing allegedly given to bleeding and to cupping and to the claim that an eight month foetus cannot be born to live, and so on, his response is the same: it is all a matter of the distant past. Alternatively, when present cases are mentioned, of obviously spurious claims for empirical backing, and we all know that to some extent these are unavoidable, then the response is equally apologetic; medicine is not a mathematical science; it is a complex matter; doctors must do something and cannot always wait for the best results of the best tests possible.

We are very far from denying the truth of these highly apologetic remarks. We consider them irresponsible, not because of their content but because of their function: when someone shows some generally admitted claim for empirical backing to be spurious, this should cause us some concern − but the apologetic remarks dispel the concern. We may be too busy to investigate the spurious evidence, or not sufficiently competent to do so, and the fact that medicine is not a mathematical science should only alert us all the more to the question, how come we have accepted spurious evidence and how should we do better in future? Yet the apologetic remarks come to calm the conscience of its user, not to awaken it.

We must stress − in order to avoid sounding censorious about empirical errors − that empirical backing is often unavoidably spurious, perhaps more in psychotherapy than in other branches of therapy. And, indeed, such backings have been severely challenged by hardliners, such as Joseph Wolpe and Hans Eysenck. But we feel that no matter how correct is the substance of the ammunition used in such attacks, some unfairness is implicit in these attacks; they insinuate, and at times marginally affirm, that medicine as a whole has more stringent standards than psychotherapy. It is this that we want to question, though not outrightly deny; we honestly do not know. All that we do know, and find a priori not surprising at all, is that in some branches of medicine — mental, physical, and particularly preventive (again, both mental and physical) — empirical backing is excellent, in some terribly shaky. Now, on the coattail of the unfounded claim that physical medicine has better backing than psychiatry, the chemotherapists claim to belong to medicine proper rather than to any other school and their studies to belong to biological psychiatry. But rubbing shoulders with the best is in itself no guarantee for anything.

Let us take the bull by its horns. Take the most fundamental requirement of any empirical backing, namely that it is done by a scientifically attested fact, which means a repeatable fact. Now if we say of a sophisticated chemical, say Tofranil, that we do not know why it works, but that it works, we refer to an alleged scientific fact. Now, in fact, we do not know who will benefit from it and who will not — and let us ignore now damage and side effects for a while; we will return to these in proper time — but this is not a difficulty since we may use statistics. But statistics applies properly only to well-defined populations, such as pregnant women; not to such vague diagnoses as those of depressed people, let alone the schizophrenias.

We do not oppose the chemical treatment of depressed people. Nor do we oppose any of the significant successes of chemotherapy, which we shall not survey here.[1] What we want to stress is the unscientific nature of the claim — all too often admitted as a matter of course — that Tofranil is a useful drug against depression, impotence, bed-wetting, or even obsessive-compulsive neurosis. We may wish readily to administer this drug ourselves, to such cases or to different ones. What we contend is an obvious truth concerning the alleged scientific — though not quite — status to empirical backings: we may have to use control groups, for example, and then take good care that the diagnosis is used laxly — and it must be used laxly since it is very lax — in a manner a priori unfavorable to the claim that the drug works. Also, we may try to test the diagnosis, make better pilot tests, etc. etc. These commonsense proposals are

---

1.   The interested reader is directed to the following two works which we find very useful. Frank Ayd, Jr. and Papa & Barry Blackwell (eds.), *Discoveries in Biological Psychiatry*, 1970; Donald F. Klein, R. Gittelman, F. Quitkin and A. Rifkin, *Diagnosis and Drug Treatment of Psychiatric Disorders*, 1969, 1980.

both insufficient (i.e., do not yet ascertain the status of scientific tests) and, as we shall now see, not yet put to practice by medical practioners as much as is desirable.

Before coming to the point we must draw attention to the poverty of the present discussion. Since this is not a treatise on the philosophy of technology we must leave it at that with most points untouched. Standards of tests of claims for empirical backing are concrete matters of forensic medicine, of research customs and traditions and of traditions as expressed by bureaux of standards, say. We hope that in future the statistics that come to validate the scientific status be examined for proper sampling methods. We shall not elaborate but soon come up with a few examples.

There is a lot to say about statistics in medicine. In the public mind, statistics have three different connotations, all having to do with science. But as far as science is concerned, these connotations are not only different, but have indeed opposite meanings. One is of statistics as a means of observing useful facts; the second, that of a pure mathematics; the third is of empirical testing within theoretical science. The first and original connotation of statistics, the 'applied' one, stems from the very etymological sense of the word: statistics means 'state'. The origin of the term lies in French fiscalism. In order to determine tax levels in a fair manner, one had to establish a way of evaluating not merely the value of the income/expenses of every single citizen, but to do more than that: to compare it to a given standard. In order to find a standard, a technique was created that consists of the summing up of the income of a numer of villagers, for example, and dividing it to the number of the villagers in question. The concept of the 'Norm' was thus created. It had an economical function. At the same historical period statistics also provided information data for the central government (the king), such as the number of births and deaths, etc., and so 'vital statistics' was born. Both the economic statisticians and the acturians (who deal with vital statistics), soon found out that there is no necessity of counting each and every villager's income in the country, nor to count the birth and death of every citizen. Samples sufficed: 'averages' were found that satisfied the needs of the state, since the statistician found a method that was simpler, cheaper, yet not less efficient than the mere 'counting', provided that the sampling was representative, i.e. statistically valid. The question, is the sample representative, is problematic and leads us to the other two senses; but practically if the sample is challenged, the very challenge can be used to create a new sample.

The state needs no more; it 'worked'. This is how statistics was born, and this simple example which demonstrates how, from an economical and administrative reason of the birth of the modern state, plus a need for 'validity', statistics came to be an applied, practical, yet considered a scientific discipline.

What we said so far accounts for the first connotation of statistics, i.e., it's connotation of an applied technique of assessment. The second connotation of statistics, i.e., it's connotation as a pure scientific discipline, lies in that it is viewed not as something dealing with practical, applied affairs, but in that it is considered to be a component of mathematics — of 'pure mathematics' that is; it is a component of 'high mathematics'. It derives it's validity from its conformity to the mathematical canons, for example from its being axiomatized. Obviously, this sort of statistics is of another kind altogether.

And, the mathematical theory of statistics also concerns the practical techniques of empirical testing of scientific hypotheses, just as the mathematical theory of differential equations concerns physics and ecology and ever so many different fields.

Yet, when we make claims that a certain treatment 'works', it is no mere observation of facts as in vital statistics; it is no scientific hypothesis since precisely these are the cases which 'work' in which we have no scientific hypothesis to offer; they are, of course, much less a matter of pure mathematics. Indeed, they more or less fall between the stools.

Here some philosophers speak of 'probability' in some philosophical sense; the more we see aspirin curing headache the more we tend to believe that it does. Now this is just stuff-and-nonsense: to say that we believe that A causes B because 75 out of 100 cases of A are accompanied by cases of B is very foolish since we know for sure that A alone does not cause B from the very same fact, namely that 25 out of 100 cases of A are not accompanied by B.

It is strange to find that physicians, who were educated on Claude Bernard's maxim, that even one negative result is worth more than hundreds of affirmative ones, practice daily completely contrary to this prescription of the person they view as the father of modern physiology, experimental medicine, etc.

Of course, cases where 75 out of 100 A's are also B's are of importance for testing of statistical hypotheses; but the theory and practice of statistical testing are a different matter altogether. At the very least we should be able to take the hypothesis that some cure 'works' as a hypothesis that in a population of patients of given sort the chances for a cure for the sub-population treated by the specific technique of cure in question are considerably higher than in the remaining sub-population. And the theory of testing tells us that the selection of the populations on whom the effectiveness of a given technique is tested must be specified by techniques independent of the specific techniques in question, and that the sampling should be reliably repeated and tested for selecting representative samples. That is to say repeatability of any (statistical) experiment under (statistical) scrutiny is of the essence before it can be viewed as scientific.

Let us stress the fact that in all medicine vital statistics is all too often taken to count as data, as result of statistical tests or experiments. Yet, we know that this is not so: not all data are results of tests and they should be ignored. No matter how much information we have about Tofranil or about aspirin or about quinine or about the pill; scientific experiment requires sampling and testing, not merely recording. This is how quinine was found to be specific, how quinine was found to be losing its specific effectiveness, etc. etc. As we shall see, the whole of the chemopsychopharmacological school of thought breaks down on the point of statistical testing. In order to show this we have to examine the most basic claims of the psychopharmacological school and see how they enable us, if at all, to use any statistics.

Let us repeat: chemotherapy is extremely widespread in psychiatry.[1] We are here to attack the chemopsychopharmacological school of thought; we are not here to attack the use of physical or chemical means, such as the use of drugs, in psychotherapy or any other place. It is proper to defend it by the (true) claim that to the largest extent, that it is easiest, cheapest, and most relieving to a hospital staff, to administer daily sedatives, tranquilizers, and aspirins. But we are speaking not of the chemical practice as of the chemical school, of those who think of mental illness as a biochemcial imbalance or disturbance to be properly and frontally tackled.

First, let us notice, most of those who administer drugs are not members of any specific school, and some of those who are, belong to the psychiatric, not the chemical school. Are there, then, clinics that practice exclusively the chemical ideas, or at least move in line with the philosophy of the chemical school? How do treatments recommended specifically by that school differ from the usual? Where is such treatment available and how efficient is it claimed to be?

The answer is most disappointing, and not only because of one by now obvious fact that even there (i.e in most of the chemically oriented centers) psychotherapy still prevails in addition to the chemotherapy administered. (Even there some form or other of psychotherapy do abound, which incidently, in itself is not necessarily a disadvantage for the patient.) The answer is

---

1.   See H.M. Van Praag, 'Tablets and Talking – A Spurious Contrast', in J. Agassi, ed., *Psychiatric Diagnosis:* Proceedings of an International Interdisciplinary Interschool Symposium, Bielefeld University, 1978, Balaban International Science Services, Philadelphia, 1981, 153-164.

disappointing because there are, the world over, only a handful of clinics of this sort, and their success is minimal.

Although mental illness is almost two centuries old, psychotherapy proper is only less than one century old − hypnosis, autosuggestion, psychoanalysis − and psychopharmacology proper is no more than three decades old. And shock therapy and lobotomy, if they merit honorable mention at all − which we sincerely doubt − precede psychopharmacology by a decade. Yet, historically, queasy as we are, we must observe, these brutal methods were biological, did make an impression on the profession, did raise hopes, did offer an impetus for psychopharmacology, and did decline though regrettably not utterly vanish. And, we cannot honestly deny even that at times these butcheries are possibily justifiable.

We must stress that the enormous progress of pharmacology is indeed a boon. But let us be brutal with this young promising branch too. Is there any novelty at all as yet in psychopharmacological treatment? Are alcohol, canabis, opium and its derivatives, barbiturates, and similar traditional drugs so very different from the new drugs? Are mescaline, amphetamines, and LSD, really new, for that matter? As we know, amphetamines were discovered by an American of Chinese origin who made use of his limited familiarity with Chinese traditional pharmacology (pejoratively titled 'herbalism') before World-War II. And it was amphetamines and tranquilizers that set hopes high and gave impetus to research. But with what results?

There is no escape from an intellectual approach to technological innovation, however practical: the defence of any new cure merely by the traditional claim 'we have no idea, but it works', with no rationale at all is always highly suspect. We must have some idea, however vague and however tentative, of a biological mechanism, of causation, of balance, of whatever else one cares to talk about. We have shown here, quite conclusively we think, that claims for novelty of either drug or its use, seem impossible without further explanation. But not only novelty of drug and use, also novelty of success or success rate: what counts as success? why? We only have one statistical criterion for success, and that is comparing two groups as to perseverance of symptoms, death rate, and other incapacity. In other words, we must have a theory of pathology, we must have an idea of what wrong is rectified, before we can say at all that 'it works' in any sense, not to mention that we should have some idea as to how we can perform repeatable statistical tests to check its truth. There may even be a partial sense to saying that a cure works without specifying the ill, but even this requires a partial pathology, and this is not known as yet (perhaps it does not exist).

Let us stress that we are not the first to hold these views about the need for pathology to make sense of any claim for success, though we have not found anywhere a straight and unapologetic statement of the problem-situation. The fact is that the chemical school was regularly concerned with the problem and attacked it with the program of psychopharmacology which is as follows. Suppose we found certain chemical abnormal characteristics, similar or not so similar to the Rhesus factor incompatibility, whether in the blood, in concentrations of hormones, in chemical qualities of secretions, in sodium/potassium balance, in the genetic mechanism, etc. Suppose we found that this abnormalcy is fairly normal in mental homes. Then we could substitute for diagnosis the chemical tests that correlate with them. Perhaps we may be luckier; we may find two abnormalcies, the one correlated with manic depressives, and the other with the schizophrenias! After all, such is the scientifically attested case of the mental retardation due to genetic factors known as Down's syndrome. Moreover, a chemical abnormality can possibly be treated. The blood of a blue baby can be replaced, the bone marrow of the sufferer of leukemia can (not really); inborn errors of metabolism may be cured by supplementing the body with a proper enzyme or even through a diet. So is the forgetfulness associated with senescence. So, if we knew what abnormality causes or is mental illness, we might know how to treat it!

Let us stress, we may have a successful cure with or without a rationale with or without a proper knowledge of the seat of the trouble; these constitute four possible cases of a cure, and ample examples for each. Yet none of them is the case of mental illness.

To specify. Serotonin. It has been claimed that the mentally ill suffer an unusual imbalance, whose end-product is a high concentration of serotonin in their urine. Perhaps the imbalance is over-production of serotonin, perhaps an excess excresion of it; the question we raise is, can we identify mental illness by excess serotonin in the urine? The answer is a resounding no! Even a high consumption of bananas may lead to this excess.

The reader may think our example frivolous, and so it may indeed be. Quite possibly we may test for serotonin after due caution concerning diet; perhaps even test all sorts of other disturbances. For, after all, this is a rather trivial matter that is handled well enough by statisticians who use sampling methods to test given hypotheses. The question is perhaps still tricky: it has turned out that in the United States all inmates, of mental homes and of prisons, show high serotonin concentration in their urine — some say it is due to the staple diet in government institutions; we do not know.

Yet this does not have to matter. What happens in jails and in mental homes is vital statistics, not at all statistics; and so not to the point at all. The point is, indeed, that we can only ascertain such matters without frivolity by proper statistical sampling methods. That is to say, we must sample mental patients properly and then test them for serotonin. But if we sample mental patients, as this school of psychopharmacology suggests, by reference to serotonin, then the test is redundant since success is assured.

In other words, the program is doomed to be refuted by frivolous arguments, like the argument from bananas, and any proper attempt to exclude any frivolous criticism will insure the program's utter success.

We do not mean to limit this severe and in our opinion deadly criticism to the chemical school alone. It is the fallacy that confuses vital statistics with statistical tests by proper statistical sampling that is our real target. Thus, for example, the same critical remarks we have made may be addressed to a psychotherapist, such as Hans Eysenck, who himself so forcefully attacks his colleagues for the absence of a scientific method in their researches. For, he himself tests schizophrenic patients, so diagnosed by psychiatric criteria which he (rightly) dismisses as not proper. And he publishes the results for his tests (the test of his hypothesis of introvertion-extrovertion) claiming that they are scientifically based upon 'raw material' that he himself deems objectionable.

But, by exposing the unscientific nature of the statistics of the psychopharmacological school we do not wish to denounce it. Historically serotonin was a bliss. When LSD was first synthesized in 1938 it had no medical use. When it was found to be hallucinogen in 1943, it was still deemed useless. After all, hallucinogens are not new — indeed not even LSD which was known to many primitive tribes as an extract not of lysergic moss but of morning glory seeds. Yet the fact that serotonin and LSD25 are members of the same chemical family, struck a chord in the hearts of all the members of the psychopharmacological or chemical or medical school.

Let us stress the importance of the chemical side of it, the heart of psychopharmacology. The connection between mental illness and hallucinogens and dreams and fantasy are old and their locus classicus is the work of Moreau (de Tours) of 1845. The psychopharmacological twist comes in the resemblances of serotonin and LSD25: here we can show a chemical imbalance in mental illness.

This serotonin-LSD-schizophrenia alleged correlate, we know now, is a mere coincidence. But it raised high hopes. Now the sedimentation is what the psychotherapists, especially the Freudians, believe it or not, said in response to the discovery: psychopharmacology, they said, may aid psychotherapy; under the influence of LSD (or of some magic concoction of both uppers and downers) a patient may be more easily pried into. This, too, was but a dream.

The last word in the chemical school's research program makes two distinctions. It first distinguishes the mental patient from the one susceptible to mental illness, since the illness itself obviously depends on both susceptability and external stresses. It further distinguishes schizophrenia as a distinct strain. It then tends to view the disposition or susceptibility to schizophrenia − the jargon for it is the schizoid condition − with some constitutional factors open to hard line investigation.

Yet, to begin with, one must establish − statistically − a strong corrolation between the schizophrenic and the schizoid. It would be easy if we could complete the program, observe the schizoid by his genes, say, and the schizophrenic by a written test, say, and correlate the two. But the program is only starting and we only wish to correlate the schizophrenic and schizoid to make sure we are are on the right track.

The correlation was made, and it was fairly successful. The question is, how were schizophrenic and schizoid identified. The schizophrenic was a certified patient. The schizoid was identified less clearly; but one of his distinguishing marks was that he could have a schizophrenic for a sibling. What the correlation showed, then, was that if we increase our willingness to view the person schizoid if he is a sibling to a schizophrenic then we are more likely to find that siblings of schizophrenics are schizoid than not. These shocking results were proven in a lengthy statistical essay in *Science,* the official organ of the American Association for the Advancement of Science, in 1963.

3. BEGINNINGS: PINEL

It is no accident that the beginnings of psychotherapy are situated at the time of Pinel, Tuke and Rush. It is anchored in the very epoch of the beginnings of psychiatry, which is contemporary with those ideas − with this Zeitgeist − the expression of which was the American and the French Revolution. It is not only no accident that these three events happened simultaneously; it has a deeper meaning. The vision of Man as freedom, the idea of liberty, is the core of these revolutions; and as understood then, liberty implies equality and fraternity. To see the mentally ill as equal human beings and to approach them with both understanding and compassion, is a natural consequence of the ideals of the French Revolution. Incidentally, a profound view of mental illness is expressed in the very name given to the patients by the French language: they were called the 'alienated'. This term implies that what is characteristic to mental illness is the alienation or estrangement of the patient from his true nature, which is freedom. Obviously freedom here is meant as it is in the context of the epoch, i.e., to be a free citizen in a society of equals which implies adjustment and conformity to science.

Let us remind the reader that the very existence of mental illness is still not beyond doubt. And so, perhaps Pinel and his coevals have invented the fiction of mental illness. No matter. They did so, nevertheless, in the name of human rights and human dignity which belong even to occupants of the lowest rungs of human society as they knew it. Even Thomas S. Szasz, the greatest enemy of this alleged fiction, who argues − at times most forcefully, no doubt − that the stigma of mental illness is an invitation to give up human dignity, even he agrees. He argues that though the guillotine is a progress over earlier methods of execution, its very swiftness and neatness cost many their lives. Perhaps; but he does not question the noble motives of Dr. Guillotin; nor of Dr. Pinel.

Psychotherapy is as old as psychopathology; with the beginnings of clinical diagnosis and psychopathology, psychotherapy began. It is very interesting to note, however, that psychotherapy was not based upon a psychopathology. Generally in medicine, a treatment is based upon the idea one has of the etiology of the disease, its pathogenesis, pathology, etc. A treatment supposedly must have a rationale. In the case of psychotherapy at the time of the 18th century (and indeed also in the 19th century), there could not have been a psychotherapy of any rationale in the medical sense, since the accepted idea by all psychiatrists was that psychopathology is organically determined. All mental diseases have organic causes, they said, though of course not all causes are presently known. (In fact none was known, of course.) It is only from Freud onwards that psychotherapy gained a rationale for its implementation; perhaps we could trace this rationale back to Charcot, Babinski and Janet. Nevertheless, the psychiatrists of the 18th century strongly argued for psychotherapy for the mentally ill. What could have been then the idea of psychotherapy for Pinel, Tuke, and Rush?

Before answering, let us examine the presuppositions of the question. They were presented in the beginning of the previous paragraph, as a matter of course. And, as an emprical fact we can report that the previous paragraph reads quite unproblematically. Yet it is very problematic. It is, of course, quite remote from the historical facts, and it is a rational reconstruction of a situation not too rich in rationality, and thus rather a beautification of history.

We wish to stress this, because we are comparing the rational reconstruction of the history of physical and of mental treatment. In both cases, as in all human cases, we find all sorts of folly, incompetence, and ignorance. Even the legendary mad doctor is not quite as rare as histories of medicine may let us suppose. But when we attempt a rational reconstruction we ignore the mad and backward, and the inept. We allow bleeding because it has a rationale − much as we find that rationale so very unappealing − but we stop at newts and lizard tails and aphrodisiacs of all sorts not because they do no good — bleeding does no good and worse — but because they lack all rationale. So do hot and cold compresses; so do bandages and even corsets and casts of all sorts. Yet we do not class them with the newts and the lizard tails. Why? Perhaps because we do have a rationale for the bandages and corsets and casts and even for the hot and cold compresses. But this is a game of being wise after the event; it is very dangerous. A highly superstitious treatment may gain rationale from researchers who have no knowledge of it and the rationale may be destroyed by later generations of researchers. This kind of rationale has nothing to do with historical reconstruction and we dismiss it off-hand. Nevertheless, we do admit that bandages and corsets and casts, professional or folk-medical, even when they are not at all to our tastes, are more rational than concoctions traditionally administered in professional and folk-medicine almost universally. The reason, of course, is dual. There was no theoretical guideline and there were empirical guidelines. There was, as a point of fact, a theoretical justification for applying leeches and not for applying diverse herbs and cups and corsets. And there was an empirical basis for all these, not very good to be sure, and now we can declare the empirical basis for corsets better than for herbs, and for herbs with digitalis, quinine, atropine or amphetamine better than herbs with nothing more than menthol and camphor.

It is important, then, for the study of psychotherapy, to ignore much of the non-rational in classical therapy, and admit into the purely empirically-backed therapy a mixed bag of treatments which were at the time not well distinguished and not separately empirically tested. And with this caution, we feel we may return to the question we have posed: what could have been the idea of psychotherapy for Pinel, Tuke and Rush?

What Pinel thought of psychotherapy is clearly expressed in the very title of his book, *The Moral Treatment of the Alienated*. When he spoke of moral treatment, he did not dismiss the physical treatment based upon the knowledge of the time about the use of tranquilizers, minerals, cold and hot showers, etc. But he insisted that these physical measures are not enough, and he advocated adjunct moral treatment which he divided into two parts. The first part of the treatment consists of the general approach to the mentally ill which should be humane. One should respect the patient — any patient — and hence never coerce him. The second part of the treatment is specific; and especially intended for the mentally ill. It consists of a variety of techniques, the aim of which is to educate or reeducate the patient or rather help him learn — learn to enter the civil life of civil society, learn to work to behave comme il faut, to obey the social order and social regulations of all sorts. It is clear that the first part of the treatment is general. It introduced the mentally ill into both medicine and society. It expresses the view that the mentally ill are both human beings and patients. As such this part of the 'moral treatment' is the basis for any further psychotherapy of any version in the future. The second part of the treatment, the special one, is based on so obvious a social demand to adjust — to conform — that we are surprised that no one ever challenged it save the antipsychiatrists of the mid-twentieth century. It is interesting to note how medical concepts changed not only according to pure medical thinking (what is 'pure' medicine?), but also in line with the developing social philosophies.

It is not our task to show the obvious, i.e., that metaphysics influences medical thinking. Of course it does. Our task here is to show that for the psychiatrists of the 18th and 19th centuries no psychotherapy was rationally possible for a disease that in their opinion could not be other than cerebral. Yet they prescribed psychotherapy for these patients. The question is, how did psychotherapy emerge? To what extent was it based on a clear rationale?

Psychotherapy indeed was prescribed; it was not the rationale that prescribed psychotherapy; it was common sense. Put generally, we say this. It was not the scientific rationale of the theoretician that provided treatments to medicine, but it was the practical sense and the good common sense of the daily practitioner that guided medical practice. A medical rationale is a principle, but the urge 'to do' is not less forceful.

And so, as physicians prescribed for most ills rest, good air and baths (to those who could afford it), so early mental healers prescribed rest, good air and baths. Indeed, in order to re-establish the feeling of well-being for either physical or mental distresses, the same physical and psychological means were applied. These means were sufficient for those mental patients whom we would today label mildly neurotics. To those whom we would call today the psychotics, the 'moral treatment', Pinel's treatment, had to be added: since the patients, due to their behavior, were outcasts, it was the role of the physician to reintegrate them into society, by modifying their behavior. To this end, Pinel suggested a new medical instrument, previously unthought of, i.e., the mental hospital. He considered the mental hospital as an appropriate set-up for the re-education of the patients if properly administered (in both the administrative and the prescriptive sense of the word).

As is known, this very special and specific therapeutic instrument, the mental hospital, the insane asylum, has been recently heavily attacked and condemned by E. Goffman, who considers it as just another kind of a 'total institution'. Did the mental hospital change from 1789 to our days? If it did, obviously it did for the better: we have today better material conditions for patients, more efficient medical treatments, a more sophisticated 'moral treatment' with the aid of psychiatric social workers and occupational therapists. In those places where things did not change for the better, at least they did not change for the worse. But if the mental hospital remains as it was in 1789, why did the commended then become so condemnable in 1960? Psychiatric knowledge did not change since 1789, at least not in principle, and the same applies for treatment. But the same 'moral treatment' seems not to fit any more. Why? – Indeed, the question is, to what does the 'moral treatment' seem unfit? Is it unfit as a medical model, to the medical view of mental illness (which did not change since 1789)? Or is it unfit only as far as a social view is concerned? Here again we see that, possibly, changing social philosophies intervene in medical affairs. Let us examine this situation. Let us repeat the question: did the attitude change towards the mental hospital (as the instrument of 'moral treatment', i.e., of psychotherapy) because of a change in the medical fashion proper, or did the attitude change just because of a change in the social climate? And let us further examine the question thus. If it was a change due to a shift in medical matters, was this shift in medical views a consequence of a general social change, or an autonomous one?

We said in the preface of this essay that in order to study the nature of contemporary psychotherapies in depth, we should have to study the different schools of psychopathology. Furthermore, the different psychopathologies should be studied in their turn on the background of the general pathology, i.e. on the background of the existing streams of medical thinking.

Let us begin with Hippocrates, then.

The facts are these. In the 4th centruy B.C. there were two rival medical centers: Cos and Cnidus. Cos was Hippocrates'. Surely both social structures and existing social philosophies at the time were the same for both schools.

The two schools differed both in physical and in mental matters, for all we know. The physical dispute evolved into the generalist-externalist dispute we have outlined above. Mental matters were then taken away from the medical profession and treated by church and/or by secular society until the French Revolution and its rational liberalism destroyed the classical tools for treating the insane, be these monasteries or 'ships of fools'. The French Revolution was scientific in orientation and hence it was materialistic and so it and its followers, up to and including young man Freud, were externalists as a matter of course. This was to no avail. In the meantime, the older asylums were replaced by the newer ones, the hospitals for the mentally ill.

We shall here examine developments in the period following Rush, Tuke and Pinel, and preceding Charcot, Janet, Babinski, and of course Freud.

4. ESQUIROL

We were at pains to stress that the therapy that can be rationally reconstructed has no theoretical background to speak of and at times even its empirical background is hardly worth mentioning. It is all too easy to condemn our predecessors for this, and even ourselves when we act likewise. This condemnation is unjust. When we notice that the condemnation is unjust we can either lower our standards which are too high or fool ourselves that we live up to these unreasonable standards. We wish to stress that in our opinion when there is nothing better available it is rational, at times even imperative, to act with no theory and in the light of rather feeble empirical experience.

Even when empirical experience looks theoretically suspect, even when it is both theoretically suspect and feeble, it may yet be rational. This is not only regarding the allegedly ignorant past but likewise regarding the allegedly enlightened present (since, obviously, enlightenment is but a matter of degree). We do administer now amphetamines which are stimulants par excellence, to hyperactive children, i.e. to children too active already and too easily stimulable anyway, and just in order to tranquilize them. This is counter theoretical as yet and empirically rather questionable as yet, yet we do it.

And rightly so, but only for one single reason: as yet we can serve patients no better. But only temporarily, since the case is under increasingly better empirical study and theoreticians keep puzzling over the diverse aspects of this paradoxical phenomenon.

With this in mind, let us glance at psychotherapy between Pinel and Charcot. We confess at once: we are not historians and we have found no histories easily offering us a picture of the situation that we can trust except Henri Ellenberger and Michel Foucault, and for the obvious reason that it took these two sensitive writers to penetrate the historians' faulty reconstructions (against which we have argued in the previous section). Let us report here the contribution of the French Jean Etienne Dominique Esquirol.

Esquirol was Pinel's favorite pupil and successor. As a liberal citizen he was largely responsible for '*la loi de 1838*' (the French 'lunacy bill' of 1838), the first of its kind in the world; the bill intended to protect society from violent madmen and madmen from society's abuses. Esquirol was kind and intelligent. His relationships with Auguste Comte may serve as an illustration of this. Comte was for some time a mental patient: in 1826 he suffered from an acute delusional state and was put in a mental hospital. Esquirol was his psychiatrist. In 1829 Comte regained his sanity. Esquirol admired Comte very much as a philosopher, and he become his pupil. He was a member of the small group of attendants at Comte's lecture-course on positivist philosophy which gathered each week in Comte's private apartment until he died in 1840.

In 1838, Esquirol published two volumes of his magnum opus, *Des maladies mentales considérés sous les rapports médical, hygienique at médico-legal*. His treatise (all quotes are in our translation) is 'the result of forty years of studies and observations' (Introduction); he says, it covers the whole of the pertinent psychiatric literature. His approach to medicine is typical for a physician: 'I rarely looked for explanations of the facts that I had observed', he continues, 'since I found the systems more seductive in their glamour than useful in their application'. Observe and do not speculate, is the regular maxim. The whole book, like so many others, testifies to the effort of its author to adhere to that maxim. How fortunate it is that they all speculated, all the same.

Even a slight glance at Esquirol's first chapter, 'On Madness', will immediately show him a thinker looking for a comprehensive view of psychopathology. First, that madness is a human condition pure and simple. Second, that many causes, physical, mental, hereditary and social, are responsible for the disease. Third, that madness is indeed a disease in that, whatever cause may produce it, the end result is always some kind or other of a damage to the cerebral matter.

First, that madness is, in the first place, a human condition. Consider the opening lines of 'On Madness': 'Each mental home has its gods, its priests, its believers, its fanatics: it has its emperors, its kings, its ministers, its courtesans, its rich men, its generals, its soldiers, and a people who obeys every impulse ... what meditations for the philosopher who, wanting to avoid the tumult of the world, passes through a home of madmen! He will find there the same ideas, the same errors, the same passions, the same misfortunes: it is the same world, except that in such a home the traits are stronger, the nuances more marked, the colors livelier, and the effects more striking, because Man is there in all his nudity, because he does not paint his passions with the charm of seductiveness, nor his vices by the appearances which mislead'. Are not these lines the seeds of Freud – and of anti-psychiatry? We shall see that the discussion of mental illness as mere exaggeration of normal traits is the most persistent trait of the literature through the ages.

Causes of mental illness: they are 'numerous and various'; they are 'general or particular [specific], of physical or of moral [mental] origin, primitive [primary] or secondary [due to other diseases], predispositionalistic [hereditary? endogenic] or excitationalistic [reactive]'. Moreover, 'not only climate, season, age, sex, temperament, profession, style of life, influence the frequency, character, duration, crises, treatment of madness; but this malady is also modified by the laws, the civilization, the mores, the political conditions of peoples; [not less is it modified] by near causes of a more immediate influence more easily assessed'. Again, the last word on the topic.

Pathology: There is no psychopathology which is not a cerebral pathology. Let us put it even in a stronger way: not only is there no psychopathology without it being a cerebral pathology, but there is also no such possibility – in principle. The early 19th century *Encyclopédie moderne* says (Art. Madness): '... But, if by not attributing the delusion [madness] to organic [cerebral] modifications which are appreciable by [our] senses, is it not attributing to mental alienation [the nature of] an abstract being, existing in [by] itself, thus finally making a step backwards, and admitting the essential mental affections [afflictions] to be maladies of the soul?' The argument goes on, with the expected pathos which always accompanies the discussions on issues of the mind-body problem to say of mentalism that, since it (mentalism) refuses to postulate the existence of an organic basis to psychopathology 'it is exposing oneself to the most absurd contradictions [problems, paradoxes]; it is to suppose a thousand changes in a spiritual being which is immutable by its very nature, it is recognizing that the intellectual and moral faculties are the exclusive product of the soul, and to deny, in the presence of the most numerous and most conclusive facts, that the encephalon is the physical indispensable condition for their manifestation'. (cited in F. Voisin, *Des causes morales et physiques des maladies mentales*, 1826.)

Psychotherapy: The sole significant idea of all 19th century psychiatry was the transformation of the mental asylum, so well symbolized by the London asylum Bedlam, into a ward in a hospital. The progress was not in new treatment but in the desire to treat, namely, the very idea of mental illness as illness proper. In his *The Myth of Mental Illness*, Thomas S. Szasz attacks this very idea, yet he admits it was progress. It is always possible to complain that small progress is not only of too little avail but also an impediment to significant progress. The symbol for such small progress that perhaps is worse than none, to repeat, is the invention of the guillotine: Szasz thinks that mental homes are guillotines. We think he slightly exaggerates.

5. CHARCOT'S EXTERNALISM

It was Jean Martin Charcot, the famous nineteenth century French neurologist, who was Sigmund Freud's most important teacher, as acknowledged so very generously by the great disciple himself. Freud began to express his indebtedness to Charcot right from the beginning, i.e. immediately after meeting him. Starting in his 1886 formal short report presented 'To The Most Honourable College of Professors in the Faculty of Medicine in Vienna', in which he summarized his four and a half months (October 1885 to February 1886) Paris study tour, and repeatedly returning to speak of the great man and teacher Charcot throughout his life. In his letters to his fiancée Freud spoke of Charcot even in more personal, warm, even emotional terms. There is no doubt; the encounter with Charcot deeply affected Freud's life.

It is therefore all the more interesting to study the differences between Freud and Charcot. The psychoanalytic domination of psychiatry and the psychiatric textbooks and treatises of history miss the difference. They speak of a difference, but miss the real significant one.

More than that: we need a consideration of Charcot in his own right and not in the light of Freud. This is almost totally absent. Symbolically, when one visits today la Salpêtrière one is invited by the young French residents to see the place of the amphitheatre where 'Freud attended Charcot's lectures' (now destroyed). It is not the amphitheatre where Charcot lectured – it is the place attended by Freud. Now, it may be that Charcot was not important on his own merits, only important because here was an 'event' in Freud's life, indeed important only because he happend to lecture in the presence of Freud. Such cases do exist of people becoming significant because they met future great individuals. There is no information about Christian Vurstitius that signifies except that he was a travelling lecturer who brought the Copernican message to Florence when young man Galileo was hanging about there as a college drop-out. But this was not the case of Charcot.

Charcot was a practising specialist in neurology and a neurological researcher. Moreover, he created neurology as a medical specialization. This specialization could not have developed as a medical discipline proper prior to the beginning of the second half of the 19th century. There were other disciplines that must have developed first. Medicine was traditionally two distinct professions, each resting on a different tradition of instruction. There was the master-apprentice tradition of medicine and there was the university medical school tradition.

Needless to say, contrary to all that we read in social history of medicine, what finally developed is a merger of the two, with the rise of the experimental medical school attached to a hospital, namely, the development of the new university hospital as an offshoot of the French Revolution and the Napoleonic reform and secularization of higher education. It is no accident that the new hospital evolved in France, and after the Napoleonic wars and their aftermath. E.H. Ackerknecht, in his classic and sociologically oriented *Medicine at the Paris Hospital, 1794-1848* of 1967 neither explains this background nor notices its significance. On the contrary, he argues that letting patients die unattended and studying them statistically may be just the right scientifice procedure at the time when no scientific medicine existed, but not a very humane procedure all the same. Be it so; yet it was the Paris hospital where academic and practical medicine met and the tradition of their meeting is kept alive. Quite apart from the clinical justification of this new technique of bedside teaching plus the normal public hospital lectures plus laboratory training, there was the pretense that this was empirical and hence scientific. We need not do more than register our disagreements: science is empirical in the sense of its search for explanation of empirical facts and for empirical tests, not in the sense of practical implementation and success. But this is of little import. Of a higher import was the fact that the scientific pretense gave rise to thinkers such as Bernard and Charcot.

This is not the place to discuss Claude Bernard. His metaphysics has been discussed elsewhere. His great contributions to physiology, and his alleged or real foundation of physiology as a proper scientific branch of medicine and even biology in general, are attested by all. We say alleged or real, because there are two contenders for the title, the contemporaries Wundt and Bernard. Oddly, though Wundt was an externalist and Bernard a generalist and though scientific public opinion always was (and still is) on the side of externalism – in somato- or in psycho-theraphy – nevertheless Bernard won in the public eye. The reason may well be in the fact that Bernard, though scientifically suspect on account of his generalism, was scientifically better than bona fide on account of his 1865 *Introduction to the Study of Experimental Medicine,* which to date is a leading classic and historically the father and grandfather of most newer classics. Nevertheless, it was Wundt's statistical method that won in practice; Bernard remained the one with the honorary titles alone.

Back to Charcot. His work replicates Bernard's along Bernard's methodology.[1] That is to say, Bernard gave general methodological rules and illustrated them with his own physiological discoveries. Charcot's starting point was to add to Bernard's physiological examples physiologico-neurological examples, utilizing the latest anatomico-pathological studies of nerves. Indeed he was a professor of anatomico-pathology and headed the anatomico-pathological society where all relevant data were collected. It was only years later that a chair of neurology proper was created for him.

A few paragraphs on the problem in general, before explaining Charcot's problem, may be of use to the reader. It is traditional in the philosophy of

---

1.   J.M. Charcot and C. Bernard were young interns in la Salpêtrière, at the same year, 1848. Already then they were friends.

science and/or technology, both professional and lay, to overlook the problem of applicability. Until recently all aspects of technology, including such complex engineering feats as building a by-pass around a metropolis, or such delicate feats as arterial by-pass operations, were viewed as parts of applied science, and applied science was viewed unproblematic, being science proper just put to obvious uses, with at most problems of deduction, certain mathematical or logical problems, to link pure science to its domains of applicability. Yet this is decidedly not the case. Most theoretical findings that found their ways to implementation did so with the aid of ingenious ideas that could be patented and at times were, yet one cannot patent the obvious.

In medicine, this view implies that merely empirical treatment is inferior and perhaps even unscientific and that the practice of scientific medicine proper is applied biology. Further, the traditional anti-speculative bent led all students in the period to study, or pretend to have studied, the anatomy of anything before going on to examine its physiology. In Paris, early in the 19th century, the accent was on medicine becoming scientific. There Trousseau invented the routine of rigorous practice which, when Freud saw it followed by Charcot almost a century later, still surprised him, of combining a university frontal lecture with actual medical practice of examining a new patient and inspecting older ones, etc., thus combining the medical school tradition with the master-apprentice tradition as mentioned. Also there, Laënnec began the tradition known as the clinicoanatomical school, and Charcot belonged to that school. The use of anatomy in medicine, namely of pathological anatomy, was diagnostic. Diagnosis and/or pathology — anatomical and physiological — are nowadays taken as a matter of course as one entity. But we shall fail to comprehend Bernard and Charcot, we shall even fail to comprehend the great advances today in medical knowledge and methodology, unless we realize that the general backward state of the philosophy of technology (which views it as unproblematic applied science) has led the physicians to demand the development of the clinical anatomy (i.e. the morphological pathology) of an entity to be the first step leading to its clinical diagnosis (i.e. its physiological pathology) as the second step, and only then leading to its diagnosis proper, i.e. as a disease entity. This is inductivist methodology applied to medical research. (The complaint of Ackerknecht, thus, is exaggerated: purely inductive studies are neither human nor scientific but both studies and treatment were in fact more commonsense.)

There is a good reason why all this traditional inductivist procedure that was so sanctioned and is still sanctioned by so many medical people is still not clear and explicit. The reason is that in psychiatry the medical school professes to adhere closely to the strict canons of scientific method, yet according to the canons just mentioned the medical school ought to center on brain or gene pathology before daring to do psychopathology, let alone diagnosis, not to mention treatment. It is thus easy to see why the pseudo-scientific pseudostatistical mock-correlation of criminality with sex gene abnormalcy so delighted representatives of the medical school; at long last they could have an instance, however minute, of a diagnosis that follows the classical inductivist canons. This, of course, is terribly apologetic. For our part, we do not advocate the classical inductivist canons in medical research, and we are not enamoured overmuch with the medical school in psychiatry: the medical school commits the worst crimes in its own books: it is pseudo-scientific any way one looks at it.

Back to Charcot. What we want to see now is how he, a member of the Paris school and an adherent to the new medical school in psychiatry, got away with it. Charcot began his career in internal medicine; had he done only what he did in internal medicine, he still would have had world-wide fame as an internal physician. Already at the age of 34 he gave the first descriptions of intermittent claudication, clinically characterised by cramp-like pains and weakness in the legs, induced by walking and relieved by rest; pathologically — as he discovered — caused by vascular spasm and/or arteriosclerosis (1859); he was reputed as one of the finest experts on rhematoid conditions; in the following decade he contributed to the study of diseases of the liver, bile ducts, and kidneys (1866). It is clear that all these conditions were studied as disease entities, but Charcot could present the fruits of each investigation in the traditionally required order and manner, beginning with the clinical differentiation of morphology for morphological pathology, leading to physiological differentiation for physiopathology, and ending with a syndrome defining the diagnosis of a disease entity. Charcot was very proud of his scientific methodological purism, which he expressed by his maxim, compare and contrast! Michel Foucault rightly sees in Charcot and his contemporaries the beginning of scientific clinical studies since they required the systematic linking of clinical matters proper — symptoms and signs — with anatomical pathology. The link is proven by physiological pathology, according to Charcot's and Bernard's classic requirement. That is to say, in their — generalist — view, there is only one pathology, and it is functional, or, in biological terminology, all pathology is physiological.

Where, then, has Charcot's externalism disappeared?

The medical view of pathology always was physiological: if a change in anatomy occurred with no physiological pathology, then there would be no clinical symptom. If the change would be a defect, then the defect would be discoverable only in a general check-up, or incidentally to other examinations or in post-mortem examinations. Examples of anatomical malformations not causing obvious troubles abound − some morbid, others not. Examples abound of morbid anatomical malformations not discoverable during their bearers' life-times but observable post-mortem; one of these is aortic aneurism that causes sudden death. The case of anatomic pathology with no physiological pathology, thus, is theoretically unproblematic. The problematic case is physiological pathology with no anatomic pathology. Is that possible?

This question is very central to medical research. Many physiological pathologies have no known anatomical pathologies. Indeed, it is this characteristic that makes us call them physiological. The question is, should the researcher seek a specific anatomical pathology that should go with the specific physiological pathology which he studies? Must there always be a specific anatomical pathology to go with each specific physiological pathology?

The answer is clear: the externalist says, yes; the generalist disagrees. Charcot worked as a generalist. He began with the study of clinical symptoms, looking for their physiological and anatomical concomitants. He thus studied certain dysfunctions of gait, speech, and eye-movement. He asumed these three dysfunctions to be necessary and sufficient conditions for what today is known as multiple sclerosis. Of course, in retrospect it is all too easy to understand the difficulty of offering a coherent diagnosis to such a multifarious disease. He sought the anatomico-pathology of this hypothesized disease and found multiple disseminated sclerosis in the central nervous system in all cases of post-mortem examinations performed on patients who had died of that disease.

Charcot further studied a similar condition: the patients complained of paralysis, muscular atrophy, and tremors. He diagnosed this condition by characterizing it clinically − with reference to the paralysis being spasmodic, the tremor in the voluntary movement, and the atrophy progressive. Post-mortem examinations revealed the concomitant anatomico-pathological lesions centered in the pyramidal tract, hence amyotrophic lateral sclerosis as differentiated from multiple sclerosis, and thus another example of the triumph of the anatomico-clincial method in medical research revealing itself.

Charcot then studied hysteria. He characterized it by the pattern which at the time evolved out of the clinical picture. For the disease he called la grande hystérie he found four characteristic stages. He was in error, as in retrospect is easy to know. He performed post-mortem examinations in search of anatomico-pathological lesions. He found none, of course. He was convinced one could be found. In a pinch, he proposed, perhaps the expected lesion is physiological: after all, a physiological spasm of a bloodvessel is the equivalent of an anatomical occlusion by a thrombus. Is there such a thing in hysteria? Externalists must, in the circumstances, answer in the affirmative.

We may also see here the great value of traditional inductivist methodology, much as we reject it; it helped introduce the physiological side of pathology even though pre-Charcot externalism forced him — as it had forced others to stress the anatomical side of pathology simply as a method of empirical verification of the connection between the clinical and the anatomico-pathological. Claude Bernard introduced both non-inductivist new canons (he calls experimental research induction, but there is nothing in carrying over a name from an old to a new tradition) as well as his generalist canon for pathology: 'there is only one pathology, and it is physiological'.[1] Yet this double deviation permits reconciliation. For, following Bernard's methodology and then presenting the fruits of research inductively, Charcot merely insisted that every physiological pathology has an underlying anatomical pathology to go with it. Which is materialist metaphysics that postulates, in cases of pathological spasms with no visible anatomical pathology, that there must be such, on the histological level or even beneath it. Charcot was very sensitive to all this and marked as defective all existing physiological pathologies not accompanied by anatomical or histological pathology: he called these cases 'functional'.

And from anatomy and physiology, to the pathology of the nervous system. Following his own recommendation to compare and contrast, Charcot saw neurological abnormalcies that he tried to diagnose post mortem. He moved from interal medicine to neurology because of the pecularity of the population of Salpêtrière, namely of that ward in the Paris hospital where the chronically ill and the invalids were concentrated. His job dictated to him which conditions to study. Studying physiology as a second step following anatomy or morphology, yet having to reverse the chronological order of the steps, forced him to study all possible second steps in the hope of finding later for some of them the proper first step. This is how Hysteria was rediscovered — especially since diagnostically it was as confusing as multiple sclerosis had been before he made sense of it.

6. CHARCOT'S PSYCHIATRY AND ITS ANTECEDENTS

It is a well known fact that the physicist honored as the destroyer of the aether was the great aetherist James Clerk Maxwell. This is no paradox: you

---

1. This view was first formulated by Bernard's teacher F. Magendie in 1836. Johannes Müller held the same idea at about the same time.

kill the aether by doing your best to revive it and by failing; for, if no one can outdo you and you fail, the failure signifies.

Maxwell's case, though not paradoxical, has no or almost no analogue in the history of science, at least not in the history of psychiatry. But the defect is in the literature, not in the logic of the living dynamic process. We view Charcot as the Maxwell of the neurological or the medical view of psychiatry. He is the peak and he is the breakdown. True, many still follow the broken down view, but then many were aetherists up to Einstein and beyond. True, just as Einstein himself was not afraid to return occasionally to the aether that he, more than anyone else, made a matter of past history, so psychiatrists, whether Freud or others, should not have feared the neurological approach and they did not.

In brief, it was the systematic search for the characterization of every disease by its symptoms as a theory based on physiopathology and the ability to characterize accordingly one given disease – neurosis – yet failing to locate its correlate neurophysiopathology that gave rise to modern psychiatry, especially Freudian.

In particular, it was Charcot's awareness of his missing link and his creation of a stop-gap that opened the way: when the stop-gap was taken for real, medical psychopathology was created.

Again the parallel with physics is obvious. The introduction of Lorentz transformations was but a stop-gap for H.A. Lorentz, but the real thing for Einstein only five or six years later.

Let us look, then, at the stop-gap. Let us consider the diagnosis, its intellectual ancestry. The stop-gap was Charcot's concept of coherence that enabled him to characterize hysteria, for the first time, as a disease entity, even though he should not have since he had no anatomico-physiological pathological findings to serve as foundations for it.

But the ancestry of the development is of the essence since it is the whole of his intellectual apparatus and prior achievement that made him decide hysteria was a disease entity anyway.

Briefly, it was the fact that hysteria had been considered a disease in earlier times that forced his hand. But, and here is the crux: in physical reconstruction of diseases he modified earlier views along the lines of new findings developed along the lines of the new scientific methodology. Here no modification was made, and this is the revolution.

In Charcot's hands a new concept emerged: coherence. A clinical entity became coherent on the background of congruent anatomy and physiology. When it became coherent, diagnostic studies were complete and the search for therapy would be undertaken. It is by finding a clinical picture for which no correlation is found between it and its supposedly etiological counterpart, i.e.

between the diagnosis and its anatomical and physiological pathology, that made this clinical condition incoherent. Everybody save Charcot could be satisfied; (like Maxwell) he called for the completion of the picture until coherence is reached.

Although already Hippocrates and Sydenham (the English Hippocrates) accurately described the clinical manifestations of hysteria, it is to Charcot's merit that he put it on the diagnostic map as a disease or a disease entity. What is a disease? What was a disease for Hippocrates and Sydenham? It had to have some coherence, to use Charcot's terminology. What was coherence for them? We do not know. In Charcot's language a disease entity was the equivalent of coherence. If we go from Hippocrates to Sydenham to Charcot and ask what the coherence of hysteria could be for a Charcot, we find the answer in Charcot's own understanding of hysteria: he could not find physiology and anatomy behind it. Had he found only physiology, he would label it derisively as functional. Yet he had not even physiology: all he had was a semblance of physiological pathology. Indeed, he declared hysteria to be 'la grande simulatrice'. Yet, it was, he said, functional: he deemed the simulated pathology a variant of physiological pathology and for a variant of anatomical pathology. He was so near to invent psychopathology that its inventor, Freud, saw himself as his disciple.

It is today accepted by all students of hysteria, that Charcot saw hysteria as a condition doubly viewed: as a mental condition on the one hand, as a patho-physiological condition on the other. How is it possible? Charcot, from the beginning of his studies on hysteria (1868) and throughout his teaching career, attributed an important role to the idée fixe which, installing itself in the mind and dominating it without being controlled, is capable of developing itself and acquiring enough power to realise itself, to objectify itself, under diverse forms − such as of paralysis, convulsions, hypoanesthesia, mutism, − all these phenomena that can appear spontaneously or when imposed on the subjects by suggestion. In this sense hysteria is casued by psychological mental representations (images). But simultaneously, Charcot admitted that mental images are products of higher nervous system centers, and thus that hysteria is also a physiological condition, and so patho-physiological even though not patho-anatomical, since no anatomical lesions were found; he could not − as nobody could, at the time − conceive of a mental phenomenon which is not a product of the activity of the higher centers of the nervous system. For example, discussing the case of hysterical mutism (silence), Charcot spoke of the clinical picture as a psychic (mental) paralysis of the verbal center, induced by auto-suggestion; he said: 'it is in the grey cortex of the cerebral hemispheres that one has to look for the dynamic [not anatomical] lesion which gives birth to this symptom' (*Oeuvres*, Vol. III). The reason, however, for the dynamic lesion, can well be, in itself, a mental one, even 'an occasional cause, such as a violent emotion, a traumatism'. The mental cuase, in its turn, acts by means of a sudden spasm (contraction) of blood vessels in a given area of the brain, thus functionally paralysing it.

One sees here the possibility of having four modes of action resulting from the four possible combinations of somatic and of psychic entities (if one accepts the body-mind dichotomy):

Physical cause – physical result (somatic diseases)

Physical cause – mental result (brain damage due to physical violence or to syphilis and drug-induced psychoses)

Mental cause – physical result (hysteria, which is simulation, as well as psychologically caused somatic illnesses, such as peptic ulcer)

Mental cause – mental result (such as Freudian phobia).

For Charcot, however, even a mental cause (idée fixe, suggestion) that may result either in a physical sign (convulsion) and/or in a mental sign (mutism), both results will have physiology (patho-physiology) as an intermediary. From here on, the roads are open in two directions: the one will maintain the body-mind dichotomy and will nourish the endless disputes between the organicists and the psycho-geneticists, the other road will lead to the attempt to overcome the body-mind dichtomy, by viewing it in terms of levels of organisation of functions, simultaneously physical and mental à la Jackson, thus bringing Ey in the focus of the dispute – yet with one level being much more physical so that normally one tends to overlook its mental aspects, and vice versa.

Was Charcot an externalist or a generalist? As far as psychotherapy is concerned, he was an externalist. By determining the important role the idée fixe ploys in the genesis, in the appearance, and in the physical manifestations of the neurosis, (moreover, reproducing it experimentally – since suggestion brings about the appearance or the disappearance of the most of the symptoms), Charcot said, we see in hysteria, 'a psychological disease par excellence' so that 'psychotherapy is essentially justified'.In other words, the cause of hysteria is external, and the remedy is its elimination.

The piquant fact is that Charcot's contribution is an externalist factor to the generalist tradition of Hippocrates and Sydenham. Hippocrates recognised hysteria as a disease, and differentiated it from mere malingering. Sydenham did the same. The first ascribed hysteria to uterine vapours (hence the name: Husterikos=uterus=womb), the second, to central nervous system activities (in his terminology, activities of 'spirits'[1.]). Similarly, Charcot distinguished hysteria from malingering, and ascribed it to activities of the central nevous system: hysterical symptoms have to do with mental images. In this he followed his contemporary, Paul Briquet, who understood hysterical symptoms on the background of the normal emotional matrix — very much in line with the idea of Esquirol quoted above. All this, however, falls short of a clear idea as to whether hysteria is both psychic and somatic or only psychic. For a true generalist this dichotomy is very unpalatable anyway. Hence the importance of Charcot who tried but failed to use physiology on the background against which to explain neuroses; he thus broke clearly away from the somatic or rather organic part of the traditional generalist view of hysteria and its pathology, but, for want of an externalist, physiological characterization of hysteria, he fell back on generalism, as we shall soon see. The picture is these days made hard to perceive since it was later further twisted by Freud: whereas Charcot attempted to bring physiology to the fore, and in failing became a generalist, Freud saw in physiology the background — and, ironically, returned to the mind-body dualism quite against his will, and turned an extreme externalist as if to prove his scientific bona fide. This is how his celebrated research project was born ('Project for a scientific psychology' (1895), S.E. Vol. 1, pp. 283-397).

Not by following Charcot, but in his teeth.

Lest this be deemed a minor change, let us amplify the point. Charcot was deemed a traitor by some of his most ardent adherents. It is one thing to approach medicine — physical or mental — unscientifically and quite another to stick to the scientific approach yet to allow a psychosis without neurosis, and even to call it neurosis prior to the discovery of any nervous disorder of any kind. Now, this is not to praise or to blame Charcot. It so happened that under the category of neurosis he included both epilepsy and hysteria, and we nowadays agree with him only about hysteria; rightly or wrongly the whole medical world goes with Charcot half way and agrees that a neurophysiopathology exists in the case of epilepsy and not in the case of hysteria. But we are not trying to be apologetic for Charcot: we only wish to make sense of his development. And the development we try so hard to make

---

1.   In the medical literature of the Renaissance, especially the high Renaissance, including Descartes, (animal) spirits are material, not mental. See any work of D.P. Walker. Newton's *Principia* ends with reference to such spirits; see I. Bernard Cohen, *Introduction to Newton's Principia*, 1971, 26-7 and 243.

sense of is his Maxwellian switch, his recognition of his failure to provide a strict and programatic mechanism. But this change involved also another change – a change from mechanism to generalism. That he became generalist is all too obvious.

Let us survey the logic of the situation. Externalism as well as inductivism demanded that symptom be anchored in both physiopathology and anatomicopathology, not to mention etiology proper. Now the problem, of course, is even in the very description of the clinical picture. Charcot showed a certain interconnectedness by exhibiting for the first time both a coherent clinical picture of multiple sclerosis and a physiological-cum-anatomical pathology. We could argue that all his achievements vis-à-vis multiple sclerosis came together, thus defying inductivism; but we are not concerned with scientific method here. Clearly, the problem of hysteria is very similar to that of multiple sclerosis. Charcot is the person who had made multiple sclerosis into a disease entity proper, since before him it had no clear clinical picture, since its manifestations are diagnostically so confusing. To begin with hysteria is as confusing, and hence a similar challenge. Charcot made hysteria too into a disease entity, which was both his claim for fame and his downfall – since he failed to produce a disease entity in complete parallel with multiple sclerosis, as required by his own canons. In addition, Charcot made a mistake even in his clinical picture of hysteria, by erroneously presenting it as a disease which develops in four stages. We shall not discuss this here; we mention it only in order to remind the reader that rational reconstruction is always easier because writers know what they may ignore. What matters here is not any specific error of Charcot, but his desertion of his own externalist canons.

7. CHARCOT'S GENERALISM IN PSYCHIATRY

To repeat, Charcot had failed to find a physiology for the background upon which to place neuroses as he, Charcot, understood them. For he placed under the rubric of neuroses both epilepsy and hysteria. 'Epilepsy and hysteria, these are the two important classes of neuroses', he said.

We need not go into why he saw both epilepsy and hysteria as neuroses. Suffice it to say that he got this from the general background on which he was regularly operating, modifying some disease entities, uniting others, and so forth. Indeed, he attempted to unite also hysteria and epilepsy. But not enough to see them as exactly the same disease entity. Just as he saw amyotrophic lateral sclerosis and multiple sclerosis as more or less one yet still distinct – his exercise in comparison and contrast, we remember – so he wished to show epilepsy and hysteria as closely related but not identical. But how? How could he differentiate between one neurosis — epilepsy — and the other neurosis — hysteria — if for these clinical conditions no pathological anatomy at all could be found? It was not consistent with his declared canons. Even today there is no pathological anatomy to be found even in eminent cases of grand mal epilepsy, though physiological pathology is eminently established. So much so, that by definition the set of all the symptoms of epilepsy yet without any physiopathology is deemed something else — usually hysteria. For we do have electroencephalographic evidences for such cases of hysterical grand mal: there are cases where a clinical fit is a 'classical' one and nevertheless the ensuing EEG of the patient looks quite normal. Yet, as long as the physician will not deny that we deal with a case of genuine epilepsy, he will say that had he taken the EEG picture during the fit the physiopathology of the brain-waves would have manifested themselves. Now, hysterical fits can clinically be differentiated from epileptic fits proper: one of Charcot's merits was precisely his studies of the minute clinical differences he found in patients which led him and later Babinski to find the criteria for such a clinical differentiation. The importance of the Babinski sign is exactly its Charcot quality: it is neurological. Yet it is not usually neurological to the extent of being neuroanatomicopathological. The non-existence of anatomicopathological findings in epileptic patients as well as in hysterical patients, the fact that there is no anatomicopathological finding in epilepsy and hysteria, did not prevent Charcot from calling them genuine diseases, yet of different kinds. He called both neuroses (i.e. he saw them as belonging to the same family) and he considered both to be, pathologically, functional. He even suspected that it is something like electrical discharge in the brain that causes epileptic fits, but not hysterical fits; he could not say why, how, or where exactly. Similarly, for hysteria, he spoke of a possible blood vessels spasm or the like in the brain, without specifying in which vessels it happened, how and why exactly. But this was highly conjectural. In practice, too, there was a difference between 'the two important neuroses', epilepsy and hysteria, in the clinical course of the diseases: indeed, it was this practical difference that, for Charcot, indicated some neuropathological difference. As usual, the anti-speculative bent of the mechanist makes him speculate that all differences are mechanical; if not anatomical that at least functional; all the same, there was a snag: he considered them as two true diseases, but only on firm clinical grounds, since the physiopathological background was provided in order to square it with mechanism, not as an empirical finding proper. It is interesting to note here that the only concession Charcot would make in favor of hysteria as a psychological disease, and not a mere physiological one (such as epilepsy), would be in seeing its stimulus, namely its cause, in a mental act such as excitement, strong emotion, etc., rather than in a 'pure' physiopathological stimulus such as in epilepsy. This would be nice if all and only hysteria can be induced by suggestion and occur as a result of excitement or strong emotion. Yet this is not so: though admittedly epilepsy cannot be induced by suggestion, sometimes genuine epileptic fits do occur as a result of excitement or strong emotion. And so, precisely in his failure, the externalist Charcot changed into a generalist. Precisely here, and where he tried an externalist conjectural cause for hysteria (vascular spasm) and failed even in the externalist differential diagnosis of hysteria from epilepsy, he had to make a great switch. He did it in the following manner.

Let us remember that Charcot used to go at times from a diagnostic entity to physiopathology and anatomicopathology and at times the other way round. Let us notice that in the case of hysteria he was definite in the diagnosis and in the dark on the pathology. He tried then to skip from pathology to a still earlier phase, so as to turn his extrapolation into an interpolation: he looked for the etiology of hysteria.

To show the greatness of this step, let us see the peculiarity of etiology. There are disease entities which are more specific etiologically than any other way, such as malaria, whose causative agent is a specific parasite. Indeed, different malaria parasites produce different malarias. Other disease entities have no specific etiologies, e.g. anemia, that can be caused just as easily by malaria as by leukemia or all sorts of malnutrition – indeed sixty different etiologies of anemia are specified in the standard textbook of internal medicine. This, of course, may bring us to question whether anemia is a specific disease entity at all. After all, we can produce a program to say, one etiology, one disease entity; one differential etiology, one differential disease entity. But this will not do. There is a limit beyond which commonsense forces us to stop looking for differential etiology as medically utterly irrelevant and biological theory concurs. No other example is more to the point, simple in its cruel logic, than trauma; who cares how a wound was inflicted? And if this example is not biological enough, there are ample biological examples. Consider pneumonia: we readily differentiate viral from bacterial pneumonia; but we will not deem different diseases any two cases of pheumonia with different bacteria. A priori we are willing to allow diagnosis to go at times one way at times the other. Likewise, the same illness caused by the same enzyme deficiency may be genetic, environmental, or due to malnutrition; treatment only slightly differs but not insignificantly, yet it is obviously the same syndrome and one etiology – because it is truncated. Even though the genetic type demands continued treatment, it is the continued treatment that matters, not the genetics, and indeed, when irreversible damage is done then there is even no difference in treatment between the environmental and the genetic kind; they all are the same enzyme deficiency disease, one way or another.

What is the etiology of hysteria? Is it specific like malaria or is it non-specific like anaemia or trauma? If it is a vascular spasm it must be an anaemia or a trauma. Indeed, Charcot viewed hysteria as a vascular spasm, rather than, say, electric spasm, just because he knew that vascular spasm causes atrophy, that it is, thus, a kind of trauma. The idea that a trauma must be caused by a foreign object and a specific one at that, whether it be a knife or a blunt object, is a typical externalist move. Once Charcot saw vascular spasms as traumas, he was already a generalist. Whatever the case may be, the role Charcot assigned to the trauma was that of a trigger and of an occasional one. The essential point, and for Charcot it had even the strength of his dogma, was that the nature of the trauma, whatever it was, had nothing to do with the clinical picture which hysteria revealed. Whatever the cause, he said, hysteria is always the same. The trauma which has caused it was necessary in principle, since no natural phenomenon could exist without a cause, but there was nothing specific in the cause.

And so, the next move, pregnant with implications as we conjecture it was for Charcot, was futile vis-à-vis his problem: we have some irrelevant etiology, leading to an obscure pathology, leading to a vague clinical picture. How can this be further nailed down? He tried, then, a different move: perhaps, after all, hysteria is not a distinct clinical picture? The word hysteria signifies nothing in itself, it is only a designation of 'a coherent group of facts which are nosographically intertwined' (Charcot, *Leçons de Mardi,* 1888-89, p. 37).

And so Charcot's generalist concept of coherence as a stop-gap replacing pathology was born. To see its significance we can look ahead and see how crucial coherence was for Freud's diagnosis of hysteria and for psychoanalysis in general. But this is a poor kind of a game. We must look back, not forward, to see the greatness of a move.

The idea is not necessarily psychological. We have now, as followers of Charcot, knowingly or not, intuitions about the coherence of many disease entities and we have the idea of a syndrome, in physical as well as in mental condition, where a syndrome is a coherent set of signs and symptoms and even of information from deeper examination. Hence it is the syndrome's coherence that counts, not the syndrome, since we feel that an incoherent syndrome is lacking. The end conclusion from this should abolish disease as an entity, and view it as a coherent sort of imbalance, almost the way the Hippocratic school insisted and we have explained at length when discussing, in our first chapter, the historical debate between generalism and externalism. We see here, in Charcot's neglected idea of the coherence of the clinical picture, [of the imbalance], a possible bridge between Cos and Cnidus.[1.]

Paul Briquet, a contemporary of Charcot said in his work, the first in modern times on hysteria, as follows. Every hysterical symptom is but an exaggeration of an otherwise normal, common, natural emotion in animal and man. Moreover, all hysterical symptoms can be understood, he said, as if they were attempts of the patient to convey a message to others. Here we have psychological medicine emerging, not to mention the theory put forth amidst furor by Thomas S. Szasz exactly one century later.

Charcot is not popularly known to have seen hysteria as an emotional disorder; people believe Freud did, i.e. that the discovery of the psychological character of the hysterical symptoms is Freud's achievement. Yet Charcot knew Briquet's work, to which he repeatedly referred. It is clear that Charcot — before Freud — assumed some psychological factor had to be present in order to render hysterical symptoms into hysteria proper. He differed from Briquet by considering the emotional part of the hysterical symptoms as pathological. And this is the crux and the contribution of his earlier externalist program to the picture. The pathology is deformations of the normal psychological emotions and events, not mere exaggerations of them. Briquet saw exaggeration, Charcot saw deformation, Freud, further saw a deformation in the very exaggeration. That is to say, Charcot postulated a psychopathology, a deformed emotional makeup, but Freud postulated that not only the clinical picture but also the deformation was psychological. Logically, Charcot did not need Freud's hypothesis concerning psychological coherence at all; physiological coherence was sufficient for him, even if it meant coherence of a pathology.[2.]

---

1. There is almost no theory of diagnostics available. It should be said here only that the diagnostics, etiology, treatment and course of the same case seldom belong to the same school: usually course is holistically described especially due to the generalist theory of the crisis discussed above; and usually etiology is externalist, especially in the cases more easily given to externalist treatment. Symptoms are usually viewed from the viewpoint of externalist differential diagnosis and hence fit externalism with too great an ease, as noted by Hans Selye, *The Stress of Life*, N.Y. 1956, *From Dream to Discovery*, N.Y. 1966, and *Stress without Distress*, Philadelphia 1974. His own general stress syndrome which is explicitly generalist and homeostatic in the sense of W.B. Cannon's classic voodoo death, makes sense only on account of its — alleged or real — coherence. Selye notices this, but were he explicit and self-critical in his presentation he could be clearer.
2. See L.E. Trillat's Introduction to J.M. Charcot, *L'hystérie*, 1971, pp. 10-11.

8. HYSTERIA FROM JANET TO BABINSKI TO SLATER

Let us break down the complicated problem of how psychoanalysis began by putting it under the form of a few simple questions: What was psychopathology — and, by implication, psychotherapy — for Charcot? What was it for Freud? How do the two connect logically? How do they connect historically? This is the only possibility to understand Freud — both his failures and his achievements — since unless one views the problem of the origin of psychoanalysis on the background of Charcot's thinking, the only other way of understanding its origin open to us today is the genius of Sigmund Freud. Genius as it was, it was not out of a context of a given epoch. Moreover, Freud's innovations are but a step — even if a gigantic one — in the history of ideas. We stress the point, since the standard textbook of the history of psychiatry/psychoanalysis sees Freud's psychoanalysis as sui generis, as originating in the middle of nowhere; according to the textbook, psychoanalysis makes sense only in its own context; this is what Freud meant when he proudly pronounced, that psychoanalysis is not medicine; it is one discipline amongst others in the sciences. And he was right to the extent that psychoanalysis is not medicine, and despite all opposition it was soon taken by lay analysts, i.e. by experts not needing a medical degree proper, as Freud rightly demanded. Yet it is, of course, a branch of the art of healing and its thinking is geared towards this end, with the inevitable result that it never quite stood so far apart from the other healing techniques as to be utterly divorced from the Western medical tradition.

It is, thus, only on the background of the work of Charcot, medical as it surely was, that one might try to understand both how psychoanalysis evolved and how it is in part outside the mainstream of medicine and in part medicine proper at one and the same time, and both as a technique of healing and as a process of thinking.

The main thing to remember when dealing with both Charcot and early psychoanalysis, is that they dealt with classic neuroses, to wit hysteria. We shall repeatedly bump into the fact that neither physcially caused damages, such as epilepsy and aphasia, nor psychoses, such as paranoia and schizophrenia, even bothered Freud: even when he wrote about aphasia. Here suffice it to notice that we are confined by historical considerations to neuroses alone. What this amounts to is not to say that Freud was limited by Charcot's study but that he supplemented and complemented it, or even rectified it in a very important way. This can be seen when we present Charcot, with the aid of a rather illegitimate hindsight (for the purpose of clarification only) as half-way house between Briquet and Freud.

We have already mentioned above what we think psychopathology was for Charcot. He viewed hysteria, he said, as a functional disease, in which one can see that psychology plays an important and essential part. This he did not elaborate, relying on Briquet's understanding of hysteria, according to which it encompasses the whole repertoire of human and animal expression of emotions, though in an exaggerated form. Further to this, Charcot said symptoms of hysteria are outcomes of deformations, displacements of the normal, healthy emotions; that is to say, in addition to Briquet's mere exaggerations of expressions, Chacot saw a pathology in the veɪy deformation and displacement of emotions in hysteria. But whereas Briquet needed no more than normal standard psychology (in fact it was even commonsense psychology, of the common or garden variety, that sufficed for him), Freud, who accepted Charcot's view of hysterical symptoms as deformations, needed more: he needed a special – not a standard – kind of psychology, on the background of which the hysterical symptoms viewed as deformations would make sense. So the concepts of the Ego, the Id and the Super-Ego were constructed; the Unconscious discovered (or rediscovered), etc. Freud's system worked as a highly organized and harmoniously articulated mechanism (like a watch) moved by the forces which he designed, on its normal as well as deformed routes.

This is all we wish to say about Freud in this context. Whereas other writers on Charcot want Freud in – and commit illegitimate hindsights – we want Freud out. We understand why earlier writers preferred to jettison Briquet and replace him with more up-to-date psychology. Yet the fact remains; Charcot took Briquet's contribution for granted and grafted his own on that of his esteemed (younger) predecessor, and we cannot understand either Charcot's ideas or Freud's greatness unless we keep Briquet in sight. Moreover, these days of antipsychiatry may bring the whole line of great humanists from Pinel to Briquet to their own; but we do not wish to defend views of either of the dramatis personae but merely to have as clear a historical reconstruction as we can. Rather, to continue our history of the rise of scientific psychotherapy, it was Briquet who complained that his peers were not in the habit of recording, as most basic scientific medical tradition would require, the goings on in diagnostic sessions of hysterics. And the simplest way for him to start was to present, when bumped against hysteria, what he saw, in the most ordinary language he knew. This already forced him to observe – with no preconception, he inductivistically confessed – hysterical expressions of emotion as variants of known expressions of normal and presumably healthy emotions. It was his luck that his patients were unsophisticated plain folks and ones whose modes of expression – normal and hysterical alike – were plain and outright all the way. Charcot saw plain folks too, though Charcot's neurological bias drew his attention to the nervous peculiarities of his patients, particularly when his fame grew and he served all walks of French society and even foreign visitors. Displacement, in brief, is what Charcot added to Briquet's commonsense psychology or to any psychology, and an intense interest in the neurological symptoms of hysteria.

This could not succeed. Using Freudian data we know now for sure that it would not succeed: hysterical people often emulate or simulate neurological deformations the way they poorly comprehend them and much in accord with the trendy state of the fashion of the day.

Now, to say that Charcot did not need a psychological structure, is an exaggeration: he needed a psychology, but not a specific one. His metholodogical system needed it, since it was a desideratum for his view of disease, that it be described as deformation, as some pathology of the normal. This is for Charcot medicine proper − physiological or mental or anything else − to wit, medicine as pathology. The historical truth of the matter is, therefore, not that Charcot did not need pscyhopathology; the truth is that he was not interested in looking into this area: he simply delegated the investigation of psychology − including even the medical research of psychopathology proper − to one Pierre Janet, a young high-school professeur de philosophie, of all things, who, in his provincial place of teaching which happened to be Le Havre, had met a young female patient and tried hypnosis on her, and told Charcot of it. Charcot created for Janet his by now historically famed Laboratoire de Psychologie in la Salpêtrière.

Janet did not function as a physician and was assigned no duty except to follow his own researches into the psychology − including psychopathology − of the master's neurological patients. Famed as his work is now, he was marginal for Charcot and redundant for Charcot's successor who, years after the master's death, closed the laboratory so that its worker found himself unemployed.[1]

It is clear, we hope, how Janet, now so famous, was and indeed would not but be, marginal in Salpêtrière. What is not explained is why he is famous now?

For Janet, things were extremely simple. He was a Jacksonian, though he knew almost nothing of Jackson's own work: since the Jacksonian principles constitute an easy step in the development of the medical and even in evolutionary biological thinking of the time, Janet may have developed these

---

1.   This slight on Janet was not impeded by his being a professor in Collège de France.

principles independently or picked them from the air,[1] and used them at times intuitively, and in some formulation of his own: the famous lecture courses which he delivered in *Collège de France* were on this matter.

Back to the psychopathology of hysteria. Its most characteristic feature, in Janet's opinion, is the contraction of the field of consciousness: it is 'the reduction of the number of psychological phenomena which can simultaneously be present in the same individual conscience' (*Les névroses,* 1909). The hysterics cannot 'perform superior psychological operations on many things simultaneously' (*La Force et la Faiblesse psychologique,* 1930). The words of the arch-evolutionist Herbert Spencer, Jackson's mentor and major influence, are here echoed. 'The contraction of the area of consciousness, is typified by the absence of these innumerable collateral thoughts which ordinarily are provoked when scenes are successively present'. The concept of the higher degree of organization in the hierarchy of mental functions, is a typical Jacksonian idea. 'The contraction of the area of consciousness' is a manifestation, says Janet, of an activity of a lower order in the hierarchy of mental functions. This is, once again, a Jacksonian idea. The disease, then, is a result of the malfunction of the higher organizational principle. Suggestion, so frequently evoked as the originating factor in hysteria, is for Janet already the result of the hysteric's feeble higher mental capacities, not the cause of the weakness. It is the higher organization of functions which fails first. All the rest is just Jacksonian 'releases', attempts at compensation, etc.

What we have here is the first deviation from common or garden psychology – due to both Briquet and Janet. For, commonsense views suggestion as appealing to a weakness but it deems it more as the cause of the weakness. This, of course, is externalist. Nor can it be otherwise, since all normal people show similar weaknesses: the suggestible is weaker than the average just because of the suggestion which works on him. Yet, rather than accept commonsense observation of hysteria as due to suggestion in some exaggerated form, Janet saw the hysterical mind as indiginously weak, and its weakness as of the normal kind but exaggerated and thus psychopathological. This is rather generalist. And the crux of it is that exaggeration can be pathology. Let us see the contrast: for Charcot exaggeration is not enough of a pathology since the pathology of a psychological condition is physiological. For Briquet the hysteria is exaggeration and so not physiopathology and so not pathology. For Janet the hysteria is a psychological condition due to

---

1.   The French psychologist T. Ribot, to whose chair Janet succeeded in Collège de France, was also a Jacksonian independently of Jackson.

exaggeration which is pathological — hence it must be psychopathological and not neuropathological. But whether pathological or not, the indigenous weakness of the hysteric mind is common to Briquet and Janet.

There is an irony here: the mental patient began as ill, as defective, as pathological. His pathology, however, was deemed physical — in part in order to maintain his human dignity. With Briquet he was restored to normalcy; with Charcot his defect, his pathology, was deemed physiological; with Janet he was deemed, for the first time, psychological, so as to account for Charcot's neuropathology as correlated to psychopathology, yet in accord with Jacksonism and so not reductionist. It was the break with reductionism that was logically required in order to allow for the very existence of psychopathology.

Now, as always, when exaggeration becomes pathological the question arises, what is the demarcation of the normal exaggeration froom the pathological one? How weak or strong should pulse be to count as pathological? How crazy should one be to count as mentally ill? Freud says, when one can't function normally. This demarcation is no medical diagnosis.

Hence one cannot avoid seeing Janet as a generalist in his psychopathology and not medical in his psychotherapy: his proposals for psychotherapy were somewhere between Freud and Adler. In particular, it may be noted, he used free association without the couch.[1]

Janet is the person who gave hypnosis respectability of sorts and added it to the standard arsenal of mental, psychological treatments. His aim, however, was not to eliminate 'traumas' but to strengthen will-power and thus the ability to affect a reorganization of behavior on a higher level.

Charcot's innovation, we remember, the idea of the neurotic behavior as a misplaced rather than a merely exaggerated expression of emotion, was explained by Janet in a psychological theory permitting displacement. For this Janet felt the need, as Freud felt more strongly years later, to draw a map of the proper place of emotions, against which one can draw pictures of specific displacements. In order to effect a displacement, one needs some forces. He needed, then, a theory of psychic forces, again, much like Freud later on.

It is here that Janet's Jacksonism failed him. For Freud — again we use hindsight only to clarify — conflicts cancelled conflicting forces leaving weakness behind. For Janet it was weakness that caused conflict. Take the physical metaphor seriously for a while: a train climbing a mountain and unable

---

1. Freud knew that the couch was inessential for free association and justified it by personal idiosyncracy. Ironically, the couch stayed even when free association has long ceased to be of central significance or even of any significance.

to make it. For Freud we have the force of gravity and of the climb cancel each other paralyzing the train. For Janet it was the weakness of the engine that caused the conflict. This is a poor mataphor; the right one would be the train as a higher level force that is supposed to overcome gravity and even utilize it (much as hydraulic plants use the tide to create electicity for use on electric trains) but only the weakness reduces the higher power and brings it down to the level of the lower powers where they can at all conflict with each other. This will enable us to understand why Freud preferred to forget his own Jacksonianism: he wanted the Superego to conflict with the Id and create weakness. (We use here a hindsight from late Freud to early Freud; again merely as a presentational device.)

So much for Janet. His psychology was not very useful, his theories look more interesting when considered against their Charcotian background than as compared with Freud. So we shall now move on with the logic of the situation created by Charcot.

Charcot, we remember, spoke of physiological deformation, and thus stood out against his predecessors who looked for anatomo-pathologies in the centers of the nervous system. As we all agree today, most mental patients show no brain defects. But some do. It was Charcot's student Babinski who first described a sign from a sure damage in the center. It was a reflex which, when found in the patient's neurological examination (the examination is routine by now), signifies unquestionably that a real damage − anatomical or physiological − or a deformation exists in the center. By the same token, it is precisely the absence of this reflex, and similar ones, in all the patient's neurological manifestations, that indicate possible hysteria. The absence of Babinski's sign is a part of the diagnostic definition of hysteria. So far so very very good.

Now, it is Babinski who defined hysteria as suggestability − he uses a neologism 'pithiatism'. For him, suggestion produces hysteria; likewise, then, suggestion (counter-suggestion?) cancels hysteria. But what is suggestion? Why should people accept other people's opinions, ideas, commands, values, sometimes even the palpably stupid commands given in a routine humiliating show-biz hypnotic performance? Is it normal? Is it pathological? What is the pathology, then? When is it normal? When is it pathological? And, in both cases, why? These general problems of principle, in philosophy and in the psychology of thinking, the various problems of central distinctions, both relevant and not so relevant to science and/or practical medicine, such as the distinction health/ disease, normal/deviant, physiology/ physiopathology, psychology/psychopathology, mind/body − all these problems inevitably raise their ugly heads, the moment one seriouly touches psychological medicine (in contrast to physical medicine).

Babinski, we say, identified suggestion with hysteria. Accordingly, to repeat, he advocated suggestion as the therapy, and as the only one adequate for hysteria. The question arises then, whether, in his psychopathology, Babinski was an externalist or a generalist. It seems to us, that he should be classed as an externalist.

It is thus clear how to relate Babinski's views to the fact that he was not a psychiatrist, but a neurologist who showed interest in the psychopathological condition of hysteria. To complicate matters, let us mention the case of Eliot Slater, a late 20th century psychiatrist who was for many years a consultant at the famous London University Institute of Neurology. Many years after examining and diagnosing patients as hysterics, he found, in the follow-up studies, that most of them, years after being diagnosed as neurotics-hysterics, returned to the clinics as sick people, suffering from various neurological diseases proper, vascular and other systemic internal diseases, on the background of which it became easily understandable why a given seemingly hysterical symptom was placed precisely where it was and not elsewhere, that, e.g. a 'glove' anaesthesia (loss of sensitivity in a glove form rather than according to the normal anatomical distribution) was present, not necessarily from hysteria but from a lead poisoning due to the presence of lead in a glove used by the patient over a prolonged period of time. Needless to say, when Slater initially diagnosed his patients as hysterics, he closely followed the standard medical routine. He followed three concomitant procedures: (1) he determined that the complaints of the patients were anatomically not properly distributed; (2) no organic or somatic cause (i.e. one originating in the central nervous system) was found and (3) some psychological conflict could make good sense of the symptoms. Clearly Slater was struck by his follow-up studies more than anyone else. He finally concluded that there is practically no hysteria as a psychological, neurotic, disease. There are, admittedly, here and there, some Freudian-type cases of hysteria. But, by and large, he is convinced that what we call today hysteria is a misdiagnosed condition of a proper physical medical nature, a misdiagnosis due to our general neurological ignorance: symptoms appear here and there before the whole clinical picture is established. Calling it hysteria is but the concealment of our ignorance. If Slater is right, then this may be the death of hysteria.

We have traced hysteria from Janet, who was the first to give it a psychological pathology − in line with Charcot, through Babinski who separated to the utmost the purely physiological on one side from the purely psychological on the other side. Finally to Slater, who meant to give the purely psychological its coup de grace. We have skipped the most celebrated phase in the study of hysteria — that of Breuer and Freud. Let us glance at the chief peculiarity of their approach.

9. FREUD AS A DISCIPLE OF CHARCOT

It is pointless to write another history of psychoanalysis or intellectual biography of Freud, whether brief or long. Rather, we wish to complement the existing ones, perhaps to add a correction. Freud repeatedly declared himself a follower of Charcot from whom he had heard the passing remark, it is all sex. Were this all, we would consider this debt of his to Charcot to be exactly nil — perhaps in accord with his intention. There are many cases of a great thinker who took a well-known idea or an idea he heard from this or that person and made it central to his new edifice. The borrowing of an idea, small or even big, is not to be confused with the edifice built with its aid. Hence, Freud's story is a myth and a red herring.

What, then, did he gain at la Salpêtrière, assuming he gained something there?

Freud learned from Charcot that hysteria is a deformation. To begin with he thought it was physical, but already in his first classic work in collaboration with Breuer they declared hysteria to be a defect not of the body but of the phantom body. This is more in accord with Charcot than Charcot would have accepted: For, let us remember, Janet's psychology fits Charcot better than Briquet's psychology, the one that Charcot never abandoned. In other words, hysteria may be an exaggeration and a deformation, and Charcot endorsed Briquet's theory of exaggeration in psychology yet sought deformation in physiology, whereas Janet's view enables one to view exaggeration beyond a certain limit as deformation and reject physiology altogether.

There is nothing more to tell on this issue. Once Charcot's psychology is corrected to accord with his neurology, his neurology drops out. The only use anyone after Charcot had for neurology as a diagnostic means of hysteria was to exclude neurological diagnoses proper, as so beautifully exemplified by Babinski. But, as Slater has shown, we can never exclude them all, and so we can never have a conclusive medical differential diagnosis of hysteria. Clearly, here is room for a race between diagnostician and patient, since the hysterical patient will emulate or simulate neurology as best he can and an ignorant physician will be tempted to class a kinky neurology as an hysterical emulation. Beyond this only luck and teatment can do better. And on this neither Charcot nor Janet had anything to say that we deem proper to report in our present study. And so to Freud, since he, and only he, both endorsed Janet's view of exaggeration beyond a certain point as deformation — a trauma that leads to a neurosis — including the compelling conclusion from Charcot that the pathology of hysteria is a psychopathology, and incorporated this in a whole psychology of his own to present a mechanism of the deformation.

This solves a very intriguing and vexing question in the history of the popular comprehension of Freud. Was Freud's theory a psychology proper or a psychopathology? This question comes in the literature. Our solution is, he created as much of a psychology as he needed to make a psychopathological mechanism, with the desideratum that the pathological is the mere exaggeration of the natural. The paradox of Freud is Janet's: the case being a mere exaggeration makes it natural in ingredients and in quality and thus the exaggerated is in essence human like the rest of us, yet the very exaggeration is the deformation, the new emerging quality. (Similarly, in trend, excessive neurosis is psychosis.)

What we have attempted to present here was the way psychology entered medicine. The great byproduct of this was another great innovation — the humanization the mental illness. Pinel and others tried to humanize the patient; Freud tried to humanize the disease. Were Freud a generalist, contending that there is no illness and a fortiori no mental illness, he would be nearer to the truth (as we see it today) yet his very externalism enabled him to put forward the message that sent a shiver through the whole profession of mental healing.

There is a major line of progress here, from Pinel to Freud to-date, that might very well be noted here. All revolutions have a common denominator: rebellion, the rejection of the accepted. Let us try to see Freud as an anti-psychiatrist. What did he do? Here comes a physician, a psychiatrist, raises his voice and emphatically dismisses the medical model of his time. Now, is he a psychiatrist or an anti-psychiatrist? Surely, he is the anti-psychiatrist of his time, and dearly did he pay for it.

No doubt, Philippe Pinel rebelling against the approach current in his day considered, like others, the mental patients as brain-diseased; yet he rebelled because they overlooked another dimension of these brain-diseased people, something which they were deprived of, i.e. freedom. Was then Pinel a psychiatrist or an anti-psychiatrist?

Ronald D. Laing, the arch-anti-psychiatrist, surely has views about freedom different from Pinel's. Indeed 20th century ideas of freedom differ from those of the 18th century. Yet Laing is not an anti-psychiatrist at all. He is a true Pinelian.

Already Michel Foucault attacked Pinel harshly as a mere 'prison reformer'. From our point of view today, he was surely a prison reformer. Yet the very view of him as a prison reformer is very advanced 20th century view, which owes much to him.

From this vantage viewpoint, of the process of humanization of the mental healing profession, we think, a few landmarks are worth observing together: Pinel the prison-reformer as it were, Freud, the humanizer of the illness by normalizing it, and contemporary anti-psychiatry which denies the very existence of mental illness. In between stands Charcot, the physician, who wished to present mental illness with its natural physiological mechanism, which Freud replaced with a natural psychological mechanism.

IV. TRENDS IN 20TH CENTURY PSYCHOTHERAPY

1. FREUD

Let us declare this at once. In our view, nobody did so much for psychiatry as did Sigmund Freud. If we may speak for ourselves, though we do not mean to distinguish ourselves from other commentators, but rather in order to specify as our own responsibility as authors, we would say this. However strange it may sound, those of us who consider Pinel, Tuke and Rush to be the true and significant founders of psychiatry can appreciate Freud's contribution all the more. It was they who returned to their patients their human dignity, yet they did so only in principle, whereas Freud has managed to employ their humane attitude in the service of his patients. They created this very branch − psychiatry − as a branch of medicine; yet those of us who sympathize with their humanism may well find that today they sympathise more with the challenges of modern antipsychiatry than with any other aspect of the profession. In such a frame of mind, throwing a detached glance at Freud, we can hardly fail to come up with a strong appreciation of the spirit of psychoanalysis coupled with a strong criticism of different aspects of psychoanalysis, not to say even very strong criticism of it.

It is not that the authors of the present volume are very idiosyncratic here. The very fact that almost a century after the publication of the *Interpretation of Dreams,* in which the psychoanalytic concept is already fully enough presented, no modern writer can say anything in psychiatry − and, obviously, more so, in psychotherapy − without indicating the profound impact that Sigmund Freud has on him. Even Freud's most pronounced opponents, some of them founders of their own schools, are no exception. To paraphrase the famous anti-McCarthy joke about communism: 'I am an anti-Communist', protests the victim; 'I do not mind which kind of Communist you are', replies the investigator. So, you may be a Freudian, a neo-Freudian, a post-Freudian, not to say an anti-Freudian! Some sore of a Freudian you still are. This is similar to the expression common amongst philosophers concerning Immanuel Kant: you can be a Kantian, or an anti-Kantian, but you cannot avoid Kant.

What is it that made Freud's contribution so special?

Let us emphasize the question, in a quasi-anecdotical way, though it is not anecdotical at all, since it is very commonly heard amongst teachers and students in classes of psychiatry, and in hospitals and in clinics: 'After Pinel came Kraepelin, and then came (Bleuler and) Freud.' Now, from the point of view of the history of ideas, perhaps this is defensible. Yet, it is somewhat puzzling, to say the least. Pinel died in the year 1826. Freud was born in 1856, and so was Kraepelin. Bleuler was slower by one year only: he was born in 1857. So far for biographical data. As to the intellectual advancement of these three persons, Pinel's magnum opus is his 1798 *Nosographie philosophique.* Freud published his studies on hysteria in 1895, i.e., in the same year that Kraepelin was preparing the sixth edition of his *Lehrbuch* (1896). When Bleuler published his 1911 monography on *Dementia Praecox oder die Gruppe der Schizophrenias,* the four volumes of Kraeplein's eighth edition were successively appearing (1905-1915). Freud's famous *Introductory Lectures on Psychoanalysis* were delivered in the amphitheatre of the University of Vienna in the winter/summer semesters of 1917 and of 1918. Pierre Janet, Freud's contemporary — born in 1859 — and Charcot's pupil, died in 1947. We quoted above a significant 1930 publication of his. Who, then, came 'after' whom, if all of them were contemporaries?

(We must mention here the forgotten Nobel Prize laureate Julius Ritter von Jauregg — 1857-1940 — Freud's only intimate in the whole of Vienna, grand generalist, and grand organicist, inventor of the cure for syphilis, even in the stage of paralysis progressiva, by artificially raising the body's temperature so as to kill the treponemas. (His means was the malaria parasite.))

But if the logic of scientific discovery seems stronger than historical facts (dates), it is still a mistake to think that from the point of view of the history of ideas, i.e. from the development of the acquisition of medical knowledge, Freud superseded Kraepelin. He just handled different matters. For Kraeplein, no psychology was needed, since every mental disease was organically determined. Freud looked for psychopathology. Here lies his novelty — his greatness. Let us now complete what we said about Freud above.

Freud's work was directed, initially, to show how hysterical symptoms evolve on the background of a psychology that can explain the very fact of their deviation from ordinary psychology (i.e. to understand what makes them pathological), and so to give a sense to the seeming incoherence of the symptoms. He further found that the same psychology applies for semi-pathological deviation, such as slips of the tongue and of the pen, etc., thus rendering *Psychopathology in Everyday Life* possible; *Interpretation of Dreams* already makes even normal and healthy people seem to act and react according to the same psychological construct, that initially was intended to explain pathology proper.

So, from Briquet to Charcot, from Charcot to Freud, we find ourselves in one sense back with Briquet. But whereas Briquet found a human context for them all, normal emotions and pathological cases alike, he could not explain the pathological cases but as exaggerations, and this did not fit the idea of psychopathology à la Charcot; Freud, when suggesting a human context for them all, normal emotions and pathological cases alike, could explain the pathological ones as deviations, but by now he could have also shown that the same case of pathological deviation of the hysteric patient really does exist in the normal individual too, though in a less pronounced manner. Yet, at the same time we have in Freud for the first time a dynamic theory of both health and neurosis, a theory answering to our desideratum that the theory should give coherence to a disease (akin to health proper which is coherence, of course) with some kind of a rationale, yet without overdoing it so as to render all mental disease impossible. Freud so proudly distinguished psychoanalytic treatment from suggestion and hypnosis, by reference to the status he ascribed to psychoanalytic theory − the status of scientific theory which he granted it − precisely since he meant, by the label 'scientific', that psychoanalysis is the discovery of true causes. Thus, he said, when it is applied it becomes a scientific psychotherapy − the one that operates on true causes; the technique of psychoanalysis has a rationale upon which it is based; and it has the best rational directives to be guided by. Here we have classical, traditional, and obvious scientifico-medico basis which neither those who used suggestion nor the hypnotherapists had claimed to have at their disposal. Freud's claim for the scientific status for both his theory and treatment, be it accepted or not, certainly was novel.

So far, so good. Yet Freud's novel and ingenious construction, be it scientific or not, surely was not medical. This does not mean that it was not a scientific or even the correct construct; it only means that it went beyond the traditions of scientifico-medical canons. And, to repeat, Freud himself said so.

There is no doubt that the most scientific electronic engineering is not medicine, nor scientific animal breeding veterinarian medicine. What makes scientific medicine scientific is one question we can now leave open. What makes scientific medicine medicine is by no means treatment alone. It is the complex of diagnosis, treatment, follow-up, post mortem, etc.; all, of course, in the light of theory. If theory is scientific and technique in accord with the recognized rules of procedure, then the technique is scientific; what makes the technique medical is another aspect of the self-same rules and purpose of healing. Granted − for the moment only − that Freud's theory is scientific, no one can reasonably argue, no one ever tries to argue, that psychoanalytic treatment follows the canons of medical treatment. Moreover, as a first approximation, the difference between medical treatment and Freudian treatment of mental patients is no matter of theory but of the canons of medical treatment. The question, whether free association is the center of psychoanalytic treatment method, is secondary to the question, can it be subsumed under the normal recognized canons of medical treatment?

The major reason why no physician can use the psychoanalytic technique while applying the medical canons proper is not related to his belief, or disbelief, in Freud's theory, nor to his ability to put the patient on the couch and let him free associate. It lies elsewhere: first the doctor himself must be psychoanalyzed. The canons of physical medicine once were altered to include the requirement for the disinfection of the doctor's hands and instruments. Were they altered again to include the disinfection of his mind, and were the disinfection to be performed by the very same technique when applied to medical people proper as when applied to lay psychoanalysts, then psychoanalysis would be a step closer to becoming a medical technique. But not fully so.

We recognize the patient's need not only for recovery but also for convalescence and recuperation. The line dividing the two cannot be drawn. Orthodox Hippocrateans may say recovery equals recuperation. Most of us decline viewing physiotherapy as therapy proper except on a rare occasion such as arthritis, and even then for want of a stronger medicine. Now, we contend, at least post-Freudian psychoanalysis is much a matter of a synthesis, to use Freud's own term, rehabilitation, recuperation and so on; these surely resemble physiotherapy much more than an open-heart operation.

Suppose a part of the Freudian treatment is psychosynthesis; is there any process akin to a heart operation properly to be viewed as psychoanalysis (analysis = dissection, i.e. surgery or an operation with the scalpel)? If there is anything like surgery in psychoanalysis then there must be a moment of its termination after which the patient recuperates or walks away. The claim that a similar thing happens in the process of psychoanalytic treatment, is the catharsis theory in some variant or another.

We contend that the catharsis theory gave the process of psychoanalytic treatment the scant ground for its spurious claim to be medicine; that the catharsis theory was given up by Freud almost as soon as it was invented and when relinquished it left Freud utterly unwilling to view psychoanalytic treatment as a part of medicine in any sense whatsoever.

2. PSYCHOTHERAPY: THE CATHARSIS THEORY

What distinguishes psychoanalysis from any other form of psychotherapy, was the cathartic method, or rather the belief that the cathartic method necessarily had the desired curative impact. Whether Breuer was the initiator of this method, or Freud, or both, matters little. Whether the principle says of catharsis that it is the process of emotional discharge, and whether it was Aristotle, matters no more. What is important is that Freud introduced this principle into psychoanalytic practice, succeeded in it, and indeed had it as the starting point of the whole edifice; the culmination of the treatment and its successful outcome, he said, was this total emotional discharge that felt so rejuvinating.

Freud's first (1895) theory of hysteria is as follows. Some external event happens; it is usually an event which happened in early childhood. It is unpleasant in the extreme. It is damaging or traumatic. Being unpleasant, its memory is repressed and seemingly forgotten. Later on in life, for an unknown reason, the memory of a traumatic event refuses to stay put (like a child thrown out of the classroom who bangs on the door). It disguises itself and surfaces or emerges not into consciousness but as an aspect of one's conscious life: it is unhealthy and indeed identical with hysterical symptoms. Sometimes it does stay put, until a current external event, structurally or in content similar to the old trauma, revives the old traumatic memory, which then quickly goes into disguise so as to evade repeated suppression, and thus the hysterical symptoms appear. A hysterical symptom constitutes two kinds of elements: first, elements of the traumatic event itself (though in a disguished form, which analysis supposedly unmasks), and second, elements of an attempt the psycho-organism makes to suppress the unpleasant memory – as well as the memory of the still unfulfilled wish involved in it. 'One portion of the symptom corresponds to the unconscious wish-fulfillment and another portion to the mental structure reacting against the wish' (*S. E.* Vol. 5, p. 569). Incidentally, since in the very act of repression one knows of the repressed wishes, the whole process of repression is one of self-deception, or, if you will, of bad faith. We have here the idea of Sartre, decades before he published it. Who knows where Freud would have arrived, had he developed this idea brutally to the end, as Sartre tried to do or as Szasz did. In a way, Freud viewed the symptom as a compromise between the two forces: the repressed and the repressor. On the whole, it is an attempt at self-cure; but it is misplaced: the patient does not completely face the unpleasant memory and so he cannot solve the problem; his symptom, then, does not cure, but, on the contrary: it becomes precisely a disease, namely, hysteria.

Since neurosis, being an incomplete cure, is a disease, real cure must be complete. Thus, though Freud equates humanity with neurosis *(Totem and Taboo; Civilization and its Discontent)*, he wants both analyst and cured patient completely free of all neurosis and perfectly well!

Now as to the complete, real cure. The cathartic method supplements Charcot's — or it may be regarded as Charcot's discovery inverted. Charcot had shown that by instilling suitable ideas it was possible to cause hysterical symptoms. Breuer showed that hysterical symptoms vanish when the pathogenic idea can be 'disinterred from the unconscious' (F. Wittels, *Freud*, 1924; p. 38). The way to purge the pathogenic ideas from the unconscious is to help the patient to consciously remember them, either by hypnosis (Breuer) or by free associations (Freud). The patient vividly remembers, reexperiences the unconscious, suppressed events, and displays a cathartic phenomenon: cries, laughter, exclamations, emotional discharge, etc. The hysterical symptoms vanish. The patient is cured. He is perhaps as weak as a patient after an open heart surgery; but the operation is over and time will do the rest. All this is externalism to the extreme.

It is easy to quote from Freud's writings many passages, some contradictory, to substantiate or undermine a claim. Since Freud urged his colleagues to model themselves on surgeons (*Introductory Lectures*, 1918, Last Lecture; *S. E.*, Vol. 16, p. 459) and since surgery is the paradigm of externalism, we may very well view it as Freud's intent to present psychoanalysis as externalist. The same, of course, can be said of his hostility to symptomatic treatment.

There are two critiques of Freud's theory of the catharsis, both Freud's own. He was not as clear about them as we hope we are. First, the catharsis theory operates on an externalist model yet some psychopathology may be general or non-specific. This is not a criticism pointing at a falsehood, but one limiting applicability. The second critique concerns falsehood: we have cases where catharsis takes place yet the patient remains uncured. Perhaps this is so because only specific cases in the end are curable by catharsis. If so, we may ask, what makes a case specific to begin with? No answer.

Let us take this slowly. Let us view purely medical situations that exemplify externalism and generalism respectively. We would call them specific and non-specific cases; in medicine, to repeat, a thorn in a leg, or a bullet, a broken arm, are specific cases; physical collapse, heatstroke or even sunburn, poisoning (global or local), indeed any loss of equilibrium or damage to the homeostasis other than the trauma that initially caused it, are all non-specific cases. Very clearly, the trauma is the focus of cure in the specific case, and of no interest to the healer in the non-specific case. Of course, we are all too clear about there being no pure case at all: the thorn is a trauma both because it is bothersome to the system as a whole (or else it is no trauma, as when it stays in the thick sole of one's foot) and since no restoration of balance is possible while the irritant keeps destroying it (or else the system adjusts to it and good doctors just leave it there).

Now to Freud. The catharsis theory appeared in 1895. Already in 1897 his first criticism occured, and after then Freud began to move from an specific theory to a non-specific one. He then understood that he should change his theory of the etiology of hysteria. He began with an externalist theory of the trauma: painful events, such as of sexual overtures to children, especially those made by their parents. He then moved to a generalist view of the trauma: the reported memories of traumas are not always memories proper, i.e. ideas reflecting real events of erotic or sexual seductions, these seducation tales now appeared to Freud to have been at times fantasies, products of incestuous infantile desires, understandably distorted in the circumstances in general, rather than products of actual events. From now on, a new kind of therapy for the non-specific case was under way: not the cathartic one, based upon the view of the trauma as caused by specific external events. As Paul Roazen words it, 'the inner world of Freud's patients, rather than external events, was seen as the chief source of neurotic difficulties. 'Traumas' acquire their character through the way in which seemingly innocuous incidents can be experienced subjectively as distressing crises' (*Freud and His Followers,* 1971, p. 88). It is here that the way to generalism was open; all that was needed to add was that the non-specific case was the rule. But Freud hardly ever noticed a breakthrough, since, as we have already mentioned in Chapter II, inner life, for Freud, constitutes essentially of reflections of Father/Mother which obviously are external figures, objects (here one should add 'constitution', but since by constitution Freud meant 'everything that is not psychological', Roazen, p. 140, we shall leave out of the discussion these problematic issues of predispositions). So in the last resort the inner world is a residue of identifications with libidinal objects, or, more technically, with libidinal cathected objects, namely those on whom the subject wishes to bestow love or libidinal energy. And so, in the last resort, the patient's inner life à la Freud constitutes but a highly complicated organization of external figures and events: father and mother are but thorns in the patient's side.

Some of Freud's disciples, sometimes Freud himself in his later years, opted for a more boldly generalist approach. But more on this, later.

3. WHAT IS PSYCHOLOGY? OR: THE UNIQUENESS OF FREUD, REGARDLESS

What is psychology? Janet, Freud and others, such as Adler, Jung, Pavlov, Piaget, etc., all created psychologies; each and every one of those great psychologists was a creator of a psychology. It is strange to find psychologies and not Psychology as scientific disciplines. It makes our question, what is psychology? require a preliminary discussion on, why psychologies? But let us still stick for a moment to the first question, what is psychology? The preliminary question, then, will be clear: the different schools of psychology also differs about the question, what it is.

Now the textbook answer to this question is very simple. In Greek, 'psyche' means soul, mind; 'logic' means study, 'the science of'. Thus psychology is the 'science of the mind'. But, more seriously, what is psychology?

The most recent view, or demarcation of psychology, which we shall accept, is Piaget's. Psychology is the study of behavior. Now, of course, physiology too is the study of behavior. And isn't physics? To specify: human behavior? Physiology will again fall into the domain of psychology, at least whatever is specifically human physiology – such as human bipedalism. Moreover, if we specify human behavior, emphasizing the human, then animals (and ethologists) might justifiably object. Piaget enlarged his demarcation of psychology, taking as a starting point his theory of intelligence. Psychology is the study of behavior which transcends (goes beyond) the given, the intially hic et nunc. So he included animal behavior in psychology proper, as far as animals behave not directly as responding to immediate stimuli, but as if by mediation (in space, time, anticipation, etc.). Here, and fortunately so, Piaget also easily went beyond the body-mind dichotomy: every immediate action is thus deemed physiological; every mediate behavior is the field, the realm, the kingdom of study for the psychologist. By using Piaget's demarcation we do not exclude his predecessors, some of whom intuitively, some explicitly, said the same thing. We simply use Piaget because to date he has the most elaborated view of psychology as the study of mediate behavior. Incidentially, Piaget's demarcation of psychology includes all his predecessors' as good first approximations.

But as much as we value Piaget (we also highly value his predecessors, Wundt, Binet, Janet, Pavlov, etc.) we still consider his view unsatisfactory. There are physiological delayed effects and there are pre-programmed machines etc. So let us leave the demaraction and go the subject-matter. Here we think Freud is the greatest. Genious apart, what is it in the very work of Freud that makes him a Copernicus and not merely just another contributor?

The first reason is very simple: psychology before Freud was utterly dull. Love, hate, friendship, envy, sex, loneliness, even the normally observed urge to know, the pleasure we take in all those wonderful books we read, in the music we listen to,, etc., not to mention the love of God. Who did not introspect, experience, slowly or by spurts, about oneself, others, the enigmas of life, beauty? Who was not in this way an active psychologist in his/her teens? Yet classical psychology kept all of this out: all this is part of life, it was admitted, but it must be ignored by psychology since it is not science. Psychology is scientific, then, and hence, not real life! Consider, for example, Wilhelm Wundt. Tradition has him as the first scientific psychologist, the father of experimental psychology, i.e. of scientific psychology, i.e. of psychology as a science, i.e. of psychology. Since Aristotle, psychology was part of philosophy. There is hardly a philosopher, let alone a writer, a poet, an artist, who did not deal with psychology as part and parcel of normal life, yet they were worth nothing, since they were not scientists/scientific. The standard textbook sees Wundt's opening the first laboratory for psychology in 1879 as the real breakthrough, the act of birth of psychology. But, with what did Wundt concern himself? What did he study? Thinking, learning, emotions. Fascinating subjects. But how did he study them? He did it as distantly as possible — he wanted distance from the subject and so also he got distance from real thinking, from real learning, and from real emotions. The most immediate subjective experiences were studied under the guise of objectivity. Introspection was the cold light for centering on minute dull detail, on the pretext that only then can it be grasped with complete assurance. Now, here is the catch. Can one objectively study subjective experiences? The mystification of a science as objectivity could not better manifest its silliness than in the domain of psychology. The culmination in 1912 of Wundt's principle — its own reductio ad absurdum — was Watson's behaviorism, followed today by Skinner and the Skinnerians. Admittedly, the psychologists have taught us something we did not know about thinking, learning and emotions. But we were taught by alienating techniques, by eluding all direct touch with life. We learned by statistically pseudo-scientific procedures, and from rats and mazes while ignoring the terror they were in, from dogs and guinea-pigs who share nothing with pets we may keep in the household, from chickens and doves and all that. Modern traditional ethology, which tried to approach animals more directly, shamefully failed. Even the more direct and fresh variant of ethology, the most modern variant of it, is indebted less to who its acknowledged father is, than to Sigmund Freud. And even modern ethology is often dry and remote. The phenomenon of 'imprinting' found in birds is very impressive, to be sure, and is of great significance, but what exactly has it to do with human life? They evade this question, even those who derive political moral from animal aggression. So, either we learn about the nature of animals and/or humans – and this is fair enough (it is biological/natural science) – or we learn about experiential life, which is something different altogether. In short, in traditional, experimental, scientific psychology we learn about the statistical correlation between certain events with others, period. And about the correlation between some different events with others, period. And finally, then, about the correlation between both the aforementioned correlations. Can anything be as remote from real experience, let alone existential experience? Can anything be more alienated and alienating than this? One begins to wonder how scientific psychology gained respectability at all. Or did it? History tells us that universities were indeed very reluctant to encourage the development of departments of psychology. The first laboratory, Wundt's, created in 1879 in Leipzig, had to wait for the creation of its twin, Binet's laboratory in the University of Paris, until 1895. It was only in 1912 that Watson in the U.S.A. and concomitantly the Gestaltists in Germany could begin to work in laboratories in the universities. Eduard Claparède opened his Laboratoire de psychologie experimentale only in the early 20's, in Geneva, and he studied indirectly the power of the will by directly measuring muscular/physical power (effort). Later on, with Piaget, the laboratory turned to be the centre of the study of perceptions. In 1928, C.A. Spearman, in the University of London, turned from his chair of logic to psychology, and began to apply factorial analysis to psychological phenomena/events. We learned a lot from all that, Spearman using statistical methods, very sophisticated and interesting ones, and finally, again, we are still (back) with statistics, however intelligent, and not with life. Already in 1877 Cambridge was asked to create a psychological laboratory; is it accidental that this request was granted only in 1931? The foundation of Oxford's psychological laboratory had to wait until 1947. Did not universities feel that there is something wrong with scientific psychology? And who else, other than universities can these days grant scientific status?

In brief, the main-stream of psychology sought to make psychology scientific and empirical by turning away from problems of psychology as known to any old layman and gained status as such and only very, very slowly; it is still of a relatively low esteem.

Against the background of this stands Freud. He, too, was not very respected, and never had a university post. He even declared his American hosts childish on account of their esteem for him which they freely expressed when he visited Clark university (see his autobiography). Yet his impact on the general public was like wild fire. He, firstly, touches experienced life in its very flesh, he deals directly with most problems of actual psychological human life. He is there with no intermediaries, no statistics, no laboratory artificialities. Yet he made a real splash in his wild claim or pretence to scientific responsibility. On what grounds? Every patient is unique; every anamnesis is a biography; one cannot reproduce the events he studied − least of all in the laboratory. And yet Freud found (discovered? created?) laws about human (and about animal?) psychological nature, laws of behavior which he declared to be unquestionably universal.

It is not easy to sum up our image of Freud in an uncontroversial manner, since Freud is still controversial. It is hard even to pinpoint the uncontroversial part of his teaching without becoming thereby quite controversial. For example, we think Freud has made us all aware of the prevalence of ambivalence, of the existence of complex yet subconscious chains of reasoning,[1] of neuroses as the vicious circles our minds get trapped in, of anxiety as fear without overt cause, as phobias as projected anxieties, etc. Are these scientific? We do not know and frankly we do not much mind. It is hard to see what psychological insights, prior to Freud, are so very applicable day to day as his, all the valid severe objections to his ideas and claims-staking and quarrels notwithstanding. Above all, his claim to have been free of all neuroses is not a mere poor joke in poor taste, it is the severest impediment to the progress which his fertile mind should have initiated.

4. THE NEO-FREUDIANS

We said Freud criticized his catharsis theory twice: first, it applies only to (more-or-less) specific cases; secondly, it does not always work. To make both criticism one we can say, as a hypothesis, catharsis works in all and only in (more-or-less) specific cases. But why should it be so? In an attempt to answer, we must bring in Freud's theory of self-deception. Indeed, in our opinion for what it is worth, self-deception is the very key to Freudianism.

The specific case involves a very simple form of self-deception: censorship. The local character of the trauma is retained in the local character of the neurosis. It is what the Adlerian Allen Wheelis calls symptom neurosis

---

1.   All discussions of the unconscious before Freud illustrate the triviality of claims for the bare existence of the unconscious; Freud's contribution was to show, (a) that we may reason at great length and high degree of sophistication, yet quite unaware (this looked to his contemporaries a contradiction), and (b) that we do so often, perhaps all the time. See L.L. Whyte, *The Unconscious Before Freud,* London, Tavistock, 1968.

(The Quest for Identity). For Adler, in particular, the very function of the censorship is the cornerstone upon which his theory is most characteristically based and where he differs from Freud. Since we consider central the idea of self-deception, as it appears in the works of Freud and his followers, of Adler and his followers, as well as of Sartre and most anti-psychiatrists, we should elaborate.

Freud's metaphysical bias expressed itself in mechanism, which he relegated to the background, and in Darwinism, which expressed itself in his view of all drives as animal, namely (this 'namely' is surely one of Freud's greatest errors) the craving for food and sex, traditionally called by those who were at the time 'afraid' of sex, the two great instincts of self-preservation and of the species' preservations. A variant of Freud would be the replacement of the sex-drive with another drive, or the expansion of the list of basic drives. Now the question as to which drive is basic, or essential, has lost its flavor for us. It seems to us quite arbitrary that in principle Freud will view a man's boasting as an attempt to win a woman's heart and that Adler will view the winning of a woman's heart as a cause for boasting. We think it is not a matter of principle but of fact, and facts go sometimes hither sometimes thither. Moreover, Freud's criticism of Adler is correct: whereas the sex drive is in accord with psychologism, biologism, or mechanism, not so Adler's inferiority complex which, being social in character, cannot be basic enough and accord with them, since for any of them sociology cannot be an autonomous science (Freud, *The History of the Psychoanalytic Movement*). And, contrary to much misconception, Freud expressly admitted the very existence of inferiority syndromes, but not as basic, since social rather than psychological at bottom. Yet most of the neo-Freudians have given up, in particular, the psychologism he held so dear: they took sociology to be autonomous (like Adler, many of them are socialists), and thus turned philosophically Adlerian rather than Freudian on the very issue that Freud presented as crucial.

Yet here we are not concerned with any reduction of one motive to another or of one science to another. So we concentrate on the Freud-Adler idea of self-deception.

For Freud, the unconscious (the Id) is the biological source of all drives, and on the border of which in the sub-conscious the censor dwells. The sub-conscious is the seat of the Super-ego and of the censor who, obeying the Super-ego and trying to prevent an open clash, keeps the sub-conscious drives unconscious. The inevitable failure of doing so smoothly is, still according to Freud, neurosis, mild or severe as the case may be.

Adler opposed the splitting of the soul into compartments. But we deem both the splitting and its opposition to be minor technical matters. Rather we deem it significant that Adler admitted the censor (even though as a part of the whole) and even granted him — it — a much more active role than Freud: the censor not only represses but also intentionally performs diversion tactics. Whereas Freud describes the bridgegroom as fearful of matrimonial responsibility, so that he may forget the date of his own wedding, according to Adler more likely the bridegroom will fall ill, have a car crash, or use any other ploy. Yet, of course, this is only a stone's throw from Freud's analysis of hysterical paralysis as an escape from the unpleasant. (It was Henri Baruk who rightly criticized Freud for using unpleasant situations instead of heavy responsibility; this, of course, is again Freud's biologism or reductionism.) Be that as it may, be responsibility or anything else that a patient escapes; and though the idea of escape mechanism or of defence mechanism is Anna's generalization of the idea of Sigmund, based on his own instances (experiences ?), it was Alder who made it stick; neurotics, he said, fear failure and therefore dodge challenge and do this by a defence or escape mechanism, usually that of stepping up the stakes. Add fear of responsibility as both fear of success (noblesse oblige) and fear of failure (loser pay all), and we have all that is so stressed by the modern schools and all that Freud and Adler have given us for keeps.[1]

Adler's specific central point — his view of the desire to excell and thus be distinguished as the source of all psychopathology — is by now submerged: it is the censor that signifies in concealing from the patient his fears and drives — just as much as in Freud's view — and it matters less what exactly is the patient's fear or drive.

Adler's view of Man as 'aspirations', (= values) is, as Freud contemptuously observed, a social view; his view of Man as the creator of his own neuroses — mostly intentionally, even if, perhaps while using the unconscious as an originator of excuses — is the view of Man as a self-deceptor. We have here, in a nutshell, a whole view of things: a psychopathogenesis leading to a psychopathology, together strongly suggesting a psychotherapy and a mental hygiene — both based upon Man's free will and Man's passion for self-deception, as the two pillars of Man's mode of existence. Adler did not speak explicitly in these mock-existentialist terms; nor did he put it in the language of the structuralism of Claude Lévi-Strauss; he often used 'constitution' and other modish technical terms, but it is nevertheless what we

---

1.   Walter Kaufmann's *Without Guilt and Justice* of 1973 beautifully sums up the picture in
     his description of upping the stakes as a set of techniques of decidophobia, which he deems an
     erroneous moral attitude, not a pathology, much less a psychopathology. Yet he thinks he is
     very Freudian and anti-Adlerian (see his *Discovering the Mind,* Vol. 3).

attribute to him here that we think he did say. And, obviously, Adler's metaphysics is in direct conflict with that of Freud.

To conclude: though Freud had the idea of fear of consequences of some desires as the reason for repressing these desires – which repression may lead patients to their desired goals by all sorts of patients to their desired goals by all sorts of diversion tactics – the idea settled only later, as a synthesis (Karen Horney) of views of Adler and Anna Freud in the form of the view about neurotic conduct best exemplified in the punchline of the classic Edwardian comedy: this is so shocking, Darling, says Auntie, I think I am going to faint.

5. POST-CATHARTIC PSYCHOANALYSIS IS ADLERIAN

It is an acknowledged fact that a considerable portion of the middle-class population of all affluent societies are regular customers of some sort of psychotherapy or another. Some patients go only for periods of stress – one or a few in a lifetime – some go on a more or less permanent basis; yet they go. They lie on a couch, they sit in an armchair, or they have violent rows with the therapist or in his presence. The question is, what techniques are used in such sessions, and with what rationale and to what avail? We do not know. We do not even know how many patients lie on couches and how many patients lie with the psychiatrist's help-maids and have therapeutic sex, whether real live sex or in sheer phantasy.

Of course, as is true of any set of rules, the rules a psychiatrist upholds are not exactly the ones he follows. Even the Grand Master himself admitted to have broken the rules on occasion and instantaneously diagnosed a newly ushered patient instead of offering him/ her the couch. Nonetheless there is a literature on the therapeutic technique, real or alleged, and we ought to describe it, however cursorily. For, even the schools which recommend catch-as-catch-can declare rules valuable, at least for beginners and as guidelines to deviate from in order to find one's own style and play with throughout one's career.

What, then, are the alleged therapeutic techniques now in vogue? First and foremost we must observe the fact that practically all treatment today, no matter which, is eclectic. Of course the psychoanalytic society is fighting a losing battle – not to keep practice pure, as this is conceived to be utterly impossible and even undesirable – but to keep it as pure as possible. And even this, to repeat, is a losing battle.

Secondly, eclecticism needs no father – quite generally, and not only in medicine as a whole but in human practice. Even witch-doctors know of western wonder drugs and even western doctors know how to witch doctor though they call it bedside manners. An example we like for its openness and its antidogmatism is that of Henry Yellowlees who belonged to no school and was trained by his father who was an old fashioned Pinellian.

Nevertheless, if a person is to be named for inventing the grand concoction, it is, as we shall mention again, C.G. Jung. But his was based on anti-scientific, anti-commonsense philosophy, and frankly so. The ideology behind the mish-mash, insofar as it exists, is Adler's. And, we contend as a historical hypothesis, Adler's role was of a supreme though not always acknowledged importance. Let us explain.

Adler's philosophy was not only the height of commonsense, it was a philosophy demanding commonsense. That is to say, he was a socialist, he was an empiricist, and he objected to Freud's reductionism, to Freud's humbug of not influencing the patient by sitting behind him, and even of Freud's purist free associationism, i.e. the couch. Adler demanded of the analyst frankness, not a fake non-interference. He was appalled by the very idea of transference, of a healer pretending to play father by playing harsh unresponding father etc. Commonsense was for Adler part and parcel of his social philosophy and of his philosophy of social science.

We need not describe it. Like much of Freud's and of others' inventions, it is now shared by people who have never heard his name. This is true immortality. Moreover, people most directly indebted to him in the Freudian camp, such as Karen Horney, spoke of him very seldom and then derisively. We cannot blame her. She was a bit of a heretic and confessed this frightened her — as well it might. We may remember that Ernest Jones was almost excommunicated because he once wrote a friendly remark about Melanie Klein (as he tells in his life of the Master).

What is particularly dramatic in Adler's technique is that rather than let the patient slowly become expert in the psychoanalytic technique and analyse himself the way his analyst would approve, the analyst just frankly consults the patient about his suspicions and possible diagnoses thus openly initiating the patient into the theory and the practice of analysis. This meant that: (a) all healing is active self-healing, not the passive instantaneous cure described by the defunct catharsis theory, and (b) all progress is interpersonal. From this to the views of all the contemporary schools of interpersonalism is a very small step.

We do not claim that were Adler alive he would approve of all that is going on today or even that he would approve of these pages. Nonetheless we pay him the tribute. But, to regain some balance, let us mention one other contribution not due to him, and which led to important developments, namely group therapy.

Group therapy was invented in Vienna by the orthodox Freudian – Henri Ezriel. Ezriel was apologetic for his invention. He excused himself on purely technical grounds: group therapy is ever so much cheaper. This, perhaps, is particularly why the technique first got going in jails. Yet, he observed, it is the best means for interpersonal relations – even when patients get at each other's throats, and in the nastiest manner betray confidence, as they are known to do quite regularly. The vast proliferation of group techniques speaks for itself.

Similar things can be said of all the variants on group-therapy – of psychodrama and art-therapy, of family therapy and Organizational Development, of T-groups and of sex-therapy, of all sorts of do-it-yourself autopsychocybernetics performed in groups, including scientology and Est, and including the therapy aspect of social activities that are only marginally therapeutic, such as sensitivity training and consciousness raising. They are all concoctions with the same major ingredients and different trace elements. The major ingredients are, in more or less the same order, Freud, Adler, Skinner and Buber, with the accent on the ancient and pervasive religious doctrine of rebirthing or rejuvination or fresh start which is implicit in all psychotherapy anyway. The trace elements are diverse, and borrowed from diverse religious, philosophical, social and political traditions. The borrowing seems rather indiscriminate, and of little consequence. The long and the short of it amounts to two points. First, these activities replace traditional techniques, themselves designed to enhance social integration, and in modern society are neither desirable nor viable. Second, these activities that are so popular these days relate to psychiatry as medicine the way run-of-the-mill somatic self-treatment and self-medication that go on in all societies relate to somatic medicine: they all reflect only in part the state of the medical arts proper; in part they reflect the state of health of society and of the state of social medicine, which is a technology in its infancy at best.

6. JUNG IS BEYOND OUR COMPREHENSION

We intend to make this section brief and rather disjointed. We take it as read that Jung was primarily a Freudian and that he was intentionally gullible to the point of being willing to write a laudatory preface to any odd off-beat mystic text.

The best-known contribution of Jung is his idea that we all share a universal unconscious or sub-conscious. It is this contribution that, more than any other, has earned him the title of mystic, charlatan, pseudoscientist, etc., etc. The idea is best expounded in science fiction literature. For our part we do not find it exciting — positively or negatively — and we have no arguments for or against it. There is certainly much similarity between all humans, and we do not know whether this similarity constitutes, or is indicative of, or is explicable by, Jung's postulate of the existence of a universal sub-conscious. No doubt, his idea of universal symbolisms is for him a cardinal element of his idea of the universal sub-conscious, as is his idea of primal archetypes. Yet these can be examined separately.

That universal symbolisms exist, in some sense of another, we think is unquestionable: you do not have to be a Jungian or a Kleinian in order to see a female breast as pregnant with meaning — deeply emotional, erotic, symbolic, even mystic.

The new theory of imprinting and of trigger mechanisms in animal-behavior studies make it likely that the universal symbolism, to the extent that it exists, is primitive, atavistic and rather remote from all refined mysticism (though in accord with the primitivist variants of mysticism).

The idea of archetype is very similar to that of ideal type of idealisation. Mathematics and natural science are full of idealisation, and Max Weber introduced ideal type into sociology. Describing an ideal type is at times interesting and even scientifically testable. Not so typology: the division of any universe of discourse into major groups to be further sub-divided is by now passé on the ground that logic permits any such categorisations and so dismisses the claims of uniqueness made by all of them as equally arbitrary — though in light of a given theory one typology may be more convenient than another and so preferable to it.

Yet, usually, typology is seldom offered in the light of theory. It is often offered in lieu of a theory. It then hints at a theory, but so vaguely that the hint can alter under the pressure of empirical criticism. It is this kind of typology, suggesting vague and shifty doctrines, that we find pseudo-scientific. In psychology we think that such are the typology of psychological kinds, whether the one due to E. Kretschmer, W.H. Sheldon, or H. Eysenck. Though Eysenck is a defender of hard science against pseudo-science and an enemy of Freudianism as pseudo-science, we deem his work pseudo-scientific — it relies on vague classifications of patients, on the hope for cure, on sermons about science.

Yet, unquestionably Jung did contribute to psychotherapy. His comments on patients' paintings are puzzling; his interpretations of dreams are far-fetched now as they ever were. And yet, he started a crazy catch-as-catch-can, and he tried the oddest techniques. In this, and in this alone, we greatly value him. On little of the rest we suspend judgment on the basis of a claim of ignorance, and of most of what he wrote we cannot but say that in it quantity was achieved at the cost of quality.

Jung came to his catch-as-catch-can technique by way of his craziest ideas; he could not possibly implement them and rather than articulate them and draw corollaries from them in the time honored scientific manner he followed the time honored mystic manner − mediaeval and oriental alike − of looking for hints and clues everywhere. And he found many − simply on account of the poor state of the art.

Incidentally, not that it matters overmuch, Jung was a generalist by the mere virtue − or vice − of his mysticism.

7. THE PSYCHOANALYTIC TREATMENT OF PSYCHOTICS: BACKGROUND

This is a misleading title. First, a psychoanalytic treatment for psychotics, at least for schizophrenics, is by definition either forbidden or impossible. According to Sigmund Freud's theory of psychosis, the psychoanalytic treatment of psychotics is, firstly, forbidden, since the psychoanalytic procedure − free associating − will further dissociate the already highly dissociated patient, whose Ego defence mechanisms (or, the Ego forces in general) are already broken down. Secondly, the treatment is impossible since the schizophrenic is so deeply narcissistic, that he is incapable of developing a transference relationship with the therapist, yet transference is one of the major psychoanalytically necessary therapeutic tools. When transference is unattainable, all attempts at treatment are bound to fail, useless, and even (since dissociational, as we say) counterindicated. Yet such psychoanalytic treatment has been attempted, even, some say, with some measure of success, and, at least, hardly very harmful: nobody became more schizophrenic than he was to begin with as a mere result of psychoanalytic treatment. Incidentally, all this is all too vague for a discussion: what does it mean at all, to be more − or less − schizophrenic?

Some say, the allegedly psychoanalytic treatment provided to schizophrenics was not psychoanalytical at all; it was admittedly psychotherapy but not psychoanalysis proper. So be it; if it helped the patient, it need not be damned just because of the different label. But is psychoanalysis, as Freudians claim, the only 'real', 'deep', 'intensive' treatment? Does 'real' mean radical, i.e., causative, and hence scientific? Does 'deep' mean that the cure is less open to relapse? What then is 'intensive'? Is five times a week for four years more intensive treatment, more deep and real then one interminable session that lasts as long as the patient can be forced to stay awake, or less? It is hardly believable that such claims are seriously discussed in professional circles. But should Freud – or the psychoanalytic method – be blamed for its use (or misuse) by fools, by excessively zealous devotees, or those he blamed who cling to old ideas that were once new? Freud expressly declared that progress must be made and some sort of treatment of psychotics must be attempted and successfully so. Were any psychoanalytically inspired psychotherapy for schizophrenics helpful in any way, yet without being 'orthodox', or psychoanalysis proper, would he not have given it his full blessing? We think he doubtlessly would and we are at a loss to see some of his sycophants think otherwise.

Indeed, if no psychoanalytic treatment proper was provided to psychotic patients, and by psychoanalysts at that – not by heretics – how did this treatment begin at all? Who was it who dared disobey Freud's ruling?

As a matter of fact, those who began to apply psychoanalysis to schizophrenics were proper Freudians, paradoxical as this may seem.

The paradox is somewhat ameliorated by the fact that treating psychotics meant risk of loss of favor of the Master (unless spectacularly successful): both Tausk and Jung were persecuted by Freud partly because, we suggest, they attempted treatment of psychotics.[1] But this is no resolution of the paradox. Many others tried, had a mere modicum of success, yet stayed both orthodox and accepted by their peers. They were, no doubt, helped into this by sympathetic outsiders – which is how, historically, the paradox got resolved. There were those physicians who learned from Freud to observe, to change theoretical opinions if facts forced them to do so, those who admired Freud for his creativity, who learned to act intuitively, who had passion and compassion toward the enormous suffering of their patients, who felt that schizophrenics do not choose to deceive themselves by neurotic complaints and symptoms. Frieda Fromm-Reichmann, Marguerite A. Sechehaye, Alberta B. Szalita, Otto Will, Harold F. Searles, Herbert Rosenfeld, Ruth Jaffe – all these were true Freudian sympathizers, and they began to administer psychoanalytic treatment to psychotics.

So far for practice. For the theory, it was definitely not Freud who offered it. Was it Harry Stack Sullivan, Clara Thompson, Carl Rogers or perhaps followers of Martin Buber? Who gave the lead? These three cannot be

---

1.   Y. Fried and J. Agassi, *Paranoia: A Study in Diagnosis*, Dordrecht and Boston: Reidel, 1976, p.128.

called proper Freudians, not even proper sympathizers, but what of it? If neo-Freudians, post-Freudians, etc., are accpetable as bona fide Freudians, all the better. If not, let us label them otherwise. The essence is in that, whatever modifications they provided to Freud's fundamental ideas, their treatment would not have been possible without the Freudian base-line.

Yet, we cannot go on much further without sketching the theory and relating it to Freud's general framework.

First the facts which are used in diagnosis, or even the observational tools of diagnosis. The amazing fact about psychotics is their lack of inhibition, perhaps lack of censor. We contend as a point of fact that a patient's express exhibition of the Oedipal impulse (soliciting a parent to partake in a sex act and openly threatening the other parent), his anal conduct (playing with faeces), his oral conduct (food obsession, sucking), such conduct will be at once suspected as psychotic because of the openness, not to say exhibition, of such infantile Freudian traits.

Let us stress that we are not critical of the profession, though, as we have explained elsewhere (*Paranoia,* 1976), we think these indications of psychosis are no more than mere indications. For, in our opinion they are merely secondary, and usually but not exclusively dissociational. Almost no indication of dissociation is so limited, since every indication of mental imbalance makes some good sense to the patient, in a neurotic (symbolic, local) way or in a psychotic (integrative, global) way. Indeed, in the rare case when the indication makes no sense to the patient it is then plainly regressive, and as such should count as the result or outcome of dissociation alone. And dissociation is usually psychotic, due to the global nature and the intellectual defect of psychosis, as we have explained elsewhere, yet, no doubt, neurosis at its higher stage is dissociative as well – as even physical damage and senility are.

All this is but hindsight. The historical fact is still that one who slowly and with effort learns the Freudian paraphernalia and trains the hard way to see their traces wherever possible, cannot but be struck dumb when seeing them surface so clearly and exaggeratedly as in mental homes. Paradoxically, this surfacing is both a powerful corroboration and a crushing refutation of Freud.

So much for the observable facts. Next comes diagnosis. Can a Freudian who sees the Oedipal impulses surface so nakedly ever doubt that the patient suffers from the Oedipus complex? Of course not.

For our own part, we flatly disagree. There is no doubt that the patient exhibiting a Freudian trait has at one time or another suffered from it. No doubt this suffering has to do with the surfacing. Yet the surfacing itself is dissociational and so not necessarily indicative. Nevertheless, in historical fact the people who perceived the Freudian traits of patients surface could not humanly doubt that these were indicative. The questions they asked pertained only to treatment.

And so, the first development after Freud was the (true) obviousness of Freudian traits in psychotics and the (often true) Freudian diagnosis of them. The hurdle was treatment.

In one sense, the Freudian treatment of a psychotic is like the opening of an open wound: it makes no sense. In another sense the Freudian treatment of a psychotic is like the opening of an inoperable haemorrhage, or peritonitis, or cancer: it is so pervasive that one cannot but destroy the patient by removing all the affected areas. Indeed, as we claim all along, what makes psychosis what it is, is the globality of the defect resulting from its being an intellectual fixation, namely a fixation in the integrative organisation area of the mind. (See our *Paranoia*.)

What then could the poor Freudians do with their psychotic patients? They stuck to Freud's lame excuse: we cannot analyse a person who cannot transfer to the analyst. As we say, this makes no sense. There is no need for transfer, as no interpretation is necessary, since the symptom is not symbolic of the Freudian meaning but directly expressive of it. Moreover, the dissociation of the patient that precludes transference is the root of the trouble, not the technical obstacle Freud saw in it. Still further, transference is, by definition, the appointment by the patient of the analyst to the position of father figure; perhaps and/or mother figure; and so the analyst becomes both the target of the symbolic act and able to be influential regarding it. In psychosis there is no need for a symbolic act to interpret: a true dialogue between patient and anybody, physician or no physician, is all too possible when barriers break down, and the patient is all too aware of his Freudian traits. But no one can as yet use dialogue constructively; at least not to the extent of curing patients in droves.

A word about the barriers between the psychotic and his human environment. They are real and complex. A psychotic patient is dreadfully ambivalent about communication and he refuses to communicate or inhibits his effort to communicate, or communicates by exhibiting his Freudian traits, or talks incessantly − at times past his audience for fear of not being listened to, etc. These, however, are mere technicalities. Any person, physician, gardener, or janitor, who lives with psychotics and who cares enough about them, and anyone oblivious of their condition, whether children or naive bystanders, can overcome the barriers without much ado. (This was discovered by adolescent Henry Yellowlees.) At times they are puzzled to observe others inhibited by these barriers. By now many psychiatrists know that and just potter around in the presence of their patients.

So let us overlook the technicalities involved in establishing communication with psychotics and go to the paramount question: how this can be useful? We shall then be able to say, how can the early answers to this paramount question be construed as Freudian.

8. THE PSYCHOANALYTIC TREATMENT OF PSYCHOTICS: THERAPY

We have observed that Freudians found in the psychotic syndrome and diagnosis a job all too easy, and one that left no room — neither possibility of nor need for — transference.

Now, the crux of the Freudian and the fringe-Freudian conception of treatment was a matter of transference all the same. They all referred to Freud very reverently, yet critically; they declared psychotic transference possible and the door to hope. This, to repeat, taken literally makes no good sense to us. Transference for psychotics, observed Freud, is impossible. It is, we say, neither possible nor necessary: it is impossible not because of narcissism, as Freud claimed, but because of dissociation; nor is it necessary since there is no hidden wish to discover through transferences. Of course, a patient, like any weak person, may appoint any strong person in his vicinity to the position to a father figure — but for a while only. We observe as an empirical fact that the weaker a person the more surrogate father figures he adopts, and psychotics are only an exception in the sense that they may appoint also King Solomon or Jesus Christ as surrogate father figures — not to mention inanimate objects, especially dolls and such. Now, of course, it is very important to observe that a child[1] or a psychotic[2] makes this appointment in a frank and candid manner. Therefore it cannot possibly be transference: in transference proper the self-deception of the patient is made to work in a way he could not anticipate: transference is the act by which the psychoanalyst beats the patient at the patient's own neurotic game of self-deception: the neurotic is not sufficiently fully aware of his appointing his analyst for a father figure to be able to deliberate on it until it is too late, until the moment of catharsis that is, when the whole game is up: it is important to notice the importance laid by the Master on the fact that his patients felt they fell in love with him! Indeed, knowing all this is the one important factor in the avoidance of the pitfall of counter-transference: one has to know that one is not to be flattered by the

---

1.   J. Piaget (1926) *The Child's Conception of the World,* 1929.
2.   F. Fromm-Reichmann, *Principles of Intensive Psychotherapy,* 1950.

patient's confusion of love and admiration (and similarly with their reversals) as these are mere expressions of transference.

All this, to conclude, is impossible with genuinely psychotic patients, by the very fact that a psychotic is a candid person who shows his Oedipal impulses openly. Nevertheless, the significant historical fact was that the psychotic's appointment of the therapist as a father figure was deemed by the Freudians and their sympathizers who had high hopes of analyzing psychotics as a sort of transference. It is wild and cruel irony that here the therapist provided that tinge of self-deception which the patient lacked.

Empathy, then, is for the psychoanalytic treatment of psychosis, what transference proper is for the psychoanalytic treatment of neurosis. But what is the one and what is the other? How on earth does transference help? The classic answer is, transference helps through inducing catharsis; and it is false.[1] The later Freudian answer is, transference helps by enabling therapist play the role of a benign father proper. If so, then the same can more easily hold for regressive infantile psychotics. And if the psychotic is only half regressed, let him first regress all the way to the days before the trauma — to the womb if need be.

The treatment, then, is most intensive. It is that of staying with one patient for as long as needed in order to give him the courage to regress far enough and in order to give him courage and sustenance so he can grow up fast yet by a more normal route while watching each step he takes and correcting his mistakes so as to prevent the return to his old psychotic patterns. This, then, is the answer, and its Freudian character is in its reversal to the pre-traumatic period and to the patching the trauma by a more rational view of it while building the patient's personality, ego, what-have-you, or simply his moral strength, as the term goes.[2]

Let us conclude with a cautious word of appreciation. The treatment we have in mind, best described in *I Never Promised You a Rose Garden* and in *The Autobiography of a Schizophrenic Girl,* and really wonderfully described there, is both too expensive and of too limited a success. We admire the patience and devotion of the therapists and we may well admit that all expense — in terms of time, energy, etc., — is worth it for a pioneering experiment. But the fact is that if our society depends on such intensive treatments for the cure

---

1.   In generalist cases, we have said, catharsis fails regularly. Psychosis, we have said, is non-specific. Hence catharsis is of no use for psychotics. Worse still, it is easily achieved with them, and is very harmful for them. Psychiatrists with penchant for self-deception systematically hurt patients by miraculous cures.

2.   Allen Wheelis deems all non-specific neurosis — symptom-neurosis, he calls it — nothing but moral weakness.

of our patients, then we are in a bad shape. Here, of course, group therapy wedded to the technique of these Freudians may be a way out. But even this can be done only on the condition that the technique works often and easily enough. It does not. It is no surprise that it works seldom; rather, it is surprising that it works at all, since it is rooted in hardly any theory, and even the little theory it does have is, we regret to have to repeat, largely sham. The only thing in favor of this treatment is what it shares with all teachers in the Rudolf Steiner schools for the retarded: patience and good will unlimited, as well as the readiness to take as not in the least exceptional the wildest ideas of the person in charge whom one tries to comprehend and with whom one is willing to share so much.

9. ANTIPSYCHIATRY AND ALL THAT

We spoke above about all sorts of people, normal, neurotic, and psychotic, as if they were to be put in the same bag. But, in the therapeutic context one should divide the psychotics from both the normal and the neurotic and the dividing line should be the matter of self-deception. Whereas normals and the neurotics alike, are − to varying degrees − playing with self deception − the psychotic is not. One feels that in psychotic episodes there is no fake. Authenticity, the feeling that the patient's behavior is genuine, very strongly accompanies the therapist who accompanies a psychotic patient. Frieda Fromm-Reichmann was overwhelmed by her psychotic patients' strong aversion to hypocrisy, aversion even to the slightest and most commonly recognised and practiced social fictions.

There is a difficulty here. Is the behavior of all psychotic patients really so frank and genuine? Consider the psychotic state of a general paralytic whose disease doubtless is of syphilitic origin and who displays ideas of grandeur. His is the same state as that of a hebephrenic (the etiological origin of whose state is unknown; perhpas it is psychological, perhaps not). Shall we put both on a par despite the fact that one is organic and the other functional? Do both cases belong to psychiatry? If we put them on a par, since both the luetic (syphilitic) and the hebephrenic (adolescent psychotic) are psychotic, should we equally put the epileptic patient − when in a psychotic state − on a par with the hebephrenic? Does not the epileptic 'belong' to neurology? Still, we claim that even an epileptic belongs to psychiatry, if and when and to the extent that he is in a psychotic state. In other words, it is not the diagnosis that is of import (in this respect only, of course), but the state of the patient, and by a psychotic state we mean, a state in which the patient's outlook is largely impaired: the psychotic state is a condition in which the freedom of choice is more impaired than in neurosis. The one patient's result, the limitation on the domain of one patient's freedom, may be the same as another's, even if they differ in the ways of onset and decline of the state. In general terms, one may say that the neurotic 'escapes' freedom, whereas psychotics find themselves 'trapped' by their limitation: it is as if the disease 'descends' on the psychotic whereas it is as if the disease is sophisticatedly elaborated by the neurotic. Is this fact responsible for the authenticity which the psychotic patient inspires in us? We do not know, but find it hard to believe that the luetics and epileptics are more candid when in the psychotic state than before and after it. Also, we see little frankness in the severe depression of psychotic patients who, in their behavior, are the very model of infantile black-mailers, who inspire feelings the very opposite to the feelings of genuiness and openness and committment inspired by a paranoic. Are we not mixed up in putting all psychotics in one bag? Should we not be more specific, stop speaking generally of psychotics, both of the frankness of the psychotics and of the psychotherapy to be administered to them? Perhaps we should better begin to treat singly the case of the paranoic, of the manic, of the depressive, of the schizophrenic etc.? Perhaps we should better even breakdown the list of diseases — perhaps so far as to have each patient having his own private condition. (Why perhaps? — Certainly! If Hippocrates were to be consulted, he surely would have approved!) Let us, then, go that far and consider not any specific illness but the individual patient himself; this in line with the classic Hippocratic view that there are no diseases (these are mere abstractions), only sick people. Oddly, this extreme disassociation of all illness will help us, perhaps, solve the difficulty with our view of psychotics as candid: psychosis itself has to disappear, but patients exist, and some of them are exceptionally candid indeed. However, the candid sweet personality will act sweetly, and the candid nasty personality will act nastily. Perhaps the luetic, the epileptic, the drunkard, is simply uninhibited! Indeed, their conduct is exaggerated, for better or for worse, in a way perceived by Esquirol and Briquet and Charcot, whereas other patients, far from being uninhibited and derivatively candid are inhibited and derivatively self-deceptive. We could not say that the opposite of candid is shy, because some psychotics are shy. And the reader who cannot imagine a candid shy person ought to meet one in a mental home, not to say some plain peasant folk (less exaggeratedly, of course, yet the frank suspiciousness of a plain peasant is proverbial, after all). And so, perhaps, whereas normal people and more so neurotics deceive themselves to this or that extent psychotics are those who are frank and open and candid and uninhibited.

Anti-psychiatry, then, is the tendency to look at a patient and his suffering, not at the proper label to stick on him; and anti-psychiatry can appreciate the frankness of some uninhibited patients. So much in anti-psychiatry is both admirable and straight-forward human common sense. To call the uninhibited frank is a bit of an exaggeration, especially when he loses his inhibition to the bottle. Moreover, the psychotic's usual claim that psychosis just happens to him, the alcoholic's claim that the bottle just rules him, the claim made by the patient, frankly and innocently, that he, the patient, is like clay in the healer's hand and wishes to God to see him succeed — all these are self-deceptions bordering on sophisticated lies.

But we do not insist. What we find pathetic, is the claim of anti-psychiatrists that these wretched sufferers are fountain-heads of authenticity and heroic transcendence. We admire the intent but see the execution as shallow all the same. It is really nasty of us all to treat these wretches so shabbily. But it is all too easy to counter this by the mere view of these wretches as saints; and the secularization of their saintliness is pitiful.

Nor are we a jot better when observing antipsychiatry as pathetic, unless we both admire the admirable in it and take our poor view of it as strong disinfectant: we would like to say, as strong medicine, but as yet we have none: neither strong nor weak medicine for psychosis is available as yet.

10. THE MEDICAL MODEL REVISITED

We began the present study by taking the claims of antipsychiatry seriously and by considering it as a challenge to be accepted and dealt with and not dismissed as mere claims of a 'yet another school in psychiatry'. We tried to take the challenge seriously, since antipsychiatry attacks the very foundations of psychiatry, especially the claims laid by psychiatry to be a branch of medicine.

Now, we have found, to our great astonishment, that a medical model does exist, the ancient Hippocratic model, and it withstands all onslaughts with ease — the non-discriminate criticisms of medicine — of anti-psychiatrists and of critics of both a wider scope (critics of the medical establishment as such) and a narrower scope (critics of current practices and of accepted etiquette). Moreover, the Hippocratic medical model was obviously not invented to answer these criticisms since it antecedes them by far. It is therefore not the Hippocratic school, but the non-Hippocratic school in medicine, that is the target of the attack by the diverse fashionable critics, and when so construed we endorse these attacks though we deem their expressions somewhat exaggerated: our Hippocratic bias is well illustrated in these pages. Yet, we are not strict followers of Hippocrates or of his school. And, in order to be fair let us present, in as favorable a way as possible, the non-Hippocratic school, its merits, and why it is that it has gained its influence and was even dominant during the golden age of the Enlightenment and beyond. As we have indicated, there was always a sort of pendulum of fashion swinging between the Hippocratic and the non-Hippocratic. Today, is the upper hand the Hippocratic or the non-Hippocratic school? Or is it now the resolution of the conflict by the division of the territory? Can it be that Hippocratic generalism reigns supreme today in the Royal College of Medicine (internal medicine, that is) and non-Hippocratic Externalism reigns supreme in the Royal College of Surgeons, and truce is maintained? Or was a compromise of a synthesis achieved? We simply do not know. But we cannot abide by a truce and look for a synthesis which we have not found as yet. For any school to be correct it is not enough that it has some measure of success: it also has to explain the success of the competition. If we assume medicine as a whole to have some rational kernal to its fashions, then there should be some rational explanation of alleged medical success. Moreover, we wish to explain the intellectual allure of each opponent quite apart from his success, since success does not favor only one party. It is no accident that the externalist model was popular in the Age of Reason: it was part and parcel of the mechanistic view of the age. Why was mechanism so attractive? We think the attraction of mechanism is largely rooted in the fact − in general − that it conforms to externalism rather than that externalism is attractive because it is a part of mechanism: it is not that is attractive all by itself, but that externalism is attractive in is simplistic approach.[1] So we may stick with medicine for a while.

There is nothing stronger in medicine than the sense of helplessness and frustration that attacks the healer at the bedside of a sufferer for whom nothing can be done. The sense of frustration forces the healer to try anything, even a prayer or a vain hope. Even if successful, his treatment may be only symptomatic and so ephemeral and then the sense of frustration is renewed. Hence the contempt physicians so easily tend to show towards symptomatc treatment.

There is something wonderful about externalism, somthing that lends

---

1. Holism is obviously more convincing on empirical grounds and externalism is more challenging as a research program: seek the detail which, in proper combination, delivers the goods and delivers the whole system. The Cabbalah was excessively holistic yet in its combinatorics it was excessively externalist − permitting it as magic proper. The conversion of the Cabbalistic magic to natural magic was, indeed, the very process of the development of modern mechanistic science.

power to the researcher's curiosity, leads him to etiology, etc. In psychiatry the prime example is Freud's dismissal of the local cure of a phobia as merely symptomatic. The patient simply ceases to project his anxiety to the favored object of phobia, he observed, and seeks another object ot the same end. Nothing will do, he added, short of a cure of the anxiety.

Well and good. Yet the rejection of all treatment of symptoms as an error is quite in conflict with some current excellent medical practices. When a patient suffers from early stages of syphilis symptomatic treatment is at best irrelevant and at worst criminal and syphilis is the paradigm of wrong symptomatic treatment repeatedly marshalled by externalists who indeed declare all those who cure the early symptoms of syphilis charlatans (especially in view of the fact that the early symptoms, lesions, tend to disappear with no treatment anyhow). Similarly, Eysenck and other anti-Freudians declare Freudian treatment worthless, and not even symptomatic; and they also claim that Freudians have statistically no higher rate of success than the rate of the natural disappearance of neurotic symptoms in average patients.

But this is certainly not always so: the case of syphilis inherently differs from the case of cholera or diphtheria, and from most ills that go day in, day out, undiagnosed but treated − at times with significant results − by no diagnosis and no prescription yet with the use of over-the-counter drugs. Be that as it may, there is no doubt that we do not cure cholera, that most untreated cholera patients die of dehydration before they overcome the disease, that hence treating the very symptoms of cholera, mainly dehydration, suffices to save the patient's life: curing him is neither possible or necessary! And the same goes for diphtheria, for viral pneumonia, for the cases of meningitis that doctors manage to save they do not know how, etc., etc.

Now, the application of symptomatic treatment is traditionally defended by the slogans, nature cures; the physician can only help nature do its job; the physician only removes obstacles from nature's road to healing; etc., etc. We have explained at length why these slogans are essentially generalist.

The logic of the externalist and the generalist research is all too plastically obvious. The generalist wants to see things in vivo, to interfere least with the natural processes he observes; the externalist wants to see things work in vitro; he wants to isolate each subprocess, to identify each cause of each part of a process. Can it be done?

The usual tendency here is to push the debate to its metaphysical extreme in one quick step. But this leads fast to a stalemate. Mechanism and holism are untestable metaphysical doctrines. We do not know whether the stuff of the body is cogs and wheels or muscles and tendons. So let us push the debate to its methodological side. The generalist sees in theory a bundle of assumptions that we test together. If they collectively work, it is hard to say by what virtue; if they are collectively refuted, it is impossible to say which of them is false, whether only one of them or more of them etc. This is a point of logic. The philosophers Pierre Duhem and Willard Van Orman Quine have advanced the Duhem-Quine thesis, so-called, that since this is so, we cannot isolate and prove any single assumption in science.

Here, then, is the attraction of medical externalism in particular and of mechanism and of externalist philosophy in general: it is optimistic, looking for scientific proofs, rationalistic. This is the spirit of the Age of Reason.

Today we think differently. And so we have to explain the successes of externalism. And the explanations have to be specific − of specific successes − but the form of explanation can be general. That is, there is a general formula to try out first and deviate from, only for specific reasons. It is this: an externalist treatment succeeds as it is based on an externalist theory that under some very specific conditions is a good approximation to some generalist theory. That is, in some specific cases, as some theories attest, of all the factors involved in a situation or in a process, one factor becomes paramount in that varying it slightly makes for large differences whereas the situation or process is fairly insensitive to the variation of the rest of the manipulable variables involved.

This, to stress, is a general matrix, to be filled with details as specific as the case requires. The required details, however, are not always available: both externalism and generalism are problematic this way and thus they generate research projects.

A very obvious example can be taken from quite a few externalist successes, such as the insertion of a plastic tube to replace a damaged blood vessel or the destruction of a parasite responsible for an illness. There is no doubt that the externalist does not concern himself with a lot of intricate and vital matters involved, such as the body's absorption of the tube or of the medication poisonous to the parasite, not to mention the conditions that may make the original bloodvessel regenerate or the parasites innocuous. The victory of the externalist is all too obvious. After it, generalists seek cases where the externalist's triumph may be done without. The existence of such cases are triumphs of generalism − not only in that they render the externalist treatment obsolete, but also in that they can go further than externalism, especially in cases of patients who cannot take the harsh externalist treatment. The discovery of vitamins, of diets, such as milk-free or fat-free or sugar-free diets as solutions better than the externalist treatments, these are the glories of generalism. (In psychiatry there is the parallel, if highly controversial − method of treatment by large doses of vitamins − megavitamins − of Linus

Pauling and Humphrey Osmond.) Nevertheless, the dialogue continues: while the externalist is the only one available, we are grateful to him, yet the generalist repeatedly tries to make him redundant.

The externalist has his reply: the generalist may wish to transcend any given externalist explanation and treatment, but also the externalist may wish to transcend any given generalist explanation and treatment. And we have instances to this effect too, of course: just think of the treatment of a disease caused by a parasite before the discovery of the parasite, or of the general treatment of the whole body with the defective bloodvessel somewhere before it was possible to locate and treat such defects! And so, the dialogue continues: both externalist and generalist, one tries to outdo the other. So much the better.

The generalist will not let things rest. There is such a thing as spontaneous remission (Nature cures!) and treatment may very well prevent it! The externalist, however, will study the conditions of spontaneous remission and will emulate them when possible. In psychiatry spontaneous remission is still a focus of excitement. The generalists complain that physicians too often allow cases of spontaneous remission to drop out of their field of vision.

There is a saying, he who laughs last, laughs best. Who laughs last? This is a metaphysical question, and going into it seems to bring about a stalemate in one move. Is there any metaphysical argument in favor of one view? Yes. It is the classical reductionist view. The claim that all psychology is in essence biology and that all biology is in essence physics is what is known as reductionism. But reductionism makes externalism palatable on the assumption that physics is mechanistic or at least on the assumption that physicists find mechanism palatable. In fact some do, some do not. The corpusclarian and the field views of physics are still struggling and one is more on the mechanistic side, the other is more on the holistic side.

But reductionism too is both a metaphysics − living systems are controlled by laws of physics alone − and a methodology − try to explain biological law by physical laws. Is this methodology viable?

It was Pavlov's reductionism that has made him look an externalist despite his expressed generalism, despite the generalist characters of all his physiological experiments prior to his straying into psychology, his beautiful inventions of experiments to perceive processes in vivo. But his venture into psychology, for which he gained so much fame, has to do with reductionism.

Pavlov is not the discoverer of the salivation of dogs or humans who hear the dinner-gong: this is plain common knowledge. It is even used repeatedly in children's stories. Nor do we know him for having called this effect a conditioned reflex: naming is not a scientific activity. What he discovered was an obvious logical fact, and this is a major breakthrough: he notices that since salivation, that is, a physiological event, is caused by a psychological process, there is an error somewhere in the very conception of the hierarchy of science. It is not expected of biology to interfere with the physics of a system, nor of psychology to interfer with the physiological aspect of a system. Yet there it is in the event of salivation.

This criticism is not new. It was Bishop George Berkeley who claimed that the growth of a flower is a violation of the law of gravity: biology makes physical things go up when physics says they should go down.

There is an answer to Berkeley's critique. For example, one way a plant transports matter upwards is by capillarity, which is a physical force. And so on. (This 'and so on' hides a big assumption, but that is alright.) If so, then likewise salivation due to the dinner-gong should be explained purely physiologically. This last sentence, when properly generalized to cover all seemingly psychologically caused physiological processes, is the whole of Pavlovian psychology; it is behaviorism in its stark nakedness. And so the medical model of psychiatry is a mere preamble to behaviorism.

Let us conclude this with a fool-proof demonstration which no-one has managed to dent as yet. No matter how psychological a given pattern of behavior is, it may be influenced and altered − by alcohol, other drugs or simply a blow on the head, at least a blow strong enough to kill. This is permissible, since physics and chemistry are more basic than psychology; what is not permissible is the contrary. Yet every reader can conjure contrary instances, such as the evolution of patterns of conduct more or less influential on consumption of drugs and their rate of metabolism and influence on the body, etc. The attempt to eliminate such cases eliminates all psychology and forces all behavior patterns into physiology at once: into the behaviorist mold.

11. BEHAVIOR MODIFICATION AND ITS DERIVATIVES

In a nutshell the behavioristic therapist's view can be put thus: Let us treat the symptoms, since the symptoms are the very disease. This is a wonderful, deep statement, on which we would like to philosophize. Indeed, we already dealt with it in Chapter I and again in the previous section, on the medical model. Yet, we can give our verdict right away: when we closely examine what the therapists of the behaviorist school really do we find that they confine themselves to neurotic phobias (sometimes also to neurotic obsessions) alone. And this is a serious defect. When they also treat a schizophrenic symptomatically (as they should, given their own view), then they only sometimes achieve anything, and then only a superficial external conditioning of his behavior, only some sort of domestication. And this is not treatment, let alone healing.

It seems that treating symptoms alone is very superficial and thus, for the generalist, the paragon of externalism. Indeed, behaviorism is regularly viewed as extremist externalism. But, as we have explained, treat symptoms! is a generalist slogan. Except that the generalists have no monopoly over this slogan. As we say, the question of efficacy always transcends the controversy because the success in treatment by one school imposes on it the attention of the opposite school and challenges it to explain and broaden that success.

Where is the success of behavior therapy? It is confined, to repeat, almost exclusively to the treatment of neurotic phobias and sometimes it includes also neurotic obsessions. It may be advisable then to deal with the behaviorist claim that psychiatry should treat symptoms only by examining the behaviorist treatment of phobias, and stay with that, and not argue with the behaviorists about the nature of symptoms and diseases in general.

What is according to the behaviorists (and, of course everybody else) the main symptom of phobia? Fear. What does the behaviorist do in order to alleviate the fear? (How does he operate?) We think that, in analysing both the nature of the fear and the ways behaviorists handle it, we shall understand their success in the treatment of phobias and, as a corollary, their confessed failure (for which we do not blame them) in the handling of all the other psychic ills (depressions, mania, paranoia, schizophrenia, and even simple cases of 'classical' hysteria) which seems to refute their view.

The question is that of a rationale. The generalist's rationale for symptomatic treatment is, at times – but only at times – symptoms are obstacles to nature's attempt to heal. Fear, we are convinced, is such a symptom. If and when the behaviorists suggest that they allay fears so as to allow nature to heal, then they are generalists.

Example: fear of women becomes a serious problem for young men in late adolescence, or fear of touch, etc. Allaying this fear is no cure for the adolescent's sexual problem. But life in adolescent society can smooth up things, allow the adolescent to develop a flexibility, to adjust, to get healed – on the necessary condition that he overcome his initial fears that keep him out of the company of his peers.

A therapist allaying an adolescent's fears in the hope that normal living will help him adjust is generalist par excellence. If he is a behaviorist or not matter not; whether his methods of allying fears are based on behavioristic theory, are methods of deconditioning, or what have you, matters not.

Joseph Wolpe holds a different view. He allays fears as a preamble to deconditioning, and deems deconditioning as a cure. The allaying of the fear in the clinic, by way of relaxing the patient, drugging him or hypnotizing him, is merely the anesthetizing of the patient in the clinic so as to weaken on his fears that are symptoms so as to be able to work on his wrong conditioning, to undo his wrong conditioning. This looks like externalist par excellence, as not generalist at all.

But whether this is so we cannot say, and on principle. For, a generalist will have to explain the success of Wolpe, and this explanation may or may not be endorsed by Wolpe himself.

The generalist explanation is simple: the deconditioning which Wolpe exercises is also simply the allaying of fears, yet these fears look like entities located in given junctions whereas they are diffuse. Is, then, behavior therapy intended as generalist or externist? This depends on one's view.

To return to Pavlov's initial insight. If behaviorism is the attempt to ignore psychology except for its physiological aspects, then viewing fear this way one sees nothing but its physiological manifestations, of course – such as the bearing of one's teeth to the enemy, trembling, secreting adrenalin and whatever else physiology can tell, including details about dilation of eye pupils, heart-beats, dry mouth and moist palms, inhibition of the alimentary tract activity and so on, no matter how long the list is. Moreover, supposing ever so many physiological functions to be triggered by adrenalin secretion, we may omit explicit mention of them from the list of activities which physiologically characterize fear as 'merely' derivative. Now, we can say, to simplify matters, the patient suffers from excess activity of the adrenal glands. If this is the trouble, then it is very much akin to excessive or inhibited activity of the thyroid gland, and then the most natural suggestion to examine is chemotherapy. Does the administration of vitamin E check excessive adrenal secretion? If so, does it cure phobias?

Answer: no. Generalist physiology tells us that normal bodily functions are normally capable of modifying themselves well within the practicable range to accommodate for external interference, even if the interfering agent is known to inhibit a gland as required. The generalist will expect the tolerance of the patient to the external controlling agent – vitamin E in this case – and warn the externalist against increasing the dosage to the level where permanent damage may result.

The question immediately arises: how, then, can generalists at all account for the fact that externalist therapy – chemotherapy in this case – sometimes does work? Why is vitamin E no good but insulin for diabetics is permissible?

The answer is frightfully commonsense and well known. First, in rare cases the externalist model is good enough an approximation to the truth of the matter. Second, often the cure is only very temporary — until the body adjusts — but when it is a case of a bothersome symptom it may cause vitally needed relief and thus may be of extreme usefulness to the body. But there is more to it. Every drug addict knows he has to increase dosage and either exceed the limit and die of overdose or play with uppers and downers to outwit the wisdom of the body. This is the tricky case, and one which the generalist George Bernard Shaw has accused the medical profession of playing with in oder to be always needed by the patient: playing against the wisdom of the body is a vicious game (end of preface to *Doctor's Dilemma*).

It is amazing what tricks the wisdom of the body can play and outwit us: smoking raises the sugar level of the blood, but the body adjusts and the regular smoker needs his tobacco — at the accustomed frequency — to reach normal sugar level in the blood! In other words, the question whether chemotherapy works, much depends on whether the body in its wisdom recognizes the ill chemotherapy is meant to cure! For example, the body resists tobacco but welcomes small doses of insulin to regain balance lost due to sick pancreas. But, and this is the limitation of Cannon's theory, the body homeostasis much depends on mental states. This is well-known to diabetics and more so to those who share their lives. It has been empirically illustrated most beautifully by the injection of adrenalin to people and other animals in and out of fear. Now that chemotherapy is disposed of in a strongly anti-Pavlovian way, should we expect other physiological functions to abide by Pavlov's theory? Why? On what rationale?

We do not know. That conditioning at times works and at times not is ancient knowledge. Why, is still a mystery. Some conditioning has been shown to be age-dependent; some to be dependent on general constitutions that Pavlov himself tried to clarify towards the end of his long and rich career. Some depend on trigger mechanisms that seem utterly unrelated as Lorenz and other imprinting theorists have claimed — rightly or not, we cannot say.

So, some conditioning works under some conditions and it behooves behaviorists to discover which. (They could, in particular, study carefully the interaction of behavior therapy with the improved efficacy of insulin intake in neurotic diabetics.) Instead they are busy defending their doctrine. Pity.

To conclude, we have no theory as yet as to why some behavior modification works, some definitely not, and some are still terra incognita. We do not know under what conditions does the conditioning that works work. But we do know that the removal of fear during deconditioning is of extreme significance. We do not have an alternative theory to explain the success of behavior modification, but we do think fear is a major inhibitor and we do think fear is the central focus of trouble in all mental ills as we shall soon explain. And so we do think the removal of fear, by chemicals, by behavior modification, and by friendliness, of supreme importance in therapy.

The critique of behaviorism can turn savage. Fear is specific and reasonable; anxiety is non-specific; phobia is specific but unreasonable. Behaviorism, so the savage criticism averes, cannot differentiate the three. This savage criticism may be answerable. But, no doubt, the answer will not come easy.

Behaviorists cannot even add that much; for behaviorists fear is one of three or more basic response-elements, each of which can manifest itself poorly and destructively in ever so many response-patterns. Yet, they center first on fear, and then on phobias. We explain the presence of fear here as the result of its ubiquity in mental ills and we explain phobias by their being deeper fears though not as deep as the fears of psychotics, i.e. easier to handlesymptomatically yet without diagnosis. For, these are the remaining two themes of this study before it comes to a close. First the ubiquity of terror in all mental ills as the root source of the trouble. Second, the proper treatment of all ills, physical, mental, and combined, is best achieved by making a proper diagnosis leading to proper − well-tested − mode of treatment; and usually preferably, and in ignorance always, merely symptomatic treatment. We take these two points in this order.

V: CONCLUSION

1. A MEDICAL VIEW OF PSYCHIC ILLS

Supposing we have physical or mental mechanisms that may be broken, restored, and retrained, then, in line with our previous discussions, the breaking will be the illness, the restoration medicine, and the retraining no more medical than physiotherapy, i.e., a border-line case of medical treatment. Also, restoration is the physician putting things together and enabling nature to cure plus nature curing. Suppose, further, that we have a mental mechanism that is not broken, but gone practically irretrievably the wrong way; its restoration to the right way or to the point of departure to the wrong way, will be as much medical as plastic surgery meant to remove a scar, or to remove the slant in slanted eyes or sweat glands, to mention plastic surgery practiced at one time or another in Japan.

Consider, further, sexual impotence; let us begin with sexual impotence among cocks and deer. Before the discoveries of ethology and under the impact of Freud, it was taken for granted, though never to our knowledge stated, that mental castration is a sophisticated process, on the much more advanced level of intellectual and/or technological development than physical castration. There is a subtlety here, to be sure, since according to Freud the beginning of manking/civilization equals the creation of the Oedipal syndrome, including incest taboo, guilt, and all that; but these are tolerable whereas sexual impotence is not tolerable, perhaps less tolerable than physical castration. It turns out, then, that mental castration is common in the animal world. The extreme example is certain small tropical fish, all born female, who move in small schools, and whose leader changes sex and becomes male. When the male is removed, the female on top of the pecking order begins to alter her sex and within two weeks becomes male unless the original male is returned beforehand. At the other extreme there are the cocks who are lowest in the pecking order who suffer complete sexual impotence unless removed to other barnyards where they fare better on the pecking order and then start normal sexual activity. It is reported that in many animal species sexual impotence is a function of territorial conditions, but, we understand, with certain species of deer it is permanent and results from the loss of leadership in the combat that young male deer engage in prior to any sexual activity. Finally, some homosexual activity is explained not as sex but as expression of social superiority or pecking order, in some monkeys, dogs and other species.

We do not know, then, whether sexual impotence in animals is entirely permanent or always the result of environmental conditions. But suppose it is naturally permanent in a given animal, and suppose someone can find a process that nevertheless reverses the situation, for example by administering a shock. After all, in 1924 Pavlov found that shocks cause animals to forget very strongly impressed lessons. We would certainly consider such treatment as medical. Even if the animal, as a result, will be behind its peers due to loss of time between onset of illness and cure, and so will not function normally, at least unless some further training is dispensed, even then we will consider the treatment medical and the further necessary treatment actvity convalescence akin to physiotherapy.

Thus, we do not know even with lower animals, what damage is more of a reflection of unfavorable circumstances, what a mental scar. Can we say more about humans? When is the damage repairable by changing circumstances? Are scars removable? With all human mental ills, we suggest as a general hypothesis, neurotic, psychotic, borderline, and mixed, light and severe, local and global, the trouble has three aspects.

First, etiology: the main source of trouble is anxiety in Freud's original sense: deep-seated uncaused fear; it may be permanently felt like the permanent pain of the slipped-disc or the arthritic or the neuralgic, and it may be triggered like allergy by some signal, usually not known to the patient but discoverable by observation, trial and error, etc. and it may be permanent fear triggered to high pitch by some unknown or known signal. Indeed, we suggest, all fear is both permanent and triggerable to a pitch, but when on an unusually high level or unusually sensitive to triggers raising it to a very high level, or both, it is illness. Though we admire Freud's study of the causes of the fear, we consider that study no more etiological than the study — also important — of what causes most of the cuts and bruises in battles, in motor car accidents, or in a given accident-prone industrial plant; the cuts and bruises belong to etiology, their causes do not; likewise, the fear, the anxiety, the numb incapacity of the patient, belong to etiology, their causes do not. There may be a slight difference between a shrapnel and an open cut: the shrapnel must be removed. But the shrapnel itself is different from its presence in the living flesh. The catharsis theory sees the Oedipal original event — or whatever else caused the initial trauma — not as a knife, but a shrapnel, and the catharsis to be the flushing that flushes it out. To the extent that the catharsis theory does work —

on a local level and with intelligent patients, etc. − we may still see the cause of trouble as a shrapnel. Otherwise, our slogan is, medicine looks at the cut, preventive medicine looks at the knife that has caused it!

Second, course: the main development in mental ills is the attempted self-cure, that can be likened to the scarring of an infected wound or the healing of a broken bone not properly set. That is to say, usually a patient learns to handle his fears in his own way, without destroying them. If the treatment leads to his own satisfaction he is obviously not a patient, or no longer a patient. Of course, just as a medical examiner may easily find something wrong with a healthy person − complete health is most improbable − as, for example, an untroublesome hernia, heart murmur, high blood pressure, so a medical examiner may find neuroses and even minor psychoses that are hardly worth noticing. Yet self-cure is not always to the patient's satisfaction − which is what makes him a patient. The most obvious and common example for that is oedema, where excess fluid goes to one's legs rather than lungs. It is a form of self-treatment, satisfactory unless excessive yet never pleasant. When excessive it fails: the oedema, caused by high blood pressure causes, in its turn, increase of blood pressure. What is common to all such failed self-cures, whethr troublesome enough to call for medical interference or not, is that self-cure is reinforcing its own pattern.

Third, the most harmful side-effect is the loss of contact with others. All attempts to return the mentally ill to common humanity, Pinel and Rush and Tuke, Freud and Adler and Jung, Laing and Szasz and Foucault, all prove he is outside the bale of common humanity only partly by society's choice, only partly by his own choice, but mainly due to a tremendous terror. Here the model is shyness − be it normal, neurotic, or psychotic. The shy person fears initimacy since one is doubtlessly more vulnerable to one's intimates than to strangers, and the fear of hurt keeps sensitivity high and vice versa. So shyness is self-reinforcing à la Freud and is likewise self-reinforcing by keeping others away from trying to help or from being able to implement their good-will. In other words, fear and distrust reinforce each other and spell autism. Autism is the chief side-effect of all mental ills, local or global, both in that it hurts (even local autism may be unbearable) and in that it prevents healing.

So, to repeat, our hypothesis is, all mental ills are caused by fears, and constitute self-treatment that is self-reinforcing without fully overcoming the fear, and the fear breeds suspicion that clogs channels of communication, particularly to those who may help − thereby causing autism.

We should add two items. First, the motive or need. The reason the illness keeps bothering one is that one keeps away from what one desires strongly. Usually it is sex, food, friendship, worldly success, independence, autonomy. But it can be anything. It really is not a matter of the illness. If we must stress one factor we would choose neither sex nor anything concrete but, for our modern society, just moral autonomy in the abstract. Following Henri Ey we say, mental illness is illness of freedom. Second, we should say a few words on one of the most important ingredients in all mental illness; self-deception. It permeates everything we have named thus far; not only self-deception precludes autonomy, it precludes contact with other people, self-reassessment, facing fear and looking it in the eye; the lot. So much to our description of all mental ills, of the normal, the neurotic, the psychotics, the autistic, the borderline and combined. To illustrate this, let us show how self-deception permeates all mental ills by discussing the demarcation between neurotic and psychotic.

In our *Paranoia* (Chapter IX) we admitted that both neurosis and psychosis have both intellectual and emotional foci, but declared the intellectual fixation characteristic of psychosis and emotional fixation as characteristic of neurosis.

This is somewhat unsatisfactory. First, why should both components be ever present? Second, how come a person decides on an emotional fixation or on an intellectual one? He thinks it out; hence the decision is also intellectual. What makes it diagnostically more emotional than intellectual if originally both neurosis and psychosis seem identical?

We propose the following. First and foremost, all mental ills are originally identical. They are fixations under stress. Both fixations are psychological as any conduct of any animal under stress is fixated and clinging to (regressive) patterns.

We propose further — very much in Freud's lights though put very generally — that when the stress disappears and the fixation remains, the fixation itself may slowly relax and vanish as a clinical remission. Otherwise it may remain and prove unproblematic for ever or until the next moment of stress, and the patient may survive the next moment of stress or have a breakdown leading to an unusual episode or even to a different mode of life. Or the different mode of life may ensure the earlier fixation. The new mode of life has to do with two facts. First, anxiety and fixation go on reinforcing each other, so the fixation does not relax. Hence, every success in relieving anxiety after stress may be an act of self-administered preventive psychotherapy. Second, the fixation clashes with reality.

This clash may be tackled in various ways. In the normal way a patient may wish to jettison the fixation, consult friends and relations, take a vacation, and get more or less cured. Or he may ignore the unpalatable part of reality. The paradigm for this is hysterical blindness. We propose this as a paradigm for all neurosis. For, we propose the fixation involves an atrophy as a sort of blindness and as a compensation it evolves emotionally. Contrary to our earlier – Freudian – view we now suggest that the symbolic character of the fixation is not at the point of origin but rather the very consequence of the method of self-treatment.

The psychotic, however, does not overlook the difficulty; he solves it in a facile way. This makes his fixation, in a derivative manner we have amply elaborated in our first book, into an integrative principle which, in its turn, may cause persecutionism. The psychotic is blind too, but not to the difficulties; he is blind to the popular and easily accessible criticism of his facile solution.

Hence, the neurotic is self-deceptive on the concrete level of the appearance of phenomena contrary to his fixation; the psychotic is quick to handle these and so looks open and agile of mind; but his self-deception is on a slightly more sophisticated level: he either fails to listen to criticism, or disposes of it in an equally facile and at times obviously persecutionist manner.

We offer a test. As we have said, the psychotic can under stress play normal for a little while with great effort and acknowledge recognition of public opinion he is usually blind to. Also, his blindness is an active principle that costs him intellectual and emotional effort. If our theory is true, there is an obvious parallel in the neurotic case. Thus, first, hysterical blindness is tiring, emotionally and intellectually, and this can be tested by looking for tiredness and for examining cases of greater and smaller suppression of tiredness. Second, under specific conditions, e.g. a surprise encounter with a visual cliff, a hysterical blind person should see. And so on for other neuroses.

2. PSYCHIATRY AS MEDICINE

Why is it so important to consider psychiatry as medicine proper? Had psychiatry been the biologically oriented speciality that it is in many clinics, then obviously it must be a part of medicine. But for the last decades psychiatry has been considered as some sort of psychology; in some circles it is even identified with some specific psychological school; in the lay public's opinion it is erroneously yet frequently identified with depth psychology or with the psychodynamic approach, generally equalled with Freudianism proper. For our part we would like to see psychiatry both psychologically oriented and well within the realm of medicine. We mean by psychology the theory that has to do with meaningful conduct (see p. 184 above) and we mean medicine as diagnosis and etiology (see p. 127). Our reason for viewing psychiatry as psychological is that it treats mental sufferings. Our reason for wishing to see it as a branch of medicine has to do with what we value in the medical tradition, particularly the practice of medical diagnosis. Let us elaborate.

When we speak of diagnosis, we have in mind differential diagnosis. For, after all, medicine, by definition, allows for no diagnosis without its corolary/complementary differential diagnoses; what is precisely the way of thinking characteristic of a physician, i.e. of medicine as opposed to other professions, is precisely the very way of reasoning leading to diagnostically differentiating conditions in order to arrive at the proper diagnosis – which in itself is always open to further differentiation and other changes according to the way the physicians sees the course of disease/treatment developing and according to the progress of medical science. We are here, the reader may notice, only echoing Charcot's maxim, compare and contrast!

Back to diagnosis in psychiatry. The point in the matter of diagnosis in psychiatry is to exclude all other conditions, so as to yield some psychiatric/psychological picture. For, some cases are not of psychiatric/psychological conditions proper, but rather they are psychopathological signs of conditions which are mostly somatic – e.g., hyperthyroidism, myxoedema, uremia, chemically induced psychoses, degenerative and other diseases or physical damage (wounds) of the central nervous system, and brain tumors. Indeed, the most important thing to be excluded is a tumor cerebri (cerebral tumor). All such conditions, somatic, organically induced, or physical damage, will sooner or later look diagnostically unproblematic, subject to some definite technique of medical diagnosis which will be successfull or not as the case may be Almost all the medical conditions (somatic, organic etc.) accompanied by a psychiatric picture are not severely aggravated even if not properly diagnosed at the time: the lapse of a couple of days or weeks, though if not properly diagnosed causes suffering for the patient, at least it is usually not irreversibly harmful. When a case may be near-fatal, e.g. a brain tumor or brain haemorrhage, it is seldom suspected of being of mental origin. Moreover an immediate diagnosis of a space occupying lesion in the skull leads immediately to one or another sort of surgical interference to remove the cause of the 'intra-cerebral pressure'. The rule in the medical school says, a good psychiatrist should always carry in his pocket an ophthalmoscope (the ophthalmoscope being the most appropriate tool for establishing the intracranial high pressure expressed in the bulging of the fundus of the eye).

One corollary to all this is that for diagnostic purposes a psychiatrist should be medically trained to some degree. The paradox is that once the medically trained psychiatrist has successfully excluded the somatic, the organic, etc., he is left with a psychiatric condition which if he does not consider stemming from a cause of a biological/biochemical origin (known, or as yet unknown) — and he is bound to do so in some cases — once his somatic diagnosis is completed and the cause is declared mental, he then can turn the patient to some kind of psychologist whose knowledge of medicine need not be called upon.

Now, once the somatic diagnosis is completed, and then also the proper psychiatric condition is determined, so that a proper psychiatric picture is presented to us, then — and only then — what one has to do next is to begin treatment, of course. And treatment can be administered by a skilled psychologist or nurse or social worker or even a clergyman etc. — diagnosis may, and at times should, tell us who is best capable of fulfilling this task. It happened in the past and it still happens everyday. Yet, even when administered by laymen, we still wish therapy to be part and parcel of medicine. Why? Now, we can in a way avoid the issue by saying that healing is part of medicine and if lay people, psychologists social workers, or clergymen, participate in healing of physically or mentally sick people, let alone succeeding in it, then their practice 'by definition' becomes part and parcel of medicine. This would not be a mere play on words, since we all consider healing as part of medicine; it is, after all, in the last resort medicine's very goal and raison d'être. This is sharply illustrated best by the fact that there is hardly a physician, let us repeat, who did not experience in the most profound way frustration, humiliation, impotence, despair, facing those situations which he could not treat.

Nevertheless, though usually healing is part of medicine, to say this is only a partial truth. To be exact one should say the contrary and also add its complements. For medicine has healing as only one of its constituents. There is no medicine without healing, but not all medicine is healing, and even not all healing is medicine. The most elementary common sense accepts it. If every healing were medicine, then all the witches and cranks were medical people and the mountbanks would be practicing medicine — at least on the occasion on which he meets with some success (and every practitioner sees some success) but they are not.

There is no doubt that mind healers do wish to share the prestige of body healers; do they have the right?

This is a sociological question. We are not concerned with it here. But let us assume that there is some rational kernal to the prestige of medicine. What is it? It is in its scientific nature, of course; but we have now merely traded one prestige word with another. Can we specify more directly what is of value in medicine and can it be implemented in psychiatry?

We do not wish to commend all medical practices, as we have made amply clear in various parts of this study. What we have in mind are a few of its laudable qualities. For one thing diagnosis is not as arbitrary as many other assessments of human affairs. Though country doctors vary from excellent to poor diagnosticians, medical school hospitals repeatedly check and improve standards of diagnosis, tools of diagnosis, procedures of diagnosis, and they take the idea of experimental testing for granted. This is what gives medical diagnosis the semblance of science that it enjoys. We think if in mental diagnosis we would be half as cautious and clear and honest in our expressions, and even a quarter as self-critical, then psychiatric diagnosis will at once much improve.

Second, healing is more commendable if rationally based on some ideas but can be detached from them when ideas fail though practices based on them pass tests satisfactorily. This makes medical practices as eclectic as we know them yet medical researchers are so rightly worried about this eclecticism. The trouble in psychiatry, however, is much more preliminary: in psychiatry, they say, you cannot characterize a one-to-one hour session the way you characterize drug intake or even a physical operation of a few hours. Why not? The personal element occurs in all medicine, and if it is important enough to be crucial, it should be so characterizable. The chief reason why treatment in psychiatry is so unclear to us, is that it is unclear to its practitioners. They are apologetic partisans and fail to describe any practice not stemming from orthodox doctrine. This particularly holds for psychoanalysts who pretend to practice Freudian techniques but are as eclectic as any sane practitioners are. But if we do not know the ingredients in the mixture we are unable to make comparative studies. Follow-ups, and the rest of the test procedures that have advanced physical medicine so much in the last century or so can be used in psychiatry as easily as in somatoiatry. That they are not used is partly ignorance partly poor ideology that lends incentives to defend the ignorant, and ignorance and ideology enhance each other. The profession of mental healing is thus a mental patient.

3. THE STATE OF THE ART: DESCRIPTIVE

It is not the physician who cures, but nature; and the physician can only handle some obstacles on the road to cure.

Hence the cardinal errors of almost all present day psychotherapy: (1)The neglect of diagnosis, (2) the search for the ideal healer, and (3) the attempt to attack the source of the disease head-on. We shall now elaborate on these.

We shall say little of diagnosis here since we spoke of it in our previous study, *Paranoia: A Study in Diagnosis,* and since we said repeatedly in this study, of psychiatry as medicine, that one of the chief characteristics of scientific medicine that psychiatry still wants is proper diagnostic tools. We do not mean by proper, adequate: almost no diagnostic tools are adequate, for, no matter how good the tools are, of necessity they are limited. By proper we mean such that make their limitation manifest. To the extent that psychosis is psychoanalytically admittedly untreatable, for example, to that extent psychoanalysis can be viewed as diagnostically somewhat adequate — in that it declares psychosis beyond its ken. As our earlier study has indicated, however, even by this preliminary and crude test, psychoanalysis still fails. It fails in that it does not tell us how to demarcate neurosis from psychosis — quite apart from the fact that many a respectable and respected and even leading psychoanalysts would quarrel about this limiation of psychoanalysis, since some of them report cases of successfully psychoanalitically treated psychotic patients and others retort that patients diagnosed as psychotic and then psychoanalytically successfully treated must be cases of misdiagnosis by the very virtue of their having been psychoanalytically successfully treated. There is also in medicine the tendency to view the case of any successful treatment of any hitherto uncured disease to be the case of misdiagnosis rather than of rendering curable a hitherto incurable disease. This is particularly so in all cases of patients declared suffering from incurable cancer allegedly treated by quacks or faith-healers. And rightly so. A priori it always stands to reason to choose the hypothesis of misdiagnosis in preferences to the hypothesis of a new breakthrough or of a miracle. Therefore, only the proper use of proper diagnostic procedure can motivate the justly skeptical to try the new cure on patients after careful diagnosis.

Nevertheless, we may say that much about proper diagnosis. It should, and often in medicine it does consist of measuring and/or testing and then correlating a number of more-or-less independent variables. For example, blood pressure consists of four different pressure measurements (the systolic, the diastolic; both at rest and in activity — not to mention differential blood pressure). The psychological diagnostic tools to date are defective. Some of them are vague and general and pertaining to no clear-cut variables or pertaining to non-existent variables such as personality (Rorschach tests) or intelligence quotient (I.Q. test) tests and, indeed, the diagnostic tools known as psychodiagnostic tests are pseudo-precise and only give vague and general results under the guise of giving precise values to some specific variables.[1]

---

1.   See J. Agassi, 'The Twisting of the I.Q. Test', *Philosophical Forum,* 3, 1972, 260-72.

Others pertain to irrelevant variables, such as the degree of the ability to think, whether in the abstract or in the concrete.[1]

So much for diagnosis. As to the ideal healer, as we have observed, there is the extreme case here, of the Freudian requirement that a psychoanalyst be a mentally perfectly healthy person, whose perfect mental health is attested by the conclusion of a psychoanalytic treatment of him that is declared fully successful. This has no analogue in medicine. We all agree that people whose hands tremble with surgical instruments in them should not be surgeons, that drunken doctors should not officiate in any medical capacity, etc. And we can test even a doctor for alcohol level in his blood. All those are proper means that may apply to any candidate for mental treatment. Thus, we would loathe to see a sadist as either a surgeon or a gynecologist or a psychiatrist. But to search the recesses of the mind of the candidate for psychiatry only to void it of all traces of sadism is both unnecessary and impossible. On the contrary, while proper diagnosis, as we say, need be performed by, or with the aid of, a medically trained person, proper treatment may sometimes be better administered by nurses, just as medication and injections and similar treatments are administered in almost all modern hospitals, and more so in cases of mental illness in mental hospitals, by psychologists, by social workers, etc., very much like community nurses in community clinics all over the developing world. We do not mean to prejudge the question, who should treat. We mean to oppose current prejudgment, and blame it on poor diagnostic tools.

So much for diagnosis and for personnel; now for the cure, or rather against it. We deem, as most psychiatrists do, anxiety to be the major etiological cause for all mental ills, even though it is prevalent amongst the healthy population too. Yet we think it downright silly to try overcome anxiety. On the contrary, treatment should consist in learning to cope with it; namely, learning to develop, while neglecting anxiety, other factors that normally balance it to constitute together with it a proper sense of proportion.

This prescription is usually – though decidedly not always – generalist in bias; that is to say, it is a holistic bias. Here we see again the holistic metaphysics as the link or connection between the generalist world of diagnosis – a search for a set-back in general balance that the organism aims at recovering – and the generalist world of cure – remove the obstacles of the organism's own way to the regaining of the balance but do not try to restore the balance by treatment.

We noted repeatedly the limitations of generalism. Often diagnosis can be superficial and thus at least seemingly externalist. Often, externalist or

---

1. See our *Paranoia*, Appendix II.

rather seemingly externalist treatment will do — surgery is more externalist-like the more superficial it is, and so is the ingestion of drugs and hormones and other kinds of medication. Indeed, even a laxative, the grand traditional generalist cure is very externalist for uncomplicated cases of constipation.

In line with this we have no objection whatsoever to medication that allays anxiety while cures takes place — on which more soon — but we are as opposed to the chemical straight-jackets that are so current in mental homes in the last decade or two as any humanist psychologist is.

Though the cause of the illness, we agree, is anxiety, the illness itself is not. As rather holistic we are hard-put to point at diagnostic tools that can be methodically and systematically and repeatedly be used for measurement throughout treatment. Yet we do agree, that the first thing the therapist must do, be he a doctor, a nurse, a psychologist or a social worker, not to mention a clergyman, is increasingly gaining the trust of the patient and allaying his anxiety. The degrees of trust and of anxiety can easily be assessed by common sense.[1] The way to develop them, we say, may be anything from intense heart-to-heart talk to pottering around in the patient's presence, with hypnosis, drugs, and anything else in between that shows the therapist's genuine concern for and to the patient.

On this we say no more than what reasonable therapists say to patients ever since Freud: if you find it easier to trust the next-door therapist than to trust me, then go to him.

The illness, we think, consists in helplessness, indecision and such; in brief, it is, a defect in the autonomy of a person. The end of the cure is the restoration of autonomy. Yet here, again, the function of this discussion is that of a disclaimer: it is not the task of any therapist to determine the content of the patient's autonomy, and not even to make him autonomous.

The therapist's ability to help is thus essentially limited. But so is the ability of the patient, which is limited by the means of self-deception available to the patient. The cause is obvious: the patient faces decisions his society deems normal and he deems monumental. Anxiety mounts. In an effort to allay anxiety — which is the wrong self-cure, as Freud noted — the patient confuses himself and in confusion takes recourse to one of the many textbook methods of self-treatment, from alcohol to obsessive phobia, from psychotic

---

1. In his Nobel prize acceptance lecture, Niko Tinbergen describes the successful treatment of autistic children as the investment of enormous efforts almost exclusively in the collosal patience required for the acquisition of these children's trust. No medicine is needed here, and the diagnosis of child autism is the only unquestioned unproblematic unanimously endorsed proper medical diagnosis in psychiatry to date.

breakdown to belle-indifférence. The therapist can (1) keep decision problems from mounting; also he can

(2) act as the means of allaying anxiety and help by advising to avoid the standard pattern and (3) encourage the patient to try an alternative route. All this while avoiding take over responsibility that normally rests with the patient − including defeatism.

This, we contend, is exactly what the best therapists today do. This, we contend, is exactly what they can do; alas! we have no new techniques to offer. This is why the title of the section is 'The State of the Art'. Yet we do not claim to be offering no positive contribution. On the contrary, by recommending to sift the useful grain from the useless and at times harmful chaff, we think we are making a positive contribution which we say can be assessed and ought to be assessed regularly throughout treatment, thus rendering psychiatry a branch of medicine proper, which is the declared end of the present volume as its title attests.

During treatment therapists can, but seldom do, measure (by comparison only; prescise scales are non-existent) levels of anxiety, of confusion, and of self-deception; levels of ability to develop new techniques of coping, and several levels of resourcefulness, and the growth of the life-areas under the patient's active control. More cannot be done: it is not the therapist but nature that cures.

In conclusion, two points may be repeated. First, since the function of all mental disturbances is the allaying of anxiety − yet it is poorly performed, thereby aggravating anxiety itself (as Freud has discovered) − the first steps of the psychiatrist should be a temporary − symptomatic − relief from anxiety so as to permit the patient to reconsider. Thus the psychiatrist can both respect the patient's autonomy and help heal it.

Second, the natural focus of all mental ills is the natural disposition under stress to focus attention on the way to alleviate the stress. Only in mental ills this natural disposition becomes exaggerated − obsessive and rigid. The paranoic model is that of a patient relating everything to his idée fixe − the cure and cause of his anxiety − thus making it an integrative principle by which to judge everything, itself above judgement. The hysterical model is hysterical blindness or deafness or la belle indifférence: the patient examines everything for relevance to his distress and when judged not relevent he chooses to ignore its very existence. In both cases − the paranoic and the hysterical − there is a pretence which is a form of bullying: the paranoic pretends his idée fixe to be acceptable to all as obviously rational and the hysteric pretends to be ignorant of what he has noticed well enough to decide to ignore. And self-deception is a limitation on one's autonomy that prevents any reconsideration of the chosen limitation. Hence, the role of the psychiatrist is not of one who does not impose sanity, but of one who suggests that to alleviate pain the patient may have no choice but to deliberate a possible reconsideration of his choice of a limitation and of one who further offers means to facilitate the reconsideration that might lead to a change that might help the patient regain his autonomy and thus effect a self-cure.

4. THE STATE OF THE ART: CRITICAL

It is rather easy to examine the state of the art, the contemporary stage in which the profession of psychotherapy stands, and to come up with criticisms, sometimes even extreme, and even to mortal blows. It is the easiest to come up with deadly conclusions, when psychotherapy is examined from a bird's eye view, as we tried to do in this study. Yet before we come up with our disappointments, let us state the case for the importance of psychotherapy as we see it. It is a fact that there is such a pratice as psychotherapy; and that psychotherapy has existed from time immemorial. This alone is already sufficient an argument for the claim for its relevance and importance to human life. But psychotherapy is not only an art of ancient origin and continuous existence through history. It is also, to our mind, among those matters of deep import, that go beyond mere historical records: it has to do with some of the profoundest questions we ask concerning the meaning of life, the what's and the why's and the significance of life. In psychotherapy, from primitive people's prayer (as a form of psychotherapy?) to magic, from magic to science, hope will contine to be one of the main determinants or components of our very humanity, of our nature, essence, being, existence, etc. Immanuel Kant expressed this view in his celebrated program for philosophical anthropology posed (in the introduction to his lectures on logic) in the form of his four famous questions: 1. what can I know? 2. what ought I to do? 3. what can I hope for? and finally, summing the three in one, 4. what is Man? As we know Man, hope is of his very nature. Hope is a paradoxical entity, at once a reality and an illusion, even a mirage, and a deceit; worse still, perhaps the monster of self-deceit. But it is there, and therefore, we think, it will continue to be there. And if this is true for humanity at large, it is ever so much more so for the suffering individual, particularly for the sufferer expressing his suffering, verbally or otherwise. Moreover, in a sense a painful gaze is humanly more striking and informative than the most powerful expression, poetic or scientific. By definition, almost, a painful gaze is first and foremost an expression of a call, a request for help. In other words it is directed to another, and its bearer thereby implies the assumption that some other – another person – is there from whom he may expect help or at least hope for some. The other may be a parent, the Lord, a friend, another unknown human being (sometimes a friendly animal will do, as Martin Buber reports in his autobiographic fragment). The help wanted may be physical, or an offer of company to escape painful loneliness, or help to overcome inner trouble. In these cases it is in principle a request for psychotherapy: a person is invited to act in the capacity of a healer – of a psychotherapist. What the person officiating as a psychiatrist can do need not be clear – at least at the start. For, at the very least he may be invited to share the suffering. The cry for help is, de profundis, be with me! The inner logic of human suffering not only philanthropically but almost logically implies sharing, a dialogue or a dialectic of sorts. It is in this point that we found ourselves obliged to criticise almost all schools of psychotherapy as failing to stand up to this criterion. As we understand it, the psychotherapies of almost all schools underplay the dialectical dimension. The exception are the schools we have arbitrarily labelled Buberian – to include also to some extent the Adlerians, and the Sullivanians, and others, such as Jacques Lacan. Orthodox psychoanalysts and behaviorists, surpisingly also most existentialists, even some (not all) logotherapists, one way or another (we have argued in previous sections), they all deny the existence of the dimension of the dialogue. No doubt, all of them, psychoanalysts, behaviorists, and existentialists, do somewhere make use of the dialectical dimension in their daily work (indeed, no psychotherapy – not even the crudest deconditioning – would be possible without some dialogue), yet to retain the logical consistency of their own systems they regard the dialogue as external, preparatory, incidental to the actual therapy. The fact that a dialectical dimension is inactively and unwittingly introduced, is a mark of distinction to these therapists – particularly when they do so despite themselves, and at times while dismissing the importance of their own dialogue. All the same, our strongest criticism of their intellectual conceptualizations, of their schools of thought or systems of thought, is just on this point. It was Wundt who claimed in 1879 that psychology had come of age and became an independent scientific discipline; the rise of scientific psychotherapy followed soon. No more magic, they foolishly said; let us go beyond folk-psychology and commonsense, beyond mesmerism, phrenology, suggestion, auto-suggestion, pep-talk, they solemnly declared; let us build our craft along the methodologically right course and put it on a sound scientific basis. This trend of 19th century psychology, like the trend of 19th century sociology, is childlike in its quest for adult status: let our subject come of age, they prayed, taking it for granted that with it they might grow up as well. Alas!

This is a childish hope for a surrogate maturity. Our own slogan for therapy is, for the first stage bring back the pep-talk! We should never be above pep-talk! Even for normal adults it is of some import.

It matters little or not at all what status psychology has, much less what status psychiatry has; helping a patient in his sufferings, i.e., doing what medicine is all about, is all that really matters: and this need not have the exalted status of psychotherapy. The very same pain may be alleviated in different ways and so diagnosed when alleviated by drugs (analgesics, major and minor tranquilisers), by food (in cases of peptic ulcers), by emetics (in cases of cholelithiases, cholecystitis), by purgatives (in cases of Crohn's disease) and by fasting (in cases of diaphragmatic hernia). Nor do we exclude all alleviating of pain by surgical operations (in the case of Trigeminal neuralgia) the generalist opposition notwithstanding. Yet, clearly, none of these techniques can qualify as psychotherapy. In psychotherapy, what is implied is, the psychiatrist's recognition of the patient's system of values. In psychotherapy we stick with the view of the patient as one who has values, or perhaps the freedom of choice of his own values (including his right to choose to have no values at all).

Incidentally, even a somatoiastrist at times effects psychiatry, when sharing with the patient a general view of the patient and his world with an eye on thereby improving his condition. This highly integrative view of somatioatry is the view of medicine as a whole as anthropological. Of course, usually, the generally accepted view of the freedom of choice permits people to benefit from encounters or avoid encounters, to offer help to each other or not, and to accept or refuse help. Medicine, says Szasz, is a form of service. The problem psychiatry faces, retorts Carl Rogers, is rooted in the fact that the help needed pertains to the patient's defective ability to choose, or else it is not psychiatry. The problem of psychiatry is, concludes Nethaniel Laor, can a mental patient as such be respected? Can he, that is, be simultaneously recognized both in his freedom of choice and in its defect?

To conclude, being a pseudo-science or a science, making the wrong or the right claim for scientific status, is usually of no significance for anyone but the snob, especially since usually what is ousted as unscientific in the name of science is often reintroduced through the back door. Even in the present case of psychiatry, dialogue – from pep-talk to the critique of bad faith – is introduced through the back door quite regularly. But in the case of psychotherapy this is not enough: we need to reintroduce the whole spectrum of possible dialogue through the main door, and herald dialogue with a fanfare. The dialogue should be between schools of metaphysics and of science – in medicine in general and in psychiatry in particular – between thinkers and practitioners, between practitioners and patients, between theoreticians and patients, and between patients. We plead for openness.

5. THE STATE OF THE ART: HOPEFUL

It is rather difficult to examine the state of the art, the contemporary position of the profession under scrutiny, psychotherapy; and it is no less difficult to come up with conclusions as to its open future. The future is not what it used to be. This joke is not as misplaced here as one may think: we learn from routine work in psychotherapy, that instances occur, moments of truth arise, which are spontaneous and unpredictable. Some are of such an unexpected, immediate, deep, experiential nature, that they leave a mark, on therapists as well as on patients with such an impact that is at times quite unforgettable. All this makes reasonable prediction difficult even when it pertains to nothing more than what will happen in a given psychotherapy course or even session, let alone the future of a whole discipline.

In 1961 Michel Foucault responded to a request to write a history of psychiatry. He found this task insurmountable: he could not write a history of psychiatry and he even went so far as to suspect that there was actually none. What may exist is only a history of madness: There is the phenomenon of madness from time immemorial, and each century, society, culture, etc., conceives of it as it does and deals with it the way it does. If asked what madness is, Foucault's answer would be: just study the history of madness and you will come as close to an answer to this question as possible. Perhaps the same applies in psychotherapy. Let us try and follow the line of thought of Foucault. If asked, what is psychotherapy, then we should say, it is a phenomenon that exists from time immemorial. We find it under diverse masks and guises, from primitive magic to sophisticated techniques in various ways and under various forms almost always together with, and in parallel with and complementary to this other characterizable phenomenon, its major object of treatment, namely madness. If asked what is psychotherapy, we might also invite the questioner to study its history, i.e., the history of ideas in psychotherapy. Since the very subject matter of our volume is this history of ideas in psychotherapy, it may, we hope, help us observe what makes psychotherapy what it is. Our answer, then, may be, one may find out what is the cure of madness (psychotherapy) by studying the history of madness and of its attempted cure (psychotherapy). It is with this serious intent that we say, let every psychotherapist search for himself, place himself in time and in space of his own century, society, culture, values, universe of discourse, etc. Let every psychotherapist decide for himself in the light of his knowledge of the history of his profession, who he is, and what is his chosen brand of psychotherapy.

This, however, might be added. First, if, when in a study of the history of something – psychiatric ideas in the present case – we gain some idea about that something, the idea is not thereby proven. On the contrary, the idea emerges as the very bias of that particular study. And the bias, the guiding idea, may be articulated and subjected to critical scrutiny. Yet, we think, the history adds something, if only the ammunition to the critic's weapon: we better not restrict our knowledge of something – psychiatry, in the present case – to the view from the narrow sights of one particular idea. Even if the idea 'emerges' from a historical study, we may still hope that the historical study offers a broad background to the idea that may help those who wish to improve upon it, or perhaps transcend it. We therefore suggest that if each psychotherapist will join the common traditional canons of medicine even while holding to his own theory and practice, then a proper psychotherapy can emerge, and a medical one at that. Do we deem right to dismiss as invalid any of the existing theories or practices in psychotherapy? No, we do not; at least not quite. We do not deem right to dismiss as invalid for that matter even our pet aversion the existing psycho- pharmacological schools of therapy, be their pretension for scientific respectability as inflated as we think it is. As for criticism, we have said enough in this volume; and surely some readers will reject our criticism. Others will criticize us in our turn. Therefore, we repeat, let us agree to differ and let each and every therapist continue to hold his own theory and practice, if he so thinks fit. And let him freely refer patients to practitioners of different schools if this seems to him to be in their interests. We are only suggesting one thing which we hope might nevertheless help improve upon the situation of contemporary psychotherapy. We suggest that in the future the ongoing debates should include at least statements of medical canons to apply to psychiatry. For our part we take the canons of medicine as we understand them. The Hippocratic or neo-Hippocratic canons, which are these: Nature cures. Primum non nocere. Think. Criticize and allow your own views to be criticized. Check. Take doubt to be a guiding principle (Claude Bernard). Experiment. Follow-up. Re-think. And always admit error openly and openly profess shortcomings.

The combination of two points of view, i.e., the anthropological and the medical, open a possibility of an anthropological medicine, and paves the way to a psychological medicine, an approach to medicine that may, perhaps, transcend both traditional medicine and traditional psychotherapy. This trend of viewing medicine as primarily a matter of public health goes back to the Hippocratic Code, yet is being rediscovered perennially. It is also extended from time to time and, to repeat, for our part we do not object to curing an ailing economy or a sick society by the medical canons as we understand them. After all, what we deem the canons of medicine that we so approve of, are none other than the canons of rationality. And these need no limitations.

If this indeed is the outcome of what we would wish the future of psychiatry to be, both as medicine and as psychotherapy, then this is the interim conclusion which our study indeed hints at, not only a wish but also as a probable course of events to come: medicine in general, and psychiatry in particular, should keep going away from magic and authority and scientific mystique, towards humanization, dialogue and mutual respect, and open public view; it will thus move increasingly away from defensiveness and towards genuine naturalness.

Perhaps the most harmful and least criticized aspect of immature conduct is defensiveness. People are found acting defensively in all walks of life, medicine included, psychiatry included as well. Defensiveness is, in our own view, though never totally avoidable, still the paradigm of bad faith, of self-deception, of the fear of being rejected subsequently to any admission of error, no matter how minute or how reasonable. And the lack of maturity in a psychiatrist − on this Freud was just wonderful − is extremely dangerous for his patient. Yet Freud, whose impact on the professions of psychology, psychotherapy and psychiatry is the greatest, for better and for worse, was immature in the extreme − defensive in the extreme, rigid in the extreme − and yet admirable, and compassionate, not in the least to be rejected come what may. We propose to declare both the dismissal of Freud and the defence of his folly equally out of step − for a little while, of course. There are matters of greater significance just these days, such as the application of the canons of medicine to psychiatry, wall-to-wall.

NAME INDEX